The Long Game of Joy

The Long Game of Joy

A Playbook for Grace, Faith, & Forgiveness
in the First Year of Marriage

Anna Elkins

w o r d b o d y

Also by Anna Elkins

Hope of Stones

Living Large on Little

A Children's Book of Blessings
(with Jan Elkins)

And: The Story of More

The Honeylicker Angel

The Space Between

The Heart Takes Flight

As Editor:

Deep Travel: Souvenirs From the Inner Journey
(with Christina Ammon)

Dedication

For Jared: brave man to share the adventure of marriage with me—
and to brave this book!

Table of Contents

Marriage experts call the first year of marriage "the wet cement year," because it's the time when both members of a couple are figuring out how to exist as partners without getting stuck in the murk, without being trapped by bad habits. It's a time to set and test boundaries and create good habits that will continue for the rest of your marriage.

—Jo Piazza
How to Be Married

*Now in the middle of my life
I realize that my journey is to forgive
everything that's happened.*

—Diana Marie Delgado
from "Dream Obituary"

It's not whether you win or lose, it's how you play the game.
—Grantland Rice

We Fought About *What?*

I titled this book *The Long Game of Joy,* though I'm not a huge fan of games—there's usually just one winner. But I discovered that on the playing field of marriage, *both* players can win. On this Unified Field of Love, two can become one and know joy.

Which might sound sweet....

But it's also a marvelous-hard healing process!

I confess: the first year of marriage was rough for me. And I'm pretty sure it would have been rough regardless of whom I'd married; I had too much of my own unlearning and learning to do—even though I thought I'd done it.

That's one of the many things I wish I'd known but discovered only after talking with people who'd been married 10, 20, 30, 40+ years. And after reading poems to help with mystery. And after reading books on marriage to help with practicalities. All of which I'll reference often in these pages. Like this bit of wisdom from Winifred Reilly:

> I thought of how helpful it would have been to have learned, early on in my marriage, that not every problem can be solved and not every irritant can be negotiated away, that a good marriage is a mixture of delight and disgruntlement, that unhappiness comes from expecting it to be otherwise.[1]

That's good advice for the long game.

And what is the long game?

A long-term endeavor.

A marriage.

To my surprise, I found that the game of marriage has more than one time zone. It's played not just along linear time—a procession of moments and milestones, but also across *non*-linear time—a process of healing past wounds and releasing old woes.

To make this time distinction, I use two Greek terms. *Chronos* is chronological, measured time—ticking clocks and day-planners. *Kairos* is opportune, gift time—epiphanies and revelations of grace.

I also use those terms to structure the book. You'll find twelve *chronos* chapters, one for each month of our first year, detailing some of the conversations and events I recorded in my daily journal (each section break indicates a new day). Every *chronos* chapter is followed by a shorter *kairos*—a birds-eye view of what I learned as I looked back at the preceding month.

The writing styles of the two "time zones" are a bit different. I chose to leave the *chronos* journal entries a bit raw—to share the messy, day-to-day struggles *and* how I chose to transform those struggles. The compost and what I cultivated from it. There's some embarrassing stuff in here. But I invite you to enter the muck—it's worth getting to the good harvest.

While I edited the book, I cringed or laughed—or both—at the misunderstandings between my husband and me. Re-reading our difficult discussions, I would remember something I had read or heard afterward that would have prevented a swath of angst, mostly on my part. My steadfast husband doesn't do angst— something I finally appreciate!

Revisiting past arguments, I found myself saying aloud, "Oh, I wish I'd known...." So I decided to add insight right where I wished I'd had it—interjecting my daily journal entries with revelation. *Chronos* pierced by *kairos*. I spent a year live-writing this story and then more than a year revising it. During those countless revisions, I found that editing the book also helped me edit my expectations—which had caused most of the trouble in the first place.

Ah, newlyweds confronting all the new of being wed! I would have felt a bit less crazy knowing how challenging the start of marriage can be, and I would have welcomed more advice for the play of the game—a playbook. So I essentially wrote the book I wish I'd had when I married. May this memoir be a helpful manual with its quotes and resources, and a hopeful meditation with its poetry and contemplations.

I should also mention that my original working idea and title for this book was: *The Marriage Menu: Mr. Meat-and-Potatoes Marries Ms. Kale-and-Quinoa.* It was a bit too cute. Plus, even *I* got bored with my own menu planning a few months into marriage. But two bonuses came from that defunct idea:

1. It got me writing every single day of our first year together (you'll see many food entries early on).

2. Since I'd jotted down so many menu items, I decided to use names of food as codes for subjects of arguments I wished to keep private—but which I wanted to share to show how we learned to communicate.

Turns out, it's helpful to substitute "kale" or "cake" for the subject of a fight—because a fight is never about the content anyway. (Though I am embarrassed to admit that we did spiral into fights starting with literal crackers. And jam. But I get ahead of myself.) In fact, I had so much fun using food code names, I used them for most non-private arguments, too—the better to see beyond the surface of any opinion-triggering subject to the heart of how we handled it.

When you read about our troubles, please remember this: our relationship is tremendously better now. As I write this introduction, it is late afternoon, and I'm waiting for my husband, Jared, to get home from a long week at work—hard work he does with faithfulness I deeply respect. I've loaded the cooler, and we're headed to camp at the lake with friends, where we'll eat too much watermelon and stay in the water for most of our waking hours. These friends have been married over twenty years, and their honesty has blessed us immensely.

I want this book to be like those good friends: a blessing. I aimed to write with honesty and honor, and I'm grateful to the many readers—including professional editors and counselors—who helped me with that vision. Any failures to carry it out are wholly my own.

I can now laugh at the crackers and jam. I hope you'll laugh, too, as you bear with me and my husband—who read this book, knew he had first refusal rights (and that I wouldn't publish it if he didn't want me to), and who was invited to adjust or add commentary wherever he wished. In fact, Jared would like to add that it's hard to relive one's "jackassery," but if it helps others, it's worth it. Truth.

Also true: most of what I agonized over has been not just resolved but restored.

Like a playing field in the spring rain, our marriage was a muddy mess for a season, but we learned so much, that when I look back at the sorrows, I see their purpose.

We kind of crammed a decade of lessons into a single year. (A cramming compounded by building a house together—which I do *not* recommend doing as newlyweds!) It took us a few skirmishes and time-outs, but we figured out we are on the same team and have the same goal: union.

Adam Grant writes:

> As we approach any life transition…we can pause to ask people what they wish they'd known before they went through that experience. Once we're on the other side of it, we can share what we ourselves should have re-thought.[2]

Thank goodness for the sharing, right? This book is filled with what I wish I'd known and how I re-thought much of what I knew.

And so I want to start here—in the good *now* of the future, long after celebrating our second anniversary, knowing we can *both* keep winning. That *kairos* can keep reaching into *chronos*.

Maybe that's a good way to live anyway: knowing that all of our difficulties and despair can be transformed. Can even morph into joy.

If you can fall in love again and again…if you can forgive…if you can keep from growing sour, surly, bitter and cynical…you've got it half licked.

—Henry Miller

For one human being to love another; that is perhaps the most difficult of all our tasks; the ultimate, the last test and proof, the work for which all other work is but preparation.

—Rainer Maria Rilke

You and I can turn and look
at the silent river and wait. We know
the current is there, hidden; and there
are comings and goings from miles away
that hold the stillness exactly before us.
What the river says, that is what I say.

—from "Ask Me"
William Stafford

Part I: Meet the Players

Once upon a summer in Southern Oregon, I went to the local Growers' Market. A tall man I hadn't seen before was helping at the Pennington Farm bakery stand, and he sold me a berry turnover. I don't remember what we talked about, but I do remember hoping I would see him again.

I later learned the man was a stonemason. His name was Jared, and he was like a son to the Penningtons, often helping them at their market stand the weekends he wasn't kayaking. I learned this because, behind the scenes, friends had arranged that we should meet—and had given him my number.

Jared called. We met at the GoodBean in Jacksonville and drove to the upper Applegate River, where we spent a Sunday afternoon on the water.

There were many more rivers and afternoons for the rest of that season. And when we first kissed on the banks of another river, I knew he was the one. But life had different tributaries for us at the time, and we eventually went in separate directions…largely because we had almost opposite thoughts about marriage. As in: Jared had never wanted to marry, and I always had. Which meant we also had very different expectations about matrimony. Some of Jared's were formed in childhood when his parents divorced. Some of mine were formed by historical romance novels, though I knew my deeper dream of union had more to do with divine love than vapid happily-ever-afters. And we both, though not aware of it, had internalized all kinds of cultural expectations.

We stayed friends over the years, occasionally encountering each other at church, my art receptions, or his construction sites. Then, on the eve of my spring departure to teach poetry in Switzerland, Jared sent me a message asking if we could meet up for a walk sometime. When I returned to the States, we walked together on summer solstice. And soon after, almost exactly eight years after our first date, we met again at the GoodBean and drove to the upper Applegate River to spend a Sunday afternoon on the water.

The following month, he called to ask if we could be friends.

Autumn came, and he went to kayak in Peru. Winter came, and I went to help lead a writing workshop in Mexico. In between, we spent all the holidays with each other and each other's families— who kept asking if this was just friendship. (I might have been asking myself the same thing!)

In late winter, Jared drove me out to a small town near a big river to show me parcels of land for sale. The lot we liked most was dotted with oaks and madrones and had creek access. He wanted to build a house, and he asked me to help design it. (I might have also been wondering if this was a house I would live in one day.) The hand-sketched house plans progressed to official, CAD blueprints. We met with a builder.

I was still wondering....

And I was having a few conversations with God. I reminded Him that my heart had broken when Jared walked away all those years ago. And now, here he was, back in my life in my early forties, when I finally had embraced being single and was enjoying a deep romance with God.

It seemed like Jared wanted to be more than friends, but.... It was all one big "dot, dot, dot" of elliptical confusion on my end—yet also a great opportunity to practice the power of curiosity. I was beginning to learn that "Curiosity is underrated."[3]

I now know that there is a lot more going in Jared's head and heart that he lets on. But I didn't then. So finally, I initiated the DTR: the Define-the-Relationship talk. He was surprised that I was confused. I was surprised *he* was surprised. Later, he told me that he had already decided to ask me to marry him by that point... when I wasn't even sure if we were dating/courting/whatevering. We probably should have pressed into that disconnect a bit more because it would define the first year of our marriage. But part of me knew we would figure it out—that though it would be hard, it would be worth it. And it is. Susan Cane writes: "Whatever pain you can't get rid of, whatever joy you can't contain, make it your creative offering."[4] This book is my offering.

One spring eve, Jared asked me if I wanted to meet him at the land he'd just bought. I didn't entirely want to go out—it was rainy, and I was cozy in my little loft. But I wanted to see him, so I said *yes*. When I arrived, he pulled out what looked like a wrapped frame. I opened it to find a print of the hand-drawn house plans we had sketched together. On the back, he had written, "Will you marry me." As a writer, I love that there was no question mark. Because of course—despite a very different timeline than I had expected— there was no question.

And of course, we served Pennington pies for the wedding reception.

But unlike romantic comedies where the credits roll when two people finally stand together at the altar, I want to begin at our wedding. Because that's not "The End," it's just the beginning....

Chronos: July

"I do."

We kissed, taste of corn dogs on our lips.

It begins....

The rest of our Fourth-of-July wedding at Plaisance Ranch was a beautiful blur of friends and family and fried chicken.

We are married.

Jared and I closed the party minutes before the venue's curfew. As we walked out the gate behind our friends Chris & Chelsea, they turned and said they had an extra permit to raft the lower Rogue River tomorrow—any chance we were interested?

Jared looked at me, and though I knew he wanted to go, I could tell he was preparing to thank them but decline.

I surprised him by saying, "Sure!"

He smiled at me, then at our friends, "Let's check in with you in the morning."

He later told me he wasn't sure how much wine I'd had. I kissed him and said I make very good decisions with wine!

I should add: when we were just friends long ago, Jared had mentioned that if he ever did marry, he'd like to be camping. I had laughed and suggested that his future bride might want to have her honeymoon somewhere with indoor plumbing and fluffy robes.

Well, for our first night as man and wife, we got the sunken tub and plush robes at a classy hotel.

Then for the next two nights, we get to use a portable toilet called a groover and sleep in a tent on the banks of the river. A hers-and-his win.

◆◆◆

We lingered at the hotel right up until the noon check-out, then raced back to his place (our place?) in Grants Pass to pack for the last-minute raft trip. My parents had given us a picnic backpack stocked with oodles of cheeses, salamis, olives, crackers, roasted red pepper spread, chocolates, dried- and fresh fruits, peanut butter (Jared's favorite), and carrots. We basically up-ended the contents into a massive, bear-proof RTIC cooler and headed to the river.

Jared's father, Andy, drove us to the put-in at Grave's Creek and handed us a bag with three bottles of fine wine from him and Jared's step-mother, Linda.

We have good family.

That night, after getting through the rapids of Rainey Falls, after watching a bear watch us from the banks of the river as we glided down its glossy surface, after a group on the shore tossed us a "Happy Honeymoon" strawberry (and Jared caught it), after spotting turtles on rocks in the last rays of daylight, we joined our friends on a sandy shore just in time for dinner, pulling out our appetizers, setting them on a cutting board balanced on a river rock, and making a pleasing meal from them.

A five-star hotel followed by class-five rapids.

Our new life has begun.

◆ ◆ ◆

That afternoon, while rowing me down the river, Jared asked, "What do you want to do once we're married? I'm excited to see what makes you come alive."

A beautiful question. I thought about it, watching sunlight glinting off of everything—his shoulders, the oars, the swirling surface of the water.

In all that brightness, I said, "I don't know. And that choice is such a luxury." I thought of my poetry and art—all the personal projects I've chipped away at between freelance editing jobs.

Remembering a conversation we'd had when engaged, I added, "To be able to write and paint without having to edit anymore? I think that might be heaven on earth. Thank you for the chance to explore."

In that golden moment, I had no idea of the rapids ahead—and I don't just mean the whitewater of Coffee Pot or Blossom Bar. I'd never been down that stretch of river, never been on a multi-night raft trip, and never been married. I didn't yet know the tension of learning to trust another person as we navigated the rapids of matrimony. I didn't yet know the calm-water blessing of a husband who was happy to be the main breadwinner, freeing me to focus on my not-so-breadwinning poetry. There in the raft, I just basked in both meanings of *present*—this current time and the gift of it.

The day unfurled downstream. We had snacked our way through breakfast and lunch, and by dinner, we were happy to accept our friends' offer to share their steak salad. In turn, we shared the remainder of our wedding cake. Neither Jared nor I are huge cake fans, but Cathy Pennington had made for us one in addition to the pies. It turned out to be splendid. Like so many unplanned blessings.

◆ ◆ ◆

And then there are the planned blessings. Like baking a dish of bacon mac and cheese and popping it into Jared's freezer a week before our big day, thinking it might come in handy after we were married. A blessing because....

Right before the wedding, Jared had suggested hosting his mother, Kayt, for dinner tonight—a dinner that now happened to be within an hour of returning home from our last-minute raft trip. I was truly happy it would work out—Kayt lives in Southern California, and I was glad that we'd get to connect before she flew back.

I was also glad for that mac and cheese. Minutes before we'd left for the river, I'd popped the dish into the fridge to defrost. All I had to do was heat it in the oven when we got home. *Main dish: check.*

I thanked Jared for buying a bunch of kale the day before the wedding. *Salad: check.* I silently thanked my parents for including a box of chocolate truffles in that well-stocked picnic pack. And I thanked myself for not bringing them with us on the river trip. *Dessert: check.*

It all came together, and we enjoyed dinner on the patio. So much gratitude: for Kayt, who is a kind and lovely person, and for the wonderful son she raised.

> Though your destination is not yet clear
> You can trust the promise of this opening;
> Unfurl yourself into the grace of beginning
> That is at one with your life's desire.
>
> —from "For a New Beginning" by John O'Donohue[5]

It's official. Wednesdays are date nights. For our first, we went to Ahi for sushi and sparkling saké.

We are still two strangers.

Afterward, we walked across the street to the bank, where we cashed a wedding check in the ATM.

I commented that we have a lot of financial details to figure out. Neither of us have been married before, and we're both on the brink of middle age, so we are each used to being thoroughly independent.

While Jared and I were growing our friendship redux last fall, I published a nonfiction book titled, *Living Large on Little: How to See the Invitation in Limitation.* So maybe I should take my own medicine and look for the invitation in the "limitation" of making decisions with another human. Which probably looks like being *inter*dependent. A beautiful thing.

Another beautiful thing: for our first financial decision as man and wife, we chose charities to contribute to.

I am so grateful for how wise Jared has been with his finances. I've been wise with mine, too, but as a poet-painter, let's just say that my little Roth IRA was…little.

I am also grateful for something I didn't see at the time: amid our vast differences, Jared and I share similar views on money. We're both savers, we believe in giving, and we enjoy frugal indulgences like imported cheeses from discount grocery stores and free weekends camping in the wilderness. I didn't know what a boon that shared mindset was. We would clash on most everything else, but at least we'd mostly be on the same financial page. (Past Me didn't know to celebrate that win. Future Me does.)

◆ ◆ ◆

What you might discover if you are brave enough to rummage in a former bachelor's kitchen cabinets: bulk shrink-wrapped Costco cans of tuna and black beans, duplicate BBQ seasonings, ten bottles of expired aardvark sauce (what *is* aardvark sauce?), an exploded can of stewed tomatoes, Swedish crackers that expired ten years ago, and an industrial-sized can of enchilada sauce—that hasn't expired.

Inspired by the black beans and sauce, you might decide to make enchiladas. At this point, I would advise digging through the deep freeze (below countless sausages) where it's likely you'll find some chicken.

Bonus points if you happened to have left mini tortillas in the bachelor's fridge back when you were engaged and visiting for dinner.

Voilà: a batch of enchiladas big enough for leftovers…

◆ ◆ ◆

…leftovers warmed on the car dash en route to the Kalmiopsis to camp on a secret creek I've promised not to reveal the name of.

We ate by the water's edge, talking about good food to bring camping. I mentioned my free *Bon Appétit* magazine subscription, and how I enjoyed its inspiration. I'd once cut out a little sidebar for camp-food ideas, especially liking the peanut-butter-sriracha-basil toast.

Jared scoffed. Just straight peanut butter for him.

I was surprised—he seemed almost angry about it. He then told me about being a kid. After his parents' divorce, his mom started cooking new things. They were fancy and flavorful, but as a growing boy, he had been more interested in quantity than quality.

Somehow, my mention of a new way to use peanut butter sparked all this. I suggested that sriracha toast was just a fun way to try new flavors. That you can have quality *and* quantity. But he was resolute, and I chose to feel annoyed that he chose to take the conversation that direction.

We were mostly silent for the rest of the evening.

This is a good place to insert a *kairos*, "what-I-wish-I'd-known" bit. John F. DeMartini writes:

> When someone starts to get on your nerves, that's your opportunity, again, to look inside and find that very same trait in yourself—and discover that you have it in equal measure.[6]

Though I didn't want to admit it, I have my very own storehouse of old peeves. They just look different from my husband's.

When we climbed into the tent, I realized I'd forgotten the sleeping bag, so we only had a sheet. I was less annoyed with Jared when he spooned me all night to keep me warm.

I think I'll keep him—plain peanut butter and all.

◆ ◆ ◆

Our first event as a married couple: the company picnic. Jared and his older brother, Alex, own a third-generation masonry company. It was founded by their grandfather and built up by their father. The work they do is massive and mighty; they and the men who work for them work *hard*. I love that the brothers honor their employees with special gatherings and bonuses. For the summer gathering, they hold a catered picnic at the park. It turned out to be a gentle July day, and I was glad to meet all the men and their families. I was also glad that my new niece, Noel, had brought a picnic blanket we could nap on once people started playing sports. My sport is napping on couches, but a picnic blanket beneath the leafy trees is even better!

Second date night as a married couple.

If I were to give this failed evening a title, it would be "Catastrophe Cherries."

Though I knew marriage could be hard, I guess I didn't think it would be this hard the second week in. And maybe I'm surprised at one of the many ways it's hard. I'll call it "toast."

After writing and cleaning all day, I had prepped dinner: peppered pork loin with roasted carrots and potatoes. Had hand-dipped lush, dark cherries in chocolate. Had donned something lacy from my new lingerie collection and wrapped up in a slinky robe.

Around 4:30, when Jared was supposed to be home, he called to say that he had to run by the bank to get something notarized for the new house we are building. Bummer, but important. All good.

Just before five, he texted, "See you in 15."

But the line at the bank was long. He wasn't back until six. The lingerie was a one-piece that could have been longer in the torso, and after an hour and a half in it, the fabric was irritating my skin. But my real irritation was just beginning. When Jared walked in, I showed him the chocolate-covered cherries.

With a smile, he walked past me to dump his work clothes in the laundry and said: "I hate chocolate-covered fruit."

True, he said it in good humor. Also true: I was mad. But I said nothing.

What I'd wish I'd known in that moment was the therapist's maxim: get curious, not furious. And the suggestion that a married couple adopt the motto: "How about that?"[7]

Jared wanted to go to the river, so I changed into a swimsuit and told him to pack up whatever of the dinner he wanted. I had no more appetite.

We took the stand-up paddleboard to the Applegate, and he paddled us down to our spot below the rapids. He started to sense that something was wrong. I didn't say much at the river; I was still trying to figure out my emotions. That can take me a while, and I try to do so before articulating them. But a bigger issue—the "toast"—had been growing the last couple of weeks, and that I *had* been mulling over enough to articulate. I wasn't just mad. Now I was also sad.

On the drive back to the house, I began to voice some of my "toast" woes. Starting with how I knew most of what Jared didn't like— because he told me all the time. In fact, I couldn't keep track of his dislikes. But I knew very few things he *did* like—because I rarely heard those things. So I felt like I was flailing about in trial and error—with everything from figurative "toast" to literal sriracha-peanut-butter toast.

By the time we pulled into the driveway, we'd had our first wife-in-tears, husband-with-deer-in-headlights-eyes conversation. Jared is a very good listener. And I gave him a lot to listen to.

We ended up sitting side by side on the couch in silence for a long time. I try to give him time to process what I've been processing for a while, without expecting an immediate answer. I can trust that when he does come up with a solution, it will be well considered.

He finally said, "I have a lot to think about, and I don't know what I think about all of this yet, but I do know that I love you."

How about that?

◆ ◆ ◆

Early this morning, Jared sent a beautiful text from his job site.

Actually, it was a photo of a note he'd hand-written:

> Forgive me. Thanks for bringing all of this up. I promise
> to work on all of this for our connection. I love you.
> Thank you for your grace and mercy.

Those words opened up so much in my heart. The gratitude and grace, the forgiveness. I responded with love—and probably a few too many heart emojis.

Tonight, we had burgers at Sarah & Byron's. We sat out by their pool, and when they asked how things were going, Jared mentioned that I've been cleaning his house.

Yes. Yes, I have. I didn't say that I've been spending *many* hours a day cleaning his house after writing. As I work from room to room, I've found all sorts of things, even doubles of things—like two panini makers. He used to rent out several rooms short-term, so former guests have left all kinds of surprises.

I did say to Sarah & Byron that every few days, I stack two piles, one labeled: Goodwill? And one labeled: Toss? And Jared gamely goes through them, though I'm pretty sure he'd rather not. Good man.

Byron shared a lesson he'd learned in marriage. Recently, Sarah had spent days cleaning out their garage and shed while he was away. When he returned, he couldn't find his super magnet: "I admit, it looked like garbage—an old broom handle with a magnet duct-taped to it. But I use it to pick up stuff from the bottom of the pool. I've learned to ask, 'Honey, have you seen my…?' instead of "Did you throw away my…?'"

I smiled at Jared. "You have a new line: 'Honey, have you seen my super magnet?'"

◆◆◆

Camping weekend observations: I like watching dawn begin at the base of tallest pines almost as much as other early morning activities as newlyweds. Watching my husband kayak down waterfalls? I *don't* like that. He's very good, but it looks very scary.

We returned home and put together a dinner with the rest of the camp food. We sat at the splintery picnic table I'd earlier washed clean of spiderwebs. I had covered it with a table cloth and shaded it with a garden umbrella—both of which I'd brought from my old place. Assemblage. Dinner was assemblage, too. What do we have on hand? What from the past will work in the present? What do we keep and what do we toss?

Applies to leftover camp food and previous lives.

> ...he carries what he can
> and discards the rest.
>
> —from "What We Carry" by Dorianne Laux[8]

◆ ◆ ◆

Big family dinner at our house. I love getting to know my new relatives. My oldest niece, Noel, was away volunteering at a kids' camp. At one point, someone asked the other two kids their favorite part of our wedding.

My fifteen-year-old niece, Natalie, said her favorite part was that my parents officiated.

My twelve-year-old nephew, Abe, said, "Dessert!" I had pie *and* two slices of cake."

Both very, very good things.

◆ ◆ ◆

When life (or wife) gives you lemon-bar gelato....

This date night redeemed the last one. I had found a lemon-bar gelato, remembering that Jared liked the lemon bars I made this spring from a friend's Meyer lemon bounty.

But when he walked in after work and I showed the sweet treat to him, he backed away with his hands up, "I'm not saying anything."

I laughed, "Really? You don't like lemon gelato?"

He smiled and simply repeated, "I'm not saying anything."

Wise man. I hugged him.

We ate Mexican food at El Charro Viejo.

Before bed, I thanked him for being gracious about the gelato earlier. He replied with a smile, "I'm learning." One of the things I love about him: he can be very good at course correcting. He's had plenty of practice when kayaking, and maybe those skills can translate into marriage. I'm starting to like kayaking after all.

◆ ◆ ◆

We ate dinner on the patio, and for the umpteenth time, Jared said he's never at home and doesn't want to be home. Interestingly, he says these things *while* he's at home. Since this has come up so often, and I love being at home, I've been thinking about it. And trying to practice advice from the talk, "Why You Will Marry the Wrong Person," given by Alain de Botton: "To love someone is to apply charity and generosity of interpretation."[9]

So we talked about our different childhood experiences of home. After Jared's parents divorced, home and family looked different. His idea of home became more of a base camp for other adventures.

In contrast, home to me has always been a haven—my safe, cozy place to regroup from the world's chaos. I'd rather be home than away—despite years of pushing myself out into the world. I admitted that it's been a stretch for me to go camping every weekend since we've been married, but I am trying to enjoy it.

In all likelihood, we each made judgments about *home* and *away*. Maybe we can each release them and embrace the good things that lie outside our preferences.

◆ ◆ ◆

Jared wanted to camp north of Galice before helping with the Youth 71Five Ministries' raft trip the next day. Because where we'd camp is a "sketchy" area, he didn't want to leave a good vehicle there and instead planned to take the old truck parked at the company shop that can tow a raft.

I offered to fetch the truck so we could leave as soon as he got off work, though the thing's a creaky diesel beasty, and I'm not a fan of driving big vehicles.

When Jared came home from work and hitched up the raft, I added a water jug to the cooler. He peered inside, making a sarcastic comment about how I'd loaded the food. I looked at him and closed the lid. Maybe slightly slammed it. I stewed in silence as we pulled out of the drive.

On the drive, Jared told me he wanted me to drop him off upriver so he could kayak down to where we'd camp, the place he wanted me to wait for him…where it was too sketchy to leave a good vehicle. But a good wife…?

I wish I'd known that "Your reactivity to your partner's annoying or troubling aspects is grist for your growth."[10]

My grist for growth also included Jared's driving directions, which included miles of gravel road and how not to fishtail the raft when I took the sharp right turn down to the boat ramp.

I almost missed the turn, which meant I had to back up—and not fishtail.

I was *not* happy.

I parked near the river and jumped into the cold water. I felt a bit better but was still miffed.

After scouting up- and downstream, I decided to set up camp in a hidden spot with its own private beach. I pitched the tent. Figured out how to inflate the new camp mattress Jared had bought us as a wedding gift that had just arrived. Unfurled the bedding. Set up the camp chairs near the water with the picnic basket. Laid out polenta and the red sauce I'd simmered for six hours (still warm). Anchored the beer in the river to chill.

By that point, I had manifested symptoms of the unsexy, well-adjusted-martyr syndrome, often characterized by dramatic stares off into the sky, deep exhales, and fists on hips when surveying all that one had done on her own...while abandoned in "sketchy" territory. Then the feeling of being miffed began to morph into the truer feeling beneath it: sadness.

What I didn't consciously know—but very much knew deep in my heart—was that "every day, a woman internally asks her husband, *Do you really love me? Do you really care?*"[11]

When Jared arrived, kayak over shoulder, he was impressed at the camp setup, but mostly, I could tell he had something to say. He dumped his kayak on the ground and began, "So God is trying to teach me how to be a good husband..."

I was all ears.

Apparently, while kayaking, he realized he hadn't articulated gratitude for anything I'd done—had assumed I knew he was thankful. (I had *not* known this.) He continued, "There's a list. I won't remember all of it. Thank you for making dinner. Thank you for packing the truck. Thank you for getting the truck. Thank you for shuttling..." It went on for a while.

The mad-and-sad me softened. I said with peace, "You're welcome."

We ate dinner and sat by the water until full dark, then sat there some more, until we finally retired to the tent and watched the thick stars through the tent mesh.

> The grief you cry out from
> draws you toward union
>
> Your pure sadness
> that wants help
> is the secret cup
>
> —from "Love Dogs" by Rumi[12]

◆ ◆ ◆

What to say about a day of 60+ junior-high and high-school kids rafting the Rogue? There was splashing, rock jumping, and our sweet passengers: two brothers and the boy they quickly befriended. A long, fun day, fueled by chips and salsa and sandwiches.

◆ ◆ ◆

A very good date night. We ordered Thai take-out and brought it to a shady nook near Pierce Riffle on the Rogue. The oppressive heat dissolved the second we dunked into the freezing green water. We rose up to stand in a waist-deep eddy, the late-afternoon sunlight pooling and haloing everywhere. Even the shadows glowed with liquid light.

We stood in the water a while, watching the river currents flow past us—those close to us slow, those in the middle, quick.

Some days slow. Some days quick.

We're figuring things out.

While walking in the Woodlands, I ran into my ex-boyfriend as I was going uphill and he was heading down.

Awkward.

That long-ago relationship hadn't lasted for reasons of differing spirituality. He once asked me if I had actually dated anyone in the area who believed in my "Jesus man," and I told him about Jared. He said, "Why don't you go marry him, then?"

Ah, the accidental prophet.

Later that day, I went through my wardrobe and pulled out things I doubted I'd wear again: the filmy-fragile vintage dresses I once donned for art receptions but which require dry cleaning or have no stretch—are too restricting. I kept a couple of favorites but filled a bag with the rest to take to the consignment shop.

I want the fabric of my life to have a stronger warp and weave. I want it to be flexible and ready for adventure.

Kairos: The Corn Dog Compromise

When Jared proposed this spring, he had a wedding date in mind: July 4. Beyond the general delight, I was also delighted he'd already thought of the date. I was game for the holiday wedding— we'd have anniversary fireworks forever!

The venue that first came to mind was Plaisance Ranch, a vineyard owned by dear people Jared and I both know. I had also written wine labels in poetry for all of Plaisance's vintages.

Perfect! I thought, *we'll have a wine and cheese reception.*

Thing is, my now-husband is more of a beer-and-corn-dogs guy (though we've also shared plenty of wine and cheese). Still, I thought he was joking when he said he'd like corn dogs as appetizers at the reception. Beer in addition to the wine, of course. But corn dogs? That would mean renting a deep-fat fryer, and…it kinda clashed with my vision. But I had someone else's vision to consider, too.

Enter our first compromise.

Just after the proposal, we were talking with Sam & Cathy Pennington, who had helped introduce us once upon a time at their bakery farm stand. They make a wow version of pigs-in-a-blanket, complete with honey mustard and cheese baked into the pastry crust. Cathy suggested, "How about we make little piggies and put them on a stick, and you can call them corn dogs?"

Wisdom from a woman married for decades.

The resulting elevated corn dog was our Third Thing: the thing neither of us came up with individually, but which came about by working together—kickstarted by a dear friend. We had no clue how much of marriage would be about coming up with the Third Thing. We had even less of a clue that in moments when we want to argue for My Thing vs. Your Thing, we could get excited about creating something better than either: the *Third* Thing.

In fact, "My Thing vs. Your Thing" is really "My Expectation vs. Your Expectation." And we get stuck on the versus.

I certainly had more than a few expectations about marriage that weren't playing out like I'd thought they would. Which wasn't bad or good. Just different from what I expected.

God—bless Him—hears a lot of whining from me when My Thing isn't happening. Yet marriage is exposing the holes in My Thing(s) and reminding me that neither a "thing" nor marriage is the source of my joy. Instead, as Alexander Schmemann writes: "marriage will be a procession hand in hand…not always joyful, but always capable of being referred to and filled with joy."[13]

Matrimony was also teaching my husband and me to figure out not just what worked for each of us but for *both* of us. And not necessarily what our culture would tell us should work.

But before we knew all that, we served "corn dogs" at our wedding. One of the moments I asked the photographer to capture was us biting into a corn dog together. It's more important to me than the traditional feed-each-other-cake photo. This, we made possible together.

A symbol of many Third Things to come.

May they be sweet—or at least savory!

Chronos: August

One month married. So much learning in thirty days. I keep looking over at Jared and saying, "Hey, we're married!"

For our one-month-anniversary, we went to the Growers' Market and then…dishwasher shopping. The dishwasher in Jared's house finally died, and we found one of the last new ones in the valley, due to coronavirus shutdowns and backlogs.

After, we drove to the Smith River and hiked a bit of the South Kelsey trail—which apparently continued indefinitely far above the river. Jared kept suggesting we trailblaze down through the thick underbrush to the water. I kept suggesting we didn't…until we came to a sizable creek. I figured my least thorny option was to boulder down, so that's what we did.

We emerged at river-level to find a fairytale pool of blue. We immediately stripped down, left our stuff on the bank, and swam across to a sunny rock. We spent a couple of hours there, alternating between cold water and warm stone.

Eventually, I asked: "So. One month married. How's the state of the union for you?"

He thought for a moment, stretched out on the rock, and said, "It feels like a healthy relationship."

I wasn't entirely sure how he would define healthy. But then, I wasn't entirely sure how to answer my own question, either. Maybe we are creating our own version of health, together.

> Or to render time and stand outside
> The horizontal rush of it, for a moment
> To have the sensation of standing outside
> The greenish rush of it

—from "Time and Materials" by Robert Hass[14]

◆ ◆ ◆

Whiskey & RITZ communion on the Applegate River. Jared steered me on the stand-up paddleboard to our spot beneath the rapids. He told me that rapids aerate the water, cleaning it, so being below rapids is better than above them. I love his knowledge of wild things.

Field grass lay brittle blond in late-summer heat, but the banks had stayed a lush green. We sat side by side at the shore, the river a rushing hum.

We first took communion together with whiskey back when we were dating. I don't think I'd ever had spirits for communion—just grape juice or wine. But then spirits, spirituality...why not?

I should pause here to explain communion if a reader is unfamiliar with it. A very oversimplified explanation: communion is Eucharist—the two names are mostly synonymous. And Eucharist is a sacrament of union with God—holy communion.

The act of receiving communion involves remembrance, gratitude, prayer, and the elements of bread and wine (or maybe whiskey). We remember the broken body of Jesus with bread, and we remember the blood He shed with wine. In communion, we are receiving divine forgiveness and healing. What was broken is made whole. This miracle is a great gift, and receiving it together is one of my favorite parts of our marriage. When we pray, I get to hear Jared's heart for God, and he gets to hear mine.

Communion is a time to leave all offenses behind us. I think of it as a kind of heart-reset.

Many years ago, I attended a school of supernatural ministry. One of the first things I learned there was that we can choose to become unoffendable—a supernatural miracle itself!

Communion reminds us that our offenses—and those of others—have been forgiven. Yet we can so easily forget.

In fact, here I was, about to forget and get all offended, once again....

◆◆◆

Riverside dinner picnic with Pete & Niesje at Pierce Riffle on the gravel bar...with Ron's Gravel Bar Cabernet—one of the twelve bottles Christina gave us for our wedding. Usually, Ron labels his homemade wine with masking tape and a Sharpie. But Christina had created a label for each bottle from photos of Jared and me or paintings I'd made related to us.

That case of wine was one of my favorite wedding gifts. Not least because I'd once dreamed of having my art and writing on a wine label. For my 37th birthday, I held a solo art show at a Jacksonville winery I love. I had never married, and I decided: why wait for the big party? So I invited all my friends and family. It was splendid. Live music by Jeff, a luscious chocolate raspberry cake by Hayley, and the wedding ring of my late Grandmother (I'm a hopeful romantic).

For a gift that night, Christina brought me a bottle of Ron's red wine labeled with a sticker she had made of my art show's signature painting. It was a dream come true. And though Jared and I were no longer dating at that time, he came to the gathering as a friend.

Back to the gravel bar on the Rogue River....

The wine bottle I brought that evening featured a label with the painting I'd created for our engagement: two people's faces partly overlapping. When I opened the bottle to breathe, a drop of wine rolled down the image and stopped, mid-cheek on the man's face. But *I* was the one who'd just been in tears, moments before our friends arrived.

When Jared had walked in the house from work earlier, I'd said hello with a big smile, gave him a hug, and let him decompress as needed. He hung around in the kitchen.

I had packed up the dinner picnic and was washing dishes, silently annoyed for the zillionth time at the lack of a drain cover over the garbage disposal, which sent debris flying across the sink and me every time I used it. As I was washing, a jar lid fell in, and I fished it out. Jared said that in all the years he'd lived here, *he'd* never needed a sink cover, and *he'd* never dropped anything in.

That is all he said to me after being gone all day, after I gave him space when he came home, and after had I prepped and packed up an entire picnic dinner: the picnic part being his idea—a lovely one, but a lot more work to haul than to serve on the dining room table.

I tried to focus on the last dish in the sink and not the sinking feeling in the pit of my stomach.

What I wish I'd known in that moment is this bit from *Loving Bravely:* "Your curiosity holds healing power."[15] Instead of being instantly hurt when my husband says something I perceive as critical, what if I wonder not just why he said it...but why I react to it the way I do? (Hint to Past Me: it had to do with my True Self vs. False Self. More on that later.)

We arrived to the river early. I was silent on the drive there, trying to gather myself together. Jared inflated the paddleboards for Pete

& Niesje to play with. I let a few tears slip out as I set up camp chairs and the "deconstructed salad" of grilled chicken, carrots, zucchini, green beans, and corn-tomato-basil-relish. Plus watermelon for dessert. I had just uncorked the wine to breathe when Jared returned and apologized for his comment about the drain.

I thanked him for saying so, adding, "That means so much. Especially since we don't see each other all day, and then, if the only thing I hear is negative...."

Just then, we spotted our friends on the shore, so I didn't finish my lament. Just as well. We all ended up having a real and deep conversation about relationships. Pete asked us our favorite thing about being married. I said there are big things but lots of little things—like when we kiss goodbye before Jared leaves in the mornings.

Jared said one of his favorite things about marriage was to walk into a place with me and to sit beside me. That I brought love into a room.

I found that beautiful, but I didn't understand why that was important to him. At the time, it felt more like what a friend would say than a husband.

Another thing I wish I'd known that evening: a man often feels loved when he knows a woman has his back.[16] I didn't even know what that meant during our first year of marriage. Later, Jared explained I have his back whenever I do things for him or support him—from making his lunches to sitting next to him at a dinner party.

It would take me a while to learn my husband's love languages, just as it would take him a while to learn mine.

So much mystery that eve', only a poem could help:

She aches.
And would have me think
it had to do with rivers.

— from "Living with Her" by Li-Young Lee[17]

◆ ◆ ◆

Jared invented a drink and called it a Gingerberry Sunrise. We enjoyed it at sunset with a post-river dinner on the patio. Jared reiterated what he told Pete & Niesje last night: how he loves to be with me. His blessing for the meal was full of gratitude for our relationship—in both the head-scratching times and the joyful times.

And he added, "If it gets harder, I'm good with it. If it gets easier, I'm good with it."

How about that?

◆ ◆ ◆

Saturday. We swung by Pennington Farms to say hello to Sam & Cathy on our way to camp on the upper Applegate River.

We ordered pastries and coffees and brought them out to the terrace. And then, long story short, "pastries" of a different sort came up in conversation—a kind of mixed bag of unaddressed grievances, mostly mine, and none of them sweet.

It started when I asked Jared a question. He said nothing. So I asked another question. Then another.

A generalization I wish I'd known: when you ask a man a question, give him time to respond. Don't ask another question that will distract him from trying to answer the first one. And certainly don't keep asking questions to the point that he gives up because he can't even remember what the first question was.[18]

Alas, I did not know that, so I took my husband's silence as not valuing my questions, plural.

It made for a perfect pastry storm…and I let the flakes fly.

Jared listened in silence. And then stayed silent for ten, full minutes as I waited. Ten minutes is an eternity when you don't understand that someone is processing information differently from you.

Finally, he asked what I wanted to do.

I knew he meant this literally—as in, what action did I want to take—and so I said, "Let's go to the river."

I thanked him for listening, reminding myself that he would respond when he was ready. Regardless of his future response, a weight had lifted from my spirit.

Jared found a wonderful camp spot, as always. Nearby, a creek waterfall flowed into the Applegate just above where it plunged down into boulders. We rested in a little rock pool above the convergence. Time slowed. The afternoon spread wide and kind. Jared entertained himself by tossing his stainless-steel water bottle up the little waterfall and watching which rivulet it would take as it plunged down the twelve-foot waterfall, after which, he'd jump down into the pool and fetch it.

Eventually, he came to sit beside me and said, "So, I've expedited my thought process."

He addressed each of the "pastries" I'd brought up earlier. He was considerate and asked me to forgive him. I felt heard and seen and cared for. In that moment by the water, I fell a bit more in love with my husband.

As the sun set, we listened to water and God. I imagined letting each of the "pastries" float away down the river, glad to release them. I remembered the last line of a Seamus Heaney poem I'd once memorized: "And on the riverbank forgotten the river's name."[19]

◆ ◆ ◆

Summer date-night rhythm: when Jared gets off work, I already have my swimsuit on, ready to go to the river. This time, a different stretch of the Applegate.

As Jared loaded the stand-up paddleboard into the Subaru, I noticed the thick layer of dirt on the car. I said, "I meant to wash the car but didn't get to it."

"Wash the car?" He shook his head, and on the hatchback window, he wrote in the dust: "Dirt = Fun."

I laughed.

At the river, we paddled up to a spot where blackberries hung in long vines of ripeness over the water. It was the same place we had once walked to in the brisk air of late winter. How much we'd grown since then. How much more we would keep growing.

Later, we drove to The Haul and sat on the patio. Jared's grace for the meal was a special one. He thanked the Lord for His faithfulness and for the times we've set apart to grow our union.

Amid the difficulties—or because of them?—I feel our marriage strengthening.

◆ ◆ ◆

Mindy came for coffee. I've barely seen her since Covid shut down the world, and Christina and I had to cancel the Deep Travel Paris workshop she was going to lead for us. Was that just this year?

I shared with Mindy some of the things I'm learning, the expectations I'm letting go of. She reminded me of the maxim: "Expectations are pre-mediated resentments."

Ah, yes.

After our usual hours of laughter, she headed home. As I cleaned up our coffee-and-cookie-fest, I thought about my pre-meditated marriage resentments, aka unrealistic expectations. These illusions were certainly fueled by Hollywood and historical romance novels: "You Complete Me" and "Happily Ever After." It helps to name them. And then to do a bit of heart archaeology—to dig around and see if those expectations were ever mine or if they came from invading hordes of cultural "shoulds."

From my own past research (read: casual chats with divorced friends), I found that differing expectations were at the heart of separations.

I think there are some basic expectations we *can* have about marriage: that there be kindness, that we build trust together, that we have each other's backs—even as we discover how differently we each approach those shared values. Marriage is about figuring out what works in *our* marriage. Not anyone else's.

And when my healthy expectations aren't met, I can let myself be disappointed. But I can take that disappointment to God—I don't have to barrage my husband with it.

I am learning to differentiate between what is my work to do and what is God's.

◆ ◆ ◆

Mellow Friday eve. Jared decided to wait and leave for Mill Creek Saturday morning, so he had time to install the new dishwasher. Which he did without reading any instructions. In fact, he only found the instruction manual when he opened the dishwasher *after* installing it; it was sitting there in the top rack. I love the way he can figure things out.

During our engagement, we'd talked about learning styles. Jared is a kinesthetic learner—he learns by doing, through movement.

I'm a visual learner—I need to read about it, see the words on a page, visualize the concept in my head.

Hence, I'm the one who has read way too many books on marriage since our wedding. But Jared has learned just as much.

◆◆◆

While the guys kayaked the river release at Mill Creek, I hiked the trail above. Midday, I took my lunch down to one of the boulder pools, along with my *Soul Mates* book. I am now as tan as I was while teaching in the equatorial tropics in another life.

Today, it was hotter than those tropics: 102 in the shade. When the kayakers returned, Jared saw me wilting in a camp chair and drove us further upstream to boondock on a stretch of river bank. Gotta love the rare day when your biggest annoyance is that even when it's oppressively hot outside, the water is so cold you can barely plunge into it without having a heart attack. Bonus: one dunk kept us cool until the sun went down.

Dinner was a watermelon-feta-basil salad and…corn dogs! The "real" ones. As in, from the frozen-food aisle of the supermarket. Defrosted on the car dash and heated on the camp stove. I took a participatory bite, but I stuck with the salad. I also took a photo of us and our corn dogs to commemorate our Third Thing. Jared happily ate four "compromises"—and even some watermelon salad.

◆◆◆

On my morning walk above the boulders of the river, an epiphany stopped me in the middle of the path; I married a man who likes a challenge, and he married a woman who is one!

◆◆◆

This evening, I opened a bottle of Trader Joe's bargain-brand organic rosé. I offered Jared some. He warily accepted and tasted it, grimacing, "Is it supposed to taste like that?"

I laughed and told him my friend Erin had seen the photo I'd posted of us eating corn dogs, and she had asked if my husband enjoyed rosé and brie with me. (She and I and our fellow *flâneuse*, Christina, had likely consumed our collective body weights in rosé and brie across years and countries during our gallivants in travel writing.)

After I told this to Jared. He said, "Yep. Cheap corn dogs and cheap wine. A great match."

I laughed again. The other evening, I'd had just one bite of corn dog. Tonight, he'd had just one sip of rosé. But we each gave each a try.

♦ ♦ ♦

Jared had planned to kayak after work and said he'd probably get dinner after with one of his friends. So I had planned to meet up with Hayley and Sarah, and we shared a laughter-filled evening.

I returned home to find Jared eating chips and salsa in his still-wet swim trunks. When I suggested a couple of quick dinner options I could make for him, he said, "You're gonna drive me crazy."

That is *not* a phrase of endearment.

♦ ♦ ♦

This morning, after Jared left for work, he texted that I was lovely and overly amazing—and he had been wacky last night.

First thought: Sweet of him.

Second thought: so he knows when he's acting like a punk!

"Wacky" referring to him standing in front of the fridge last night and telling me I was going to drive him crazy by offering to make him a quesadilla, while instead he grabbed the pound-block of cheddar with his dirty hands and bit into it, leaving teeth marks and black fingerprints I scraped off later.

Wacky, indeed.

Today, he didn't get home until after five, and I didn't know if he wanted to camp, so I hadn't loaded the cooler, but I had food ready.

Camping it was; Doug & Jureen would be there before us. So we loaded up and headed out after 6 p.m. To Bend. Almost four hours away. On a Friday when he's exhausted? Trying to figure this out.

On the drive up, I thanked him for the text that morning. He said he had a feeling I was mad the night before, but he wasn't sure why, and he was too tired to ask.

He apologized, in his way, by thanking me for keeping the fridge stocked with great food. How he's never had so many options before, and he was tired and couldn't think.

I reminded myself that neither of us can read each other's minds. Which is probably very, very good. And a very good opportunity to learn not just how each of us communicates, but to create a shared communication. Our own relationship language.

◆ ◆ ◆

> I am living
> a creek, writing a river.
>
> —from "Writing the River" by Luci Shaw[20]

After emerging from our tent this morning, we had breakfast with Doug & Jureen. Then the guys went off to kayak, Jureen went to a coffee shop to study a new teaching program for the school year, and I had the morning to myself. I walked five miles along the Deschutes River. Solo bliss.

We all met up for lunch at a bright little Mexican restaurant. Over margaritas, we talked about marriage—all the better because Doug & Jureen have been married for several decades. It was a magical, sunny afternoon.

Doug remembered asking Jared if he was going to marry me all those years ago. Jared had taken the question to heart because afterward he essentially told me: "If we're going to be together, it should be with marriage in mind, but I don't want to get married." And then he said, direct quote: "I'm not ready to grow up yet." Hard as that had been to hear, I'd been grateful for his honesty.

After Doug & Jureen headed home, Jared and I drove to the waterpark on the river, where he kayaked in the rapids. I spread a blanket on the lush green grass beneath a tree and read in the shade. It was an ideal, 80-degree Saturday at summer's end, with the crisp, cobalt skies of high desert.

I watched Jared fiercely paddling into the waves—a rare thing to watch him in action for more than a few, passing seconds since he's usually on a wild stretch of river. Even from the park shore, I could see his muscles working as he faced upstream, staying in the whitewater other people were inner-tubing down. When he was done playing, he walked up to my blanket. Standing there above me, his tan torso made an orange-red complement to the deep blue sky behind him. My favorite color theory.

As we drove back to our campsite, he told me that weekends away remind him how grateful he is to be married to me. I was so surprised, I closed my eyes to focus. I confess: there have been more than a few moments when I wondered why he *had* wanted to marry me.

He continued, "And that I wanted to be married to you—but I also needed to be married to you."

I thanked him for the lovely thought and asked what he meant by "needed."

His answer: "You fight for our connection with patience and grace."

The last of the horizon's apricot daylight faded, turning the pine trees into black silhouettes against the sky, and then blending them into night's gray.

All those years ago, Jared hadn't wanted to marry because he hadn't been ready to grow up. When he *was* ready to grow up, he finally found himself ready for marriage.

But now, we were both starting from marriage infancy. We both had a new kind of growing up to do that would probably mean some growing pains. My pastor parents, who have counselled countless couples, say that no matter how mature you are, when you get married, you start at "birth." Which means, in *chronos* time, our marriage isn't even old enough to walk or talk yet. And so, Marie Forleo's advice:

> To begin anything new or learn anything new means you will be a neophyte. You must go from outsider to insider. Respect that. Embrace it. Be willing to suck.[21]

And be willing to give each other grace. *Lots* of grace.

◆◆◆

On our way home, we detoured to East Lake, and I was excited to swim. But just yards in, the water blossomed with algae growing from the depths almost to the surface in a kind of underwater forest. I was wary of swimming through the slime, so I practiced using the stand-up paddleboard and just dunked in the clear shallows.

We read on the spacious beach. Picnic'd in the breeze. Speculated on a reason for the algae. Drove back toward the valley, sleepy, into a miasma of smoky skies from a wildfire far away.

◆◆◆

I invited my parents over to celebrate their 47th anniversary. After the meal, I served ice cream with some of the blackberries Jared had picked when we returned last night—berries macerated overnight in a dash of gin and sprinkle of sugar.

Mom mentioned how, in marriage, she had learned to be grateful for hard times; she knew she and Dad would grow closer. Another kind of maceration.

Things in my marriage are improving, though there are several "apples" rolling around that are keeping Jared and me from moving forward together. We need to deal with them before they start rotting.

◆ ◆ ◆

Jared texted to suggest we take dinner to the river and then head to the new house site to share communion.

I replied, "Great. I'll turn on the grill." He texted a gif of Cary Grant dancing.

Be still my heart! (I had once mentioned I love old Cary Grant movies.)

We grilled the burgers and packed up all the makings and hauled them to a tiny, sandy river spot by Gold Hill. We ate burgers with cheddar, bacon, avocados, tomatoes, sunlight.

Then to the land, where the house foundations have been set. They are so tall—I forgot what a slope the house is set on. The views are better than I thought.

We sat side by side at what will be floor level of the kitchen and shared our first communion on the land. Jared thanked God for having me beside him—and all around him—in this process.

◆ ◆ ◆

Another maybe-we-camp Friday evening. Where I prep stuff just in case....

I should note that Jared's decision to camp is often dependent on whether he'll kayak, which is dependent on river flows and the schedules of his fellow kayakers. I am learning to literally go with the flow—of rivers!

No kayaking this weekend. But after dinner, Jared *did* decide he wanted to camp, so he suggested driving to our new land and pitching the tent down by the creek. We brought drinks for the evening and coffee for the morning.

We sat by the creek in our camp chairs, ice clicking in our tin cups as the sun set. The bats flitted through the gloaming darkness. Jared asked how things were going at the old house. (I'm still cleaning it.) I said good—though I'm looking forward to the one we're building. Then I asked him what he hoped to feel when he first walks into the new house. His beautiful answer: peace and rest.

Not so beautiful: the "apples" in our marriage. And the fact we can cultivate the things he wants in the new house if we start to deal with "them apples" now. So I brought them up.

It did not go so well.

Poor guy. I know he's tired after a long week. But I've seen him drive hours after work on Friday and then stay up talking around a campfire longer than I can manage. Which I haven't understood. I later learned that his end-of-work-week energy is for *fun* things, and we can address serious things at other times.

But I hadn't figured that out yet, and when he didn't have the energy to engage intense dialogue, I indulged my tendency toward melancholy. Which looked like thinking of Pablo Neruda's poetry collection, *Twenty Love Poems and a Song of Despair,* and calling to mind a line from the single song of despair: "Oh farther than everything. Oh farther than everything."[22]

◆ ◆ ◆

In the morning, we sat side by side again, this time watching the sun rise over the mountains, lighting up the foundations of our new home.

Jared acknowledged the "apples" and that he's willing to work them out with me.

Looking out at the jumble of construction, I realized that his seemingly random suggestion to camp on our land had been divine timing. As had my unplanned lament.

There in front of us, rising from a mound of disturbed soil, was the beginning of our new house. Last spring, when we first camped here, this had all been a peaceful, lush green. Now, after the tractors and excavations and a leach field, it was a riot of ruts and dirt.

To build a house—and a marriage—we have to be willing to break ground and get dirty. It can be fun to pitch a tent in summer, but come winter, I'll be very grateful for this messy process. And for a husband who's good about playing in the dirt.

Kairos: My Hardest-Best Classroom

It's back-to-school season, but you might say I've been in summer school since July 4: the day I got married. I never knew that marriage would be my hardest classroom—but strangely my favorite. I also never knew that no matter how much reading I did ahead of time, nothing would compare to experiential learning.

And there is so-o-o-o-o much to learn. Such a variable curriculum, such a huge canon: love languages, personality styles, bathroom habits.

Still, I've never been more excited to study because what I'm learning is the heart stuff that transcends traditional education.

I couldn't prepare for marriage like I did in my student days—by plowing through the required reading list and plotting out the syllabus on my calendar.

I couldn't prepare like I did in my teacher days—by creating units and scheduling assignments all the way till Christmas.

So even though preparation is my strength, I find myself releasing the ways I thought I learned best.

And I am embracing every unplanned moment that arises. Like last Sunday. Jared and I made a detour to a lake after camping near the Deschutes River. The river was splendid, but he knows

I love lakes, so he suggested we find one.

On the obsidian-rich shore, we read aloud, napped, and played on the stand-up paddleboard. My play looks more like a wobbly attempt to not fall off. He can do a handstand on the thing… in river current.

He is learning to enjoy the stillness I love, and I am learning to enjoy the motion he loves. And we are both releasing our ideas of the "right" way to learn.

Couples' counselor Terrence Real tells his clients a truth so vital, he italicizes it in his own book: *"You can be right or you can be married."* [23]

At any given moment, we all might do well to adjust our usual learning styles. To be still when we prefer motion—or vice versa. To play in the dirt when we prefer to sweep up the dirt—or vice versa. To risk wobbling as we try for new balance.

Generally: to push the limits of our personal learning curves.

I'm starting to see that it's because of—not in spite of—our differences that we are on the trajectory for a master's degree in communication someday.

Make that a doctorate!

Chronos: September

While going through boxes of my old office contents, I found a batch of photo CDs. In an effort to clear out and condense, I'm copying the photos to my laptop and chucking the physical discs.

And so, today I dove into photos from a term at L'Abri—a theological commune high in the Swiss Alps. I studied and worked there many times, the last being winter of 2005-2006. I dubbed that season The Winter of My Discontent; I broke up with the man I thought I'd marry, then moped and coped by eating too much Gruyère cheese. In any photos from that year, I look a bit distant and unhappy. Except for one snapshot. My friend, Luz, captured the special morning she and Fallon surprised me by showing up at my chalet loft with strawberry scones and whipped cream: the day they knew I planned to reach 60K words on the first draft of my novel, *The Honeylicker Angel*. I was full-face smiling in that photo—was actually happy. I didn't remember that.

What I wish I'd known all those years ago...and what I wish I would remember on a daily basis: our brains are designed to be Velcro for the bad and Teflon for the good.[24] This old survival instinct might have served us well when we had to run from saber-toothed tigers and didn't need to "waste" energy remembering non-dangerous, good things, but it's not so helpful in the rest of life. Especially not in relationships.

That photo reminds me: my long-ago winter of discontentment

also had times of contentment—living in an incredible, intentional community of faith, working a profound, theological editing job, and writing my very own book.

I can still taste both the salty tears and the sweet strawberries. The two are not mutually exclusive. And all these years later, I'm so glad for how it turned out. And glad for the long game of joy.

I posted the photo in social-media-land with some of the above as a caption—including the phrase that came to me as I typed: "the long game of joy." My savvy writer friend, Lavinia, commented, "'The Long Game of Joy' needs to be the title of your next book!"

Aloud to myself, I said, "Hmmm, I *do* like that. I wonder what *that* book will be about?"

At the time, I still thought this book would be *The Marriage Menu.* I had no idea. (Releasing expectations everywhere—even in my own creative projects!)

◆◆◆

Jared and I double-dated with Alex & Rachael, attending Niesje's *Mountainside* album release at The Greenwood. The outdoor venue was straight out of *Kinfolk* magazine: heritage gardens, a stage beneath magnolia trees with lights strung in the branches, an open-air bar by the vineyard. I loved that Jared introduced himself to friends I hadn't seen since pre-Covid as "her husband," turning to me and smiling.

I had brought a large blanket to lay out our dinner picnic spread, and we all had camp chairs. I stayed down on the blanket. As the music began, Jared came down to sit next to me and lean his head against mine. And for a holy, gloaming moment, all was right in the world.

◆◆◆

I keep trying to let go of things—icky emotional things. What if I learned to not grab hold of them in the first place…and instead held on to what is good and true?

> But I know the hands, even knuckle hard, cannot
> hold up anyone. It is hard enough the way
> they drag their desires in front of them,
> wishing to caress or rest
> in a pocket, or simply be left alone.

—from "The Act of Letting Go" by Elizabeth Libbey[25]

◆ ◆ ◆

At a dinner with friends this evening, the topic of social anxiety came up. On our drive back home, Jared wondered aloud about why people get anxious. (He doesn't do anxiety—something that still baffles and impresses me.)

Having suffered from social anxiety myself, having friends who suffer from it, and being close to someone struggling with a far more serious mental illness, I am familiar with such things. I said our culture acknowledges our pain or injury if it's visible: like when we break a leg or gush blood. But mental suffering has often been misunderstood, dismissed, or hidden away.

I added that I got through some of my own social anxiety years ago by choosing a word before going out to a dinner or event— any positive word that I wanted to cultivate in my life. Like gratitude. If I felt stuck or had the impulse to run and hide, I could thank someone for something, or tell a story of gratitude, or mentally start a list of things I was grateful for. I was proud of that solve—it had saved me many times.

Jared tried to understand—despite also trying to argue me out of feeling anxious in the first place. Later, I saw that his way of caring was to try to fix the problem. But right then, I felt as if I had to defend my entire inner life. And I clung to my defense.

What I wish I'd known, courtesy of Alison Armstrong: "'Being able to let go of a righteous position is a key to creating partnership."[26]

That night in bed, after Jared had fallen asleep, God gave me a bit of advice: "You can be right, and you can still let it go."

This husband and wife would be wise to follow the advice of God and Armstrong.

◆◆◆

Chaos. Instead of girls' night at Hayley's, the Almeda fire. The nearby towns of Ashland and Phoenix and Talent are burning. The extreme heat plus once-in-a-century winds equaled a firestorm.

Jared offered our upstairs rooms to friends if they need a place to stay. He was working in Ashland where the fire started. Both Highway 99 and I-5 were closed at different intervals, and I wasn't sure he'd make it through.

He finally got home just after eight. We left the front door unlocked for our friends and went to bed. On the brink of sleep, we heard people arrive and slip upstairs.

◆◆◆

Jared's alarm went off even earlier than usual: 4 a.m. I couldn't go back to sleep—was checking social media for friends' whereabouts, updates, evacuation mandates, current blazes. I made blackberry scones while our guests slept. Couldn't write.

A few hours later, Mikey came down the stairs, looking far more grim than when he tells his hilarious Wisconsin stories around a campfire—a small, contained, happy fire. Not a fire that might have just consumed his house.

He situated himself with a radio dispatch device, listening for information. I made coffee and scrambled eggs. Brittany and three-year-old Ida joined us, and we all ate together. After, I went for a walk—both to let them have some space and to pick up some extra groceries if they needed to stay a while.

When I returned home, I found three more people sitting out on the patio—and a cat. I never actually saw the cat; it was on a leash hiding scared somewhere, poor thing.

Full house. Prayers for people's safety and homes.

◆ ◆ ◆

Grateful that all of our guests' homes are still standing, and grateful for our community, who stands with those who lost their homes.

Grateful to see the wooden floor joists on our new house—a blessing in the burning.

Grateful for gladness.

> We must have
> the stubbornness to accept our gladness in the ruthless
> furnace of this world.
>
> —from "A Brief for the Defense" by Jack Gilbert[27]

◆ ◆ ◆

Sunday evening catch-up. After dinner, Jared and I reconvened on the couch. He told me he'd been talking about marriage with his employee and had shared his surprise at how much the past comes up—past relationships, decisions, etc. He mentioned soul ties, which we had talked about before marriage. In fact, we had each met with a counselor to break off any past blockages to connection.* I am so grateful he values these things—which are

---

* See Resource 2 at the end of the book for information on soul ties and inner healing.

not necessarily logical or quantifiable.

I agreed that the unaddressed past can hold a lot of unseen power in our lives. And I took this opportunity to mention that I had gotten rid of the last few gifts I'd kept from ex-boyfriends.

I admit: it was a not-so-subtle hint that he get rid of the ceramic dishes his ex-girlfriend had given him.

◆◆◆

A random focus-on-the-positive: my husband's generosity. Without divulging exact figures or recipients, I will just say that his suggestion for giving to those who lost everything in the fires is most generous. I love how we can bless people.

◆◆◆

Whelp. Another catastrophe. Just relationship-level, not fire-leveled cities. Ironically, this skirmish happened the evening Chris & Shannon came for dinner to talk about their upcoming wedding ceremony, which Jared will officiate. Chris and Jared have been friends since high school, and it's a testament to Jared's loyalty that Chris asked him to do the honors.

Jared arrived home just as Chris & Shannon did. In fact, they all walked in together. I had set out a cheese board with various crackers, including Jared's favorite, RITZ. After we kissed hello, I pointed out the RITZ, saying, "I made sure to set out your favorite, since the rainforest crisps aren't your thing."

He said, "I like the crisps. At least they don't taste like the awful cardboard ones you've been setting out."

What?

I tried not to look hurt, realizing he was referring to an admittedly bland package of crackers we'd been given that I'd set out once before. Which I had not set out since…and which was why I'd set out the RITZ he loved.

So confused.

The evening was lovely, and we all shared good conversation over wild salmon. But silently, I was obsessing over the cracker comment.

I had not yet discovered this insight from Beatrice Chestnut:

> If you don't recognize the potential in others, give them credit for their good points, and appreciate the way they make efforts to love you even though they aren't perfect, how can you be receptive to the good stuff others want to give you? By focusing on what isn't there, you blind yourself to all that is there.[28]

I definitely wasn't focusing on the good stuff that was there—like Jared's loyalty I mentioned. I *was* focusing on the not-so-good stuff that that was there: the criticism and sarcasm. Which I decided I'd broach after our guests left so that it wouldn't fester.

Before we turned in for the night, I came up to Jared, hugged him, and suggested that maybe he could not criticize me, especially in front of others.

This time, he resisted. Apparently, he really *does* like the rainforest crisps (I can't keep track anymore—I thought I remembered him *dis*liking them). He had interpreted my cracker comment as sarcasm...and so had responded with sarcasm.

But I don't do sarcasm; its root means "to tear the flesh" and "bitter speech" and "to gnash teeth." In other words, it means *mean*. There's probably a place for sarcasm in satire, but it can cut into relationships.

Which is why it hurts. But Jared didn't think it should hurt. He and his friends exchange sarcasm all the time. I told him that may be fine with the guys but not with his wife.

No, we did not resolve our disagreement that night.

Yes, a fight started with crackers.

◆ ◆ ◆

Last night's ick dredged up a few more icky bits from recent communication fails. This morning I indulged in ruminating on them, mad about *all* the recent contradictions and criticism, unable to focus on anything good.

On weekends now, Jared is working on the new house, and I bring him lunch. When I arrived this afternoon, he had just listened to a Bethel Church sermon by Candace Johnson on forgiveness, and he seemed lighter.

I returned to the old house to bake shortbread and listened to the same sermon. I felt lighter, too. Ah, the beauty and power of forgiveness. Candace likened it to gravity; we can throw a ball in the air, but the law of gravity says it will fall back down. If we don't forgive, what we judge will come right back down on us. I started learning this in grade school. I am still learning it.

Tonight, when Jared and I shared communion, he thanked God for my relationship with God.

May we live this wisdom from I Peter 3:8-12, which I especially love in *The Message* translation:

> Summing up: Be agreeable, be sympathetic, be loving, be compassionate, be humble. That goes for all of you, no exceptions. No retaliation. No sharp-tongued sarcasm. Instead, bless—that's your job, to bless. You'll be a blessing and also get a blessing.

◆ ◆ ◆

Tonight: family dinner picnic on the land—specifically, on the new house's subflooring. No wall framing is up yet, so it feels like a great big, open dance floor.

I'd prepped chicken skewers with peanut sauce and had brown rice in the rice cooker—which was still crunchy when we left for the land, but which miraculously steamed to a finish on the drive, during which *I* steamed a bit because, for the third time, Jared brought up the "pickles."

Our builder, Ross, had emailed to ask if we still wanted the original "pickles" we had chosen for the house. Knowing that Jared didn't want to change any more details, I had unrolled the house plans to double-check what we had originally chosen. I then emailed Ross what I thought were the correct "pickles" according to the plans. And I cc'd Jared.

After Jared saw the email, he said to me: "We can't change the 'pickles.'"

I said I hadn't—I'd stuck with what was on the plans, as he wished. As I said this, I wondered aloud if we had printed out the new version of the plans. Aha! We had not. Solved. So I apologized for sending the wrong "pickles," said I'd write Ross again, and suggested I might get a current copy of the plans so that kind of thing wouldn't happen again.

Jared had continued to explain that we can't change the plans.

And on the drive to dinner tonight, he brought up the "pickles" *again,* reminding me that changing plans requires getting new CAD drawings, adds costs, etc. Never mind that it was over and done. That I had apologized. That I had sent Ross the correct "pickles." That my intent had been to honor the original plans.

[Jared would like to add here that he was trying to keep extra costs down. We now see how we got into a pickle about "the pickles": he was focused on the practical issue, and I was focused on the *delivery* of that issue.]

When we arrived to the land, he asked, kindly, if I needed to plug in the rice to the electrical box to finish cooking it. It had finished steaming. I had not. But I tried to because the word I had chosen for the evening was equanimity, dang it.

So I also tried to muster a good mood as we gathered to serve dinner. The setting was magical—as if we were up in the trees. Natalie and Abe took turns jumping off the creekside's eight-foot drop down onto the soft, tractor'd-up soil below.

We blessed the meal and ate. I sat cross-legged on the bare subflooring, picking at my rice, distracted.

Soon, all of what was now exposed to the elements would be sheltered with trusses and shingles. Hopefully soon, our marriage will also be sheltered with...I don't even know what. Maybe that's what we're figuring out with each of our disagreements?

Chewing on my chicken without really tasting it, I wondered: why is it that I apologized about a mistake that bothered my husband (the "pickles"), and he continued to bring it up, and yet he refused to apologize about making a mistake that bothered me (the crackers)? I admit I was still berating him for that in my head, my bad. But an apology would have wiped that hurt away. And yet my apology to him didn't seem to go through. What is blocking our exchange?

Something tells me we are acting and reacting from our own, past, private woundedness. Woundedness we are so accustomed to, we don't even notice it.

> After a while it becomes an old friend.
> It reminds you every day of how it came to be.
>
> —from "The Wound" by Ruth Stone[29]

◆ ◆ ◆

Desmond Tutu once said:

> Forgiving is not forgetting; it's actually remembering—
> remembering and not using your right to hit back. It's a
> second chance for a new beginning. And the
> remembering part is particularly important. Especially if
> you don't want to repeat what happened.[30]

The forgiven wound remains—healed, but a scar. Forgiven but *not* forgotten. In fact, remembering what we have forgiven and what we have been forgiven helps others heal, too.

When I started telling married friends I was writing a book about the first year of marriage, I universally heard, "Our first year was *hard!*"

Wait, *what?* No one told me that *before* I got married. It was as if everyone had a collective case of amnesia.

When I considered taking most of the hard parts out of the book, a wise and trusted friend said, "Please don't. Showing the mess is a kindness to people." As they say: our mess becomes our message. I did take out a lot. But I also left in a lot—with Jared's permission.

As I've mentioned, my goal was to write this book with honesty and honor. And so, over two winter months during our second year of marriage, I read an early draft aloud to Jared in the evenings. I invited him to add or subtract what he wished. That draft was far more raw than this version, and he was willing to let *that* go out into the world. Which reminds me how grateful I am for our complementary differences; if he had written this book, I likely would have suggested an overwhelm of edits!

(Despite my best attempts to get Jared to add more of his perspective to the book, he doesn't dwell on the past—another thing I can't fathom but appreciate.)

As we read through the book together, we bumped into a few things we thought we'd healed but which still hurt, so we forgave again.

We didn't want to waste our sorrows. And I wanted to share our "forgiven remembering" by writing it all out. Hence all these *kairos* thoughts dropped into the midst of our *chronos* year.

◆◆◆

I have been trying so hard to not focus on the negative all the time. Wait. Even my phrasing there reflects my negativity. Better to say: I want to focus on the positive!

◆◆◆

I remember Christina's observation about my latest poetry book, *Hope of Stones*. She said the poems prophesied my marriage—the building process of love.

Which reminds me of this passage from a lovely, illustrated children's book:

> I asked the carpenter,
> "What is love?
>
> The carpenter smiled.
> "Love is a house."
>
> "A house?"
>
> "You hammer and saw,
> and arrange all the planks.
> It wobbles and creaks,
> and you alter your plans.
> But in the end, the thing stands.
> And you live in it."
>
> —from *What is Love?* by Carson Ellis[31]

◆◆◆

Jared officiated for Chris & Shannon's wedding in a fairy-tale, forested dell. Bowery altar, wildflowers, planed-wood benches. An old clawfoot tub filled with ice and beer and wine.

Jared did a grand job. In my journal, I scrawled "ecstatic" during the ceremony…right after I almost fell off the planed-wood bench when he said that every time he looked down at his own wedding ring, he was ecstatic.

Ecstatic? I had zero idea.

How about that?

◆ ◆ ◆

We went to church for the first time since we've been married. The staff had set up a Covid-creative outdoor service in the parking lot, allowing the congregation to gather. We found a spot in the gentle morning sun.

Just before service, Jared and I were talking about the strength of kindness. Okay, maybe I was being a bit *preachy* about the strength of kindness. Then, as the worship team started their music, one of them opened with a prayer for God's mighty kindness. Nice timing, God.

After the service, Jared and I shared lunch at my parents': Dad's slow-cooker roast with potatoes on a perfect autumn afternoon beneath the walnut tree. Dad asked Jared about officiating at the wedding, and Jared mentioned what he'd said about his ring—how he was ecstatic when he looked down at it. He had also meant to add that each time he looked at his ring he knew I was *for* him. He almost teared up as he said it.

What a beautiful surprise.

I am beginning to understand that my being "for" my husband and "having his back" are what matter most to him. And a way he is "for" me and has my back is how he speaks of me with honor to others.

Some highlights from Niesje's transformational conversation about relationships:

Say: "When you do this, it affects me like this."

A riff on Brené Brown: *"I hope I'm wrong,* but the story in my head is…."

Be willing to be seen and known—even when it's messy. And not just *after* spiritual alignment. Enter into the mess *to get* aligned.

Our authority comes from what we conquer.

Expression of pain is important.

Conflict is an invitation to intimacy.

We can ask God to reveal issues to our partner—we don't always have to point them out.

Trust the nudge.

◆ ◆ ◆

Date night, and Jared was sweet—even called to see how I was and did I want Thai takeout?

Good & yes.

After dinner, we started the van conversion for our upcoming road trip—the honeymoon we decided to postpone until autumn to avoid summer heat in desert landscapes, especially since we'll be sleeping in the black van, which loves to soak up the sun.

Have I mentioned we share the van with Jared's brother? When Alex and his family use it, they keep all the seats in. When we use it, two rows of seats come out and Jared mounts a bed he built onto support shelves that are bolted into the sides and floor. It's tall enough under the bed to sit on camp chairs, though usually that space is filled with his bike and/or kayak.

As Jared assembled the shelves, one of the supports got a bit persnickety, and it took a while for him to install. And then my husband got a bit persnickety. He brought up our decision about "pineapple." Almost hilariously, we completely agreed on the "pineapple." But Jared made a sarcastic comment about *how* I agreed with him.

I addressed it on the spot without waiting to ruminate. And though I tried to do so with grace, it was a brief bravo. Because when I asked him why he'd said what he had, he was silent. And I forgot to give him time to answer. And then—you guessed it—I brought up past scenarios to illustrate my point. Rookie mistake.

It took a while to figure out that we have both failed to communicate: him by feeling comfortable telling me what he's *unhappy* about but somehow not feeling safe to tell me what he's *happy* about. Me by feeling comfortable telling him what I'm *happy* about but not feeling safe to tell him what I'm *unhappy* about.

We didn't go to sleep angry, but neither of us were happy, either. I lay in bed awake for a long while.

I'm surprised to discover how much of my mindset isn't positive. I may not *say* a negative thing, but boy can I *think* it! And though our words create worlds, our thoughts do, too.

The Passion Translation of Proverbs 17:9 would have helped at that moment: "Love overlooks the mistakes of others, but dwelling on the failures of others devastates."

This paragraph from Guy Finley would also have helped—which I wouldn't discover until later that autumn:

> Instead of blaming your partner for making you aware of

some limitation in yourself, you say—silently to yourself—*"Thank you. I didn't know that about myself."* With that, the miracle begins: as your usual resistance to whatever they've revealed in you disappears, so does their insistence that you change *because you're doing it...on the spot!* Now instead of reliving old resentments, a new kind of love grows between you. Effortless respect for one another replaces your demand for it.[32]

Goal: mutual, effortless respect.

Kairos: Serenity Now!

Throughout my childhood, the Serenity Prayer hung on the wall of my grandmother's guest bedroom. The words were carved into a wooden plaque and decoupaged with flowers. When my cousins and I had sleepovers, I always marveled at the prayer's simple, rhythmic request:

> God grant me the serenity to accept the things I cannot change, courage to change the things I can, and the wisdom to know the difference.

I wrote those lines from memory—that prayer has been with me since grade school. Even back then, I knew my life-long goal was serenity in a chaotic world.

This year, we need the Serenity Prayer not just as a decoupage over the guest bed, but as a cosmic light show illuminating our dark skies. It's been rough. The pandemic. The Oregon fires ravaging friends' homes just miles away. The upcoming elections paired with news cycles featuring Angry Everybody at fever pitch. And me over here trying to figure out how to be married. Some days, I just want to move to the Yukon without Internet, and some nights I find myself awake in the wee hours, whispering the Serenity Prayer over and over again until—much later—I finally fall back asleep.

Honestly, the more authentic version of that prayer often sounds like the character George Costanza from *Seinfeld* yelling, "Serenity now!"

We can yell two words.

We can whisper three lines over and over.

May we pray the prayers. May we also do the work to heal our own wounds so that we don't wound others from our unresolved pain and so that we can bring our healthy selves to serve a hurting world from a place of forgiven wholeness seeking to restore instead of retaliatory brokenness seeking to destroy.

And may we have a bit of serenity now!

How does a person gain the courage to love another human being? We develop it. We begin to face small challenges and we lean in. We seek wise counsel and learn. We start to face ourselves and identify our own shadow characteristics, some of which will be pointed out by our partners, whose close interaction with us will cause them to see our blind spots. This can cause us to feel terribly exposed, and we must fight the dragons of shame, draw upon the healing balm of self-compassion, and engage in some serious inner work.

—Chelsea Wakefield
The Labyrinth of Love

Your task is not to seek for love, but merely to seek and find all the barriers within yourself that you have built against it.

—Rumi

Marriage is a tough teacher, and we all have plenty to learn.

—Winifred M. Reilly
It Takes One to Tango

Part II: Marriage as Metamorphosis

Many years ago, I edited a book with the central metaphor of caterpillar-to-butterfly metamorphosis. At the time, I only knew the kindergarten basics of the process, so I researched it. I was surprised to discover that when a caterpillar is closed in its chrysalis, it undergoes a liquefaction phase—it basically dissolves. But what looks like goop retains the ingredients to transform a creature that crawls into a creature that flies.

In the first autumn of my married life, I entered a relationship chrysalis—and I oozed around in there well into winter. I have a hunch this is part of how the False Self transforms into the True Self: total liquefaction.

I should back up. I was also about to encounter the limitations of my False Self: all the constructs, illusions, fragility. All that is *not* my True Self. The wise Franciscan Friar, Father Richard Rohr advises: "Do not indulge or believe your False Self—that which is concocted by your mind and society's expectations."[33]

It was easier to indulge my False Self when I was single. I had developed plenty of nice justifications for keeping her around. But that's because I didn't have someone constantly mirroring her limitations back at me. Then…holy matrimony!

Richard Rohr also says that transformation is more about unlearning than learning.[34] I'd add that it's about unbecoming to become. Funny thing: as an adjective, *unbecoming* means unattractive. This is not a pretty process. But we've got to ask ourselves: do we want to just keep crawling along, or do we want to fly?

A part of the butterfly's metamorphosis I *did* know about back in kindergarten: just before the butterfly emerges from the now-transparent chrysalis, you can see it struggling. It looks so close to breaking through, you can even see the design of its brand-new wings. Maybe it could use a bit of help....

But if you were to "help" by breaking open the chrysalis, you would prevent the butterfly from finishing its struggle—a struggle that strengthens its wings so it can fly. And if it can't fly in the next stage of its life, it will die.

My father is a retired pastor. At one point, he stopped offering premarital counseling. He realized that there were certain struggles you couldn't prepare for before marriage—you just had to engage them. Instead, he had fiancées write a Fifty-Year Letter to themselves, detailing the values they wanted to have cultivated by their golden anniversary. Long-game thinking, that! And retired counselor Mom asked couples to take a personality test before they become man and wife. So when Jared and I got engaged, he took an Enneagram test (I'd taken one long before, though I hadn't paid much attention to it) and we wrote a Fifty-Year Letter* together.

We wrote that letter as caterpillars imagining wings. Whenever we read it, we remember that transformation is worth the goop of liquefaction. And something tells me there's more than one metamorphosis in marriage. I'll get back to you on, say, our twentieth anniversary!

But for now, we have the autumn. And lots of goop....

---

* You can find our Fifty-Year Letter in Resource 6.

Chronos: October

When I went outside this evening to dump a dead bouquet into the compost, I saw Jared stepping up onto the back porch. We kissed hello. As we hugged, I thanked him again for all his work, including assembling the van bed last night.

He pulled back to look at me with a puzzled smile and said he doesn't need thanks and doesn't get the whole thanking thing, but he's trying. And he's trying to avoid saying harsh things.

We sat outside for dinner as the full moon rose somewhere, unseen. Jared said he is fine with me sharing my pain. He is beginning to realize that his words can hurt me. He sighed, "But it's hard since I'm not into words."

I smiled and acknowledged the irony, "And you married a wordsmith."

Grace to you, my husband.

> Listen, love, I close my eyes,
> and even *that* makes sounds to reach you.
>
> —from "The Silence" by Rainer Maria Rilke[35]

◆ ◆ ◆

Let the desert road trip begin! I packed the largest RTIC cooler with…everything. Sausage and bacon and eggs. Sliced cheeses, salamis, dips. Peanut butter and cookies and brownies for Jared. For me: a fresh kale salad that will last a few days, kale pesto for when that's done, and then a bag of kale chips for the final days. "Strategery." Also, "kale'd it."

A few new trip hacks: a little basket of driving snacks under the back seat, within reach from the front. A metal bowl in the double-sided netting for washing dishes, a clothesline with pins for wet swimsuits, and a camp shower filled with water, just in case we don't find a natural water source on a hot day.

As we left, Jared asked me to grab a purple Sharpie to keep in the glove compartment. He hadn't told me, but he wanted to stop by the new house site and write blessings and Scriptures on the exposed wood framing. Hence the Sharpie—and a thick, industrial crayon, also purple, his favorite color.

While the sun set into the hills behind what will someday be our finished home, we wrote on the bare wood framing. Over the front entrance, I wrote Deuteronomy 28:6 from the NIV: "You will be blessed when you come in and blessed when you go out."

Over the kitchen window, Jared wrote Psalm 34:8 from the classic King James: "O taste and see that the Lord is good."

Only as we pulled away did I realize: the purple crayon was the one Jared had used to write out his marriage proposal to me. Which I read on the back of the framed print of our hand-sketched house plans…right where our house is being built.

◆ ◆ ◆

This morning we woke in the van bed, where we'd parked in a forest clearing somewhere near McCloud. Jared made me coffee—always sweet of him, since he only drinks coffee in the afternoon. I assembled our breakfast jars of yogurt and oatmeal and fruit, and we headed in the direction of Zion National Park.

While driving, we listened to a podcast on forgiveness. How it's not just a personal responsibility but a social one; what we don't forgive, we become…and then inflict on others. As the tall pines lining the road morphed into farmland, I thought: you could extrapolate that forgiveness principle to generational and global conflicts. Social responsibility, indeed.

Eventually, we found ourselves on Highway 50 through Nevada—accidentally. I thought Siri was routing us onto I-80 through Winnemucca. Oops.

This is the least-planned trip I've ever taken, and I used to help plan trips for a living!

But the bonus of being able to sleep in your van: no reservations or fixed destinations needed—just an old-school, hardcopy road atlas…after giving up on Siri. And the surprise of Highway 50, which turned out to be the cinematic "Loneliest Road in America." Sagebrush. Never-ending horizons. A naval base (in the desert?). Area 51 somewhere.

I had loaded up on audiobooks about relationships, unaware that this was *not* my husbands' favorite genre. [Jared would like to add that this is an understatement!] He was a good sport though. At one point, listening to *Your Brain on Love*, Jared asked me to pause the audio. The author had been explaining "the burden of gratitude."[36] Jared said that, as a bachelor, he had eaten out a lot and ordered whatever he wanted. He was learning to be grateful for a home-cooked meal, even if he might not have chosen the exact menu I prepared that day.

Ah, that explained a lot. And meant a lot. I had never thought of gratitude as a burden. A gift, yes. But then, some gifts come with a bit of a learning curve.

So much learning. Including the realization that Jared and I each had very different expectations for the day.

Jared, in a tone of excitement: "We're driving twelve hours!"

Me, in a low-key, questioning voice: "We're driving twelve hours?"

I hadn't known he wanted to drive all the way to Zion. He hadn't known I didn't want to drive more than six hours on any one day. I was impressed that we could acknowledge—even with a twinge of humor—that we can't read each other's minds...and that we can't get mad at the other if we don't communicate our thoughts.

Jared has a talent for finding camp spots on BLM* public lands. At a nice compromise of about nine driving hours, he found a dirt road up through sagebrush somewhere near the Great Basin National Park. As the sun set, we warmed a Pennington chicken pot pie in a cast iron skillet on the camp stove and started reading *The Little Prince* aloud. And then we sat and watched the seemingly endless sunset colors until the stars came out.

◆ ◆ ◆

At the Kolob Terrace entrance to Zion National Park, we found no ranger kiosk, no crowds. We hiked Wildcat Canyon Trail toward Northgate Peaks for a stunning panorama of the park's massive rock faces that we would be down at the base of the next day. A good overview.

It had been two nights since we left—and since I'd showered. When I mentioned this, Jared found the Kolob Reservoir on the map, bless him. It was at the literal end of the road, which rose far above the peaks we'd seen. Aspen groves shimmered in golden-hour sun, a visual symphony. At the reservoir, we slipped into the water—a gloss of reflective light so bright it was hard to look at. Cold and cleansing.

We drove back down to camp in a little gap just out of the park boundary on a western rise above Cave Valley. Jared found a spot with an unbelievable view, facing a massive rock wall that towered

---

* Bureau of Land Management

above the eastern side of the valley. As the sun set behind us, it lit the entire expanse of rock before us in roseate splendor.

Sausage & sauerkraut & stars. Reading *The Little Prince*.

Then lots of time to watch the sky. Earlier, we had also listened to a chapter of *Your Brain on Love* about how certain attachment styles react to commitment. That time *I* had pressed pause. I told Jared I felt a surge of relief that I wasn't crazy for feeling like he had changed his mind about "cheddar" after we married.

He said he remembered me talking about "cheddar" during our engagement—and he remembered not replying. This afternoon, he said he hadn't changed his mind; it's just that his thoughts about "cheddar" were different from mine.

I was surprised. Today was the first I'd heard of it. I said I had told him my expectations, but he had remained silent about his. So he knew both what I was thinking *and* what he was thinking, whereas I was at a disadvantage. I asked him to tell me in the future if he thinks differently—especially about the Big Things.

It took a while for the sky's light to fade. Since it's still high-risk fire season, we can't have any campfires outside of designated pits. When we're boondocking, that's a bummer, but tonight, I was glad for the full dark. I could let tears run down my face, unseen, mourning a personal dream.

Oh, how important to examine our expectations.

Well, we figured that out with a little thing like road-trip drive times yesterday, so there's hope for the Big Things, too.

> Be joyful
> though you have considered all the facts.

—from "Manifesto: The Mad Farmer Liberation Front,"
by Wendell Berry[37]

◆◆◆

Zion day: woke and went. So much for lingering mornings.

A day of emerald pools. Steep cliffs. Way too many fellow tourists.

We entered the main entrance through Springdale. Here we found all the National Park fanfare of hotels and gift shops and cafés and crowds.

We pulled into the shuttle parking lot, past a long line of people standing. I remembered reading that the shuttle up to The Narrows now required advance reservations because of Covid. But we hadn't known what day we'd be where, and we usually didn't have cell reception when we camped, so we were—contrary to all my norms—going to play it by ear.

I had a feeling....

So while Jared made sandwiches to take with us for lunch, I went to see about shuttle tickets. Sure enough: sold out.

But a rare miracle occurred, and since I was sworn to secrecy, I'll just say I got two tickets due to divine intervention. Which it was. Gratitude.

The Narrows is a canyon stretch of the Virgin River. In low-flow seasons, visitors can walk up the river into the mostly shoreless canyon—as in, literally walk *in* the river. In freezing cold water, anywhere from ankle to hip deep, slipping on rocks. I am not sure why people like to do this, especially since the river bed is crammed with other visitors, and you are all trying not to fall onto each other. *And* since there is currently cyanobacteria in the river: a neurotoxin that's hazardous if ingested, but apparently okay if you get it on your skin.

Eventually, we turned around and picked our slippery way back. When we finally scrambled onto dry ground, my numb feet hit the pavement in a flat slap—as if still trying to figure out how to balance on rocks but not needing to.

My favorite part of the river was a nondescript little cove and waterfall just off the walkway. We ignored the signs warning about cyanobacteria; we'd just spent hours in the water, what was a few minutes more? I'd worn a swimsuit under my clothes, and for today's "bath," we dunked in up to our chins. People looked at us oddly as they walked past. I was glad to be heading to wilder, less developed places.

We drove out of the park through the tunnel on Zion-Mount Carmel Highway in delicious afternoon light. By early evening, Jared had found a BLM road off the highway and a camp spot with views in all directions, broken only by a few junipers. The sand was cinnamon red and dotted with patches of miniature, sage-green cacti.

Striking desert places, these, but the elevation is getting to me. We are often at seven- or eight-thousand feet, and I've been feeling like I can't get enough air in my lungs. This evening, I got a bloody nose. But if that's the worst part of the day, I'll take it.

Dinner: sausage & kraut, silence & stars.

I woke in the middle of the night feeling like I couldn't breathe. It wasn't just the elevation. I climbed down from the bed and sat in the passenger seat with the door cracked open to the night air.

From dinner to bedtime, Jared and I had watched the sky in mostly silence. I'm learning to sit in companionable quiet in the evenings. It's just so different from my previous life of artists and writers gathering at the end of the day to talk and dream. For many years, I synced my rhythm to that night-owl set, some of whom stayed up until the early morning time Jared rises for work. I'm glad I returned to my natural morning schedule long ago. And maybe good silence is better than most conversation. Maybe.

In this landscape of canyons, I recall Terry Tempest Williams:

> I have never been as lonely as I have been in my marriage.
> I have also never been more seen or more protected. Love
> has little to do with it. Marriage is more sandstone than
> granite.... The weathering creates the redrock windows
> and bridges. Beauty is transformed over time, and not
> without destruction.[38]

On that lonely night in the passenger seat, I wish I had known that one day, I *would* feel seen in my marriage.

◆ ◆ ◆

I didn't sleep well and was glad for dawn. And for the unexpected delight of Lake Powell later that morning. We happened upon the lake's Lone Rock Beach with a whole swath of shoreline to ourselves. The air was warm and the water cool.

I announced that I was going swim out to the towering Lone Rock. I was surprised Jared wanted to join me—especially since he's told me he doesn't really swim. Turns out, it was the farthest he's *ever* swum. I was a synchronized swimmer in middle school. That was the one sport I ever liked, though I only do the breast stroke recreationally anymore—the better to breathe and see where I'm going. I might have felt a teensy bit proud of myself for doing one outdoor activity better than my husband. Especially since he's pretty much Superman.

Apparently, most people don't swim across this lake. Four different boaters and jet skiers asked us if we were okay. We saw fish flip up in the air, and Jared smiled and said he was going to be telling the story of how I tried to kill him by swimming him out to the rock. He laughed, adding that all those jumping fish were going to become piranhas in his retellings.

I smiled, "Laughing makes swimming harder."

We made it to the rock and back, *not* dying by piranha. On shore, we shared a picnic. We talked about humor: how we can use humor with love versus the sarcasm our culture has normalized.

How sarcasm often masks insecurity and an inability to find the genuine, relying instead on its counterfeit: something "funny" at the expense of others. Only a month after The Cracker Incident, and we can have this conversation. I was proud of us.

Then I washed my hair for the first time in a lake (earth-friendly shampoo, don't worry). It was strangely fun. I felt as if I'd washed away a few old ills as well.

Later that afternoon, we found a southern entrance into the Grand Staircase-Escalante Monument. We took a gravel road that went straight north through miles and miles of massive rock formations. Parts of the road were so washboard and loud, we had to turn off the audiobook—to Jared's relief.

Later in the afternoon, we came to a trailhead for Cottonwood Narrows, South. It turned out to be a slot canyon trail. We caught the last of the afternoon light dancing up on the high wall of it and took a shady walk through curvaceous sandstone striated with reds and pinks. We had the canyon to ourselves, and we ran our hands over the still-warm walls once carved by water. I've never felt such sensuous stone.

We camped beneath the sun-golden Grosvenor Arch. Again, we had the world to ourselves. Sagebrush. Red sand. *The Little Prince* at sunset. Here, the gloaming lasts an hour—the sky stays cerulean blue and the horizon line holds its orange glow even as the stars begin their nightly shine.

◆◆◆

Today we drove the last forty miles of unpaved road through regal landscape. Coming off the road corduroy onto pavement was like coming out of the rocky Narrows of Zion onto smooth paths.

A man walking his dog had told us about Lower Calf Creek Falls. It turned out to be a perfect little six-mile hike. Red-rock cliffs, petroglyphs, cottonwood-lined creek. And one of the best waterfalls I've ever seen: a 126-foot plunge down a sheer rock wall into a clear green pool with sandy beach.

I had posted a few photos of Zion yesterday when we had a bit of cell reception in a small town, and a friend commented that we should go to her sister's restaurant, Hell's Backbone Grill.

The restaurant is named for the rugged canyonland around it, Hell's Backbone, a spine-like ridge through the canyons traced by Highway 12. In places, the road *is* like a spine: just wide enough for two lanes, with endless views down off each side—a stunning, head-swiveling landscape in late afternoon light.

Hell's Backbone Grill is in the tiny town of Boulder, Utah, with only outdoor seating in the time of Covid. Hipster millennials greeted and seated us: micro-bangs-&-blue-hair, buzz-cut-&-Doc-Martens, respectively. A wiry young man with a mandala mask served us, bowing with every sentence.

I ordered a house cocktail, the Highway 12 Old Fashioned—with bourbon, angostura bitters, and juniper berries. We enjoyed scrumptious local fare and scrumptious evening sunlight shimmering through cottonwood leaves. The sun was low in the sky when we left. We decided to camp back along Highway 12; there were plenty of pullouts, and though we'd be right near the road, hardly a car drove it at night, and the views were too phenomenal to miss.

We found a spot and set out our camp chairs. Inspired by my dinner drink, I picked a few juniper berries for future cocktails.

We watched the sunset spectacle—over an hour of shifting skies as clouds rolled in, catching light and casting shadows deep into the canyons. Amber and ruby, umber and blue.

Next to my husband but alone with my thoughts, I felt as if I were watching a time-lapse film of my past and present spirit seasons: the dark swaths just as beautiful as the glowing moments. All of them brush strokes in a composition of hope.

I reminded God of all the prophetic words about my husband and marriage that I'd received from strangers across multiple continents and decades. In a way, marriage was my life-long-awaited "Promised Land."

And then God reminded *me* of something from the Book of Numbers. The Israelites were about to enter their Promised Land. God told Moses to instruct them to drive out all the inhabitants and their idols; whatever they didn't take out would become a thorn in their side. I saw a new marriage metaphor: those inhabitants we need to take out? Our False Selves.

When we enter marriage without taking out all that is false—and the idols those False Selves have created—we are going to have some serious, thorn-in-our-side trouble. Thing is, until we advance into our Promised Land, we don't even know what hindering inhabitants and idols are to be found there. Perhaps it is the very act of stepping into our promise that begins to reveal and heal all that is false. Perhaps our Promised Land also carries this promise: as we continue farther into it, we continue finding the hindrances we would never have discovered had we not kept pressing forward.

Later that night, I woke from nightmares. I think some of my False Selves were afraid the gig was up and were trying some diversionary tactics. Trying to shake off the bad dreams, and brinking between sleep and wakefulness, I suddenly had a vision of coming to a large cement wall in the dark of night, having walked a long while. Discouraged, I didn't realize the "wall" was the base of a huge bridge I was standing beneath…but wouldn't see until dawn.

Maybe what seems an impassable blockage is the foundation for crossing to higher places. And when we're standing in the dark, we can grow the grace to wait for the light.

◆ ◆ ◆

To watch the sunrise, we moved our camp chairs to the other side of the backbone road. As with last night's sunset, the clouds made a light show of the sky. And this morning, a rainbow spread across the canyonlands. Rainbow: symbol of promise.

After breakfast, we drove to Bryce Canyon National Park. We arrived to translucent, mid-morning light on the surprising rock erosions called hoodoos. These craggy red columns reach up from a curved valley floor that's shaped like a massive amphitheater. We hiked the Rim Trail along Sunrise Point to Bryce Point, the light changing as we went, the hoodoos casting shadows like a thousand sundials.

By early evening, we were back on Nevada's Highway 50. We camped just across the highway from where we had camped on the way out—another lovely, juniper-tree-encircled spot. Another evening read from *The Little Prince* facing the rim of Great Basin National Park. Another swath of silence and stars.

I decided that silence can be a good time to talk with God.

> What is essential is invisible to the eye.
>
> —from *The Little Prince* by Antoine Saint-Exupéry[39]

◆ ◆ ◆

The one relationship audiobook Jared enjoyed: Rob & Kristen Bell's *The Zimzum of Love*. The ancient Hebrew word *zimzum* refers to the space God made to create humanity, and the authors use it to describe the space love makes between two people in marriage.

I'm all about the space between. (In fact, I titled my first book of poetry *The Space Between*.)

Notes scrawled while listening to *The Zimzum of Love* on the road:

> What are you seeing that I'm not seeing, and how can you help me see that?

See conflicts as opportunities for bonding.

You are always figuring it out.

We are quantumly entangled in marriage.

Forgiving means to send away. It's a decision and a process.

Everything that comes our way is an opportunity to find God in new ways.[40]

It was the perfect point in the trip to listen to a little book that touched on all the truly Big Things—the spirit things.

And it would be part of the night's breakthrough.

Heading toward the Steens Mountains, Jared asked me to text Chris & Chelsea for things to do in the area. Among their recommendations was the Alvord Desert.

We decided to check it out. We drove north from Fields, and soon we saw it—a massive expanse of flat white. The desert is actually a playa lake, and it's magical: chalky and cracked on top but hard enough to drive on. We scoped out the shore, deciding to skip the crowded hot springs on the easily accessible side and drive clear across the playa instead. As we drove, the black van left a plume of white in its wake, like Mad Max on the moon.

We had most of the far shoreline to ourselves—the closest car barely a dot way down south of us. We hung the camp shower on the van's back ladder and tag-team showered. Up until that point on the trip, we'd bathed only in rivers, lakes, and creeks. Technically, the Alvord is a dry lake—we just bathed *at* it instead of in it.

The sunlight on the playa was so diffused, it looked like mirage-heat light—as if it should be 100 degrees. Instead, it was in the mid-70s and balmy-soft. We moved the van away from the puddle we'd created with the camp shower, noting that it was a good thing the forecast rain wasn't until the next day—it would be impossible to drive across the lake if it softened into deep mud.

My hair dried in the gentle breeze. The sun began lowering into the mountains. We ate, you guessed it: sausage—with a side of garlic green beans. After, we read *The Little Prince* as the sun set. Of all the landscapes we've seen on the trip, this lunar one was the most perfect match for a book about a boy who lived on a planet far, far away.

Before full dark, we boiled hot water for toddies to take on a walk beneath the stars. We hadn't had a single campfire on the trip. Well before we left, I'd tried to find a portable fire pit, but with Covid-related backlogs, no luck. Instead, a few nights into our journey, I'd started setting a cluster of LED lights on the picnic basket each evening. I was glad I left them on as we walked into the moonless dark. It didn't take long to turn around and not be able to see the shoreline at all, except for the tiny twinkling of those lights. And then further: nothing.

Zero light pollution meant a panoply of stars. It was otherworldly bliss to stand beneath them together. But after a few moments, Jared brought up the subject of awnings over the back doors on the new house; he wanted to know what I was thinking for them. I couldn't talk about practical house details out here in this heavenly landscape. I told him I'd think about it and then warmly suggested we enjoy the stars. He was silent. It was an odd reversal of the usual: this time, *he* wanted to talk at night and I didn't.

After a while, I got thirsty for water, so I said I wanted to head back for some. He was silent.

I started back, glancing over my shoulder to see him following. Next glance, he was several paces behind. By the time I was close enough to see the LED lights, he was nowhere to be seen. I called out, nothing. Strange. But since I had no idea where he was behind me, I continued toward the lights. Once next to the van, I called out again. I drank water and called out. I brushed my teeth and called out again. And again.

I felt sad. And then I felt abandoned. And then I started to cry.

Eventually, I saw a dark shape approach. My question came out at an almost wail, "Where *were* you?"

He reached out and hugged me but said nothing (even in my angst, I gave him silent kudos for holding me—something I'd told him helps when I feel a distance between us). But after a moment, I backed away and asked again why he'd left me out there. He said he hadn't left; *I* had left.

I retorted that I had let him know what I was doing—but he hadn't let me know what *he* was doing. As has become an annoying norm, he knows what he is thinking *and* what I am thinking. But because he doesn't tell me his thoughts, I only know my own and so am operating on limited information, and why can't he communicate already?

There were a few more dead-end rounds of this.

We were about to learn this truth from *The Labyrinth of Love*:

> In highly invested arguments, we are never arguing about what we are arguing about. We would need to look deeper to discover what the real issues are. When the argument gets heated, you can be sure that you are wrestling with ghosts of the past—shadow-boxing.[41]

After another round of our yadda, yadda, yadda, Jared headed for bed. But we were still at it. As I was getting undressed, he said from the bed, "You know what I think the issue is? I think you have abandonment issues."

I heard echoes of the *Zimzum* book and the "issue behind the issue." *Ha!* I said to myself.

Aloud, I said, "Ha! I was one of the most nurtured children I know. I have *zero* abandonment issues."

But then something in my spirit shifted. I said, "You know what?" I *do* have one abandonment issue. I felt abandoned by *you* years ago."

Shadow boxing, indeed.

I crawled into bed next to him and wrestled with the covers. I did *not* want to, but I said, "I'm sorry if I hurt you tonight."

The apology softened my heart. I continued, "And I need to ask you to forgive me. I think I'm still holding on to resentment that you walked away all those years ago. I thought I'd dealt with it all."

I guess I hadn't. Because up came a forgotten pocket of pain that burst open there in the desert. I simultaneously burst into tears. The deep, ugly, heaving kind.

I sobbed. He held me.

I told him I had known he was the one way back then. How much his leaving had hurt. How mad I'd been at him, at God.

More sobs.

Finally, quietly, came Jared's voice in the dark. "I think the greater issue behind this is that I need to ask you to forgive *me*."

When I heard those words, it felt like time expanded, like I had more air in my lungs, like a blockage in my heart had dissolved.

I took a deep breath with a new sense of spaciousness. I said I had forgiven him, many times, but I did it again.

We held each other until we fell asleep.

The Zimzum of Love mentioned that the root of the word *forgiveness* means "to send away." Earlier, Jared had said that when things came up, he brought them to God, forgave, and then "threw them away." My version is to "let go." But Rob Bell gave us a grand midline: "to send away."

◆◆◆

This morning, Jared whispered so softly, I had to ask him twice to repeat it: "I'm so glad to be married to you."

We made up and made love before the rain came.

The married authors Harville Hendrix & Helen LaKelly Hunt write about the "Space Between" man and wife. It is a sacred space:

> You might liken this zone to a river that runs between you. You both drink from the river and bathe in it, so it's important that it be free from garbage and toxins. Your interactions in the Space Between determine what you experience inside. To keep the water running clean and pure, you must stop filling it with criticisms and hurtful comments and replace them with respectful, safe interactions. You must move from self-care to caring for this Space Between.[42]

I like that river metaphor, but when I think about standing on either side of a body of water, it feels like a barrier. Maybe instead of a thing that runs between us, the river is something we each run into. I used to call this convergence. But now I like confluence better, especially since the Latin root of confluence means to "flow together." And there is still plenty of space between us when we're in the river together.

We are learning how to tend that space.

The clouds were already gathering at dawn. The rising sun shone behind us as we drove into darkening skies. On the way to Steens Mountain, the rains began. Had we stayed any longer on the playa, we would have been stuck.

Had we stayed any longer in the past, we would have been stuck, too. As with the day's rain, there would be more storms ahead of us, but slowly, we are learning how to weather them.

In the Steens, we found a trail and hiked a bit in the alternating drizzle and downpour. Jared initiated a follow-up to last night's drama. He said he doesn't get that I felt abandoned all those years ago, but maybe he doesn't get it because he didn't want me to feel that way.

It was good to listen to him, and I was glad to have learned not to interrupt when he opens up. He said that when we first dated, God had given him an open invitation to marry me. But he didn't want to get married. He said he wasn't mature enough at the time, and there might have been a lot of emotional wounding if we had married then.

I thought about wounds. Our background is the Christian tradition, which is all about the wound that heals us. Richard Rohr points out that, after His resurrection, Jesus returns to his disciples and shows them his wounds, and they are "dumfounded with joy." Rohr writes:

> Remember that resurrection is not woundedness denied, forgotten, or even totally healed. It is always *woundedness transformed.* You still carry your scars forever, as both message and trophy.... Pain transformed is no longer pain transmitted.[43]

Even if Jared and I *had* married earlier, even if we had wounded each other emotionally all these years, we still would have been able to transform those wounds. But I am grateful for what we each grew into. What we each fought for and brought to our marriage.

Back in the van, after scraping mud off of our shoes, we ate BATs (our riff on a BLT, but with cooler-friendly avocados instead of wilt-tending lettuce). The heavy rain ran down the windshield, and we were glad to be inside, even if we were a bit damp.

At some point on the trip—I forget which day—we had listened again to Candace Johnson's sermon on forgiveness. This time, another part of the message stuck: don't just forgive and release—also bless.

Chewing my sandwich, I silently blessed my husband and our marriage.

And then we were on the road again. After a long drive on washboard roads beneath roiling skies, we arrived to Hart Mountain Hot Springs.

A stroll away from the parking lot, a telltale wisp of steam rose from an unmarked natural pool, maybe ten feet in diameter. One couple was soaking there, but they welcomed us enthusiastically. I stepped in gingerly, landing alternately on black, squishy mud and hard, volcanic rock. The couple was a set of characters: he, a mason, she a self-described psychic. We were shortly joined by a golly-gee, mustachioed forester from Eugene and soon later, a firefighter from Ashland, who carried her can of mineral water on top of a can of craft beer.

Jared was game to soak for a couple of hours, even though he says he's not a hot springs fan. It was a good day for it: gray clouds, a bit of drizzle, but no more downpour.

To camp that night, we drove down a nearby golden aspen grove, the leaves making loud applause as the evening wind kicked up. We had just enough time to cook and eat dinner before the downpour came again.

I brought the twinkly lights into the van bed and read the last of *The Little Prince* by their starry light on the final night of our trip.

Our destination
is between suffering and joy, everything else is a road

filled with unending patience.

—from "Flyway" by Romeo Oriogun[44]

◆◆◆

Before dawn, Jared suggested we drive up out of the valley to the mountain ridge and watch the sun rise from there—and that I stay warm in the van bed. It was a childlike delight to be snuggled under the covers as we rode through the cold aspens and up the hill. He parked facing east and then made coffee in the van for me while I clumsily dressed in the finger-stiffening cold. Together, we watched the sun spangle across the entire wilderness plain. It was perfect except for the fact that the washboard roads yesterday had curdled the last of my half-and-half, turning it almost to butter—which was almost funny enough to make up for black coffee.

And then the long drive down the mountain.

We were back in the valley by midday, so we swung by the new house again to find more blessings written on the framing by friends and family. We walked around reading them, like the one my Mom had written: "Be revived and refreshed with promise," inspired by Song of Songs 2:4-5.

When we pulled up to the old house, Jared announced he was going to kayak after helping bring in things. So off he went, and I started the cleaning process.

When he returned, he said he'd checked in with Alex, and he'd be working a job site in Chiloquin all next week. He looked excited and started enthusiastically re-packing.

I stood there for a second before starting dinner. Well, not the return to rhythm I'd expected. But then: I'm surrendering expectations, right?

◆◆◆

Jared called from Chiloquin after work. Let's just say it was *not* the most romantic conversation.

> Love means to learn to look at yourself
> The way one looks at distant things
> For you are only one thing among many.
> And whoever sees that way heals his heart.

—from "Love" by Czeslaw Milosz[45]

◆ ◆ ◆

As I held my morning coffee, I told God I wanted a big, extravagant love—and though I know that's first with Him, I also hope to enjoy the flesh-and-blood version.

I acknowledged the fruitlessness of the yadda, yadda, yadda—both when Jared and I talk and in my own head. God suggested *yada*, instead, a Hebrew word that means "to know, to become known." To know Him and be known by Him: this is our deepest longing. This is the God-shaped hole in our hearts, and if we try to cram anything or anyone else into that space, disappointment is guaranteed. But the joy behind that disappointment becomes visible when we remember the only thing that *can* fill us: God.

So I guess I can be grateful for anything that falls short of my expectations. I can choose to say, "Well, here's a chance to invest in the truest, purest union—union with God."

Back to wanting the flesh-and-blood version of Big Love.... Though I don't have that now, God reminded me of the small but mighty word, *yet*.

And he extended this invitation: *yada, yada, yada.*

Then Jared texted me:

> Love you
> Psalm 139:5: He encompasses before and behind.
> His hand is upon you.

89

Marriage. What a way to grow our faith!

◆ ◆ ◆

Fun spontaneity: Jared came home a day early.

Fun planning: I'd prepped all the dinner makings.

He looked happy to see me and enjoyed the meatloaf, mashed potatoes, and apple pie.

Zero negativity all evening. Wait: I want to reframe that. Full positivity!

◆ ◆ ◆

This afternoon was a delight of a picnic and watercolors with my creative niece, Natalie. Achingly beautiful autumn day, maple leaves in their mid-October scarlet, skies bluest blue. We walked and sipped bubbly water and sketched the crimson leaves.

◆ ◆ ◆

While baking a batch of chocolate-chunk cookies, I listened to *The Seven Principles for Making a Marriage Work.* The author listed open-ended questions that spouses should be able to answer about each other. I don't think Jared and I would score so well! But I remembered that little word, *yet.*

And then I jotted down a few of the questions we can ask to get to know each other better:

> What are the three most special times in your life?

> What are your major hopes?

> What is your world like right now?[46]

But pragmatics first. This evening, Jared and I sorted through brick samples, gutter colors, wood stains, and railing options.

We are building a house. And we've only been married a few months. That might be crazy.

◆◆◆

Pork roast and root vegetables in the slow cooker—the last of the bachelor appliances I scoured clean. Then coffee and sunshine at GoodBean with Mindy. "Like old times," she'd said when suggesting it.

So much laughter when we meet. After talking art, we talked about men and women. How men are often black and white when it comes to emotions—with anything from anger to happiness. But women are often like the entire spectrum of gray paint chips at Home Depot where I was headed afterward to look for a good exterior gray for our house trim.

For all the women we know (ourselves included), even "moody" gets at least five colors, ranging from slightly moody to murderous.

An aside here on male-female stereotypes. By definition, a stereotype is an oversimplified, widely-held belief about a group, often based on unexamined assumptions. But sometimes, after examining those assumptions, we find that the stereotypes do apply. In the case of my husband and me, he is stereotypically male and I am stereotypically female. We each have plenty of friends who don't fit into those gendered stereotypes. But for the record, when I talk about male and female tendencies in this book, it's because those are very much our experiences.

In fact, many of our first-year marriage struggles came from male-female stereotypes. And as we grew, we learned how to expand and redefine those roles for ourselves. To be whole is to know both the strength associated with the masculine and the tenderness associated with the feminine.

Back to the GoodBean with Mindy....

I shared the beautiful story of forgiveness in the Alvord desert. There is power even in the retelling of it. Forgiveness runs so deep, so wide.

Julian of Norwich said that our wounds are our glory. Maybe showing and sharing them helps others heal their own wounds, too.

As I drove to Home Depot, I thought about how hard I've worked to know joy even while living with a constant longing. Am I more in love with the longing than what I long for?

Oh, the longing in belonging.

◆ ◆ ◆

I've been thinking about how the rough realities of marriage can remind spouses to keep their joy sourced in the divine and not in circumstance.

Thankfully, today's circumstances were good. When Jared hugged me goodbye this morning, I told him I'm so glad we chose each other. He said, "Yes—past and present."

"Good distinction. We keep choosing."

"An addition," he said, smiling in the dark.

That afternoon, Niesje came for lunch. We sat out on the porch and talked about the Enneagram.*

A PSA here: if you are unfamiliar with the Enneagram, it is a personality typology composed of nine different but interrelated numbers. It's also a relationship lifesaver, and I really wish I'd started diving into it before marriage. It doesn't just help us

---

* Resource 3 lists helpful books and websites for further Enneagram study.

understand ourselves, it helps us understand others. As we learn to use it, we identify our wounds. And it's the wound that heals us.

Niesje also shared how all relationships go through a continual cycle of infatuation, learning, disappointment, and decision. And then start back at infatuation.

Seems to be so.

I mused aloud that while Jared lifts physical cinder blocks, I lift emotional cinder blocks. His lifting is productive—the work of craftsman. My lifting is only productive if I alchemize my emotional work into art—build with it. If I do, I can also do the work of a craftsman. If I don't, I'm just an emotional ruminator who gets mired in the disappointment phase.

I admitted that my thoughts can often go nowhere. Second metaphor of the day: my over-active thinking is a spiral of thought-vultures circling the heart, looking for any dead thing to dive for.

Here's to aligning my thoughts with divine ones.

> as you walk inside the house, hope swallows you.
>
> —from "before the dark," by Adedayo Agarau[47]

◆◆◆

Poetry & pie date with my twelve-year-old nephew, Abe. While the pies baked, he asked me to teach him some poetry, and we shared several writing exercises. One of my favorites is the metaphor generator, and he came up with this fine example: "The awe-inspiring cottage of forgiveness."

May that be our home.

This evening, Jared and I took communion and prayed for friends and family. Long, thoughtful prayers from him. He humbly thanked God for everything from eternity's perspective of time to God's faithfulness. Very tenderhearted.

I feel a good shift happening. Jared mentioned he's been writing in his journal the things he's grateful for in our marriage. Ah, the power of gratitude!

It brings to mind Dr. Amen's advice:

> Focus on the times you have enjoyed with each other. The limbic system stores highly charged emotional memories. When you focus on the negative in a relationship, you feel more distant from each other. When you focus on the positive in your relationship, you feel more connected.[48]

Maybe, when we focus on the positive, it's a way of giving each other grace. Though I have a hunch there's something more to this....

◆ ◆ ◆

After a morning of writing, I had Jared's stepmother, Linda, over for lunch. She brought a bag of lovely little gifts—such a treat. It's good to get to know her more, and I like her can-do attitude.

Oh, another focus on the positive: I emptied the dishwasher and, as I was loading plates into the cupboard, discovered that Jared had removed his ex-girlfriend's ceramics.

How about that!

◆ ◆ ◆

Then my focus-on-the-positive fail.

Date night dinner was nice enough. We ate at the River Station, just half a mile from where we'll soon live. Over Jared's ribeye and my bacon-wrapped dates, I suggested we could be a cookie and

Cookie Monster for Halloween. He liked the idea and said I could get an ugly taupe dress and draw brown chocolate chips on it.

I laughed, raised an eyebrow and said, "I don't do ugly."

It was a great evening except for the fact that we somehow didn't get a chance to address "butter."

And I focused on that lack instead of all the other goodness.

◆◆◆

Okay. Instead of focusing on lack, I am going to focus on the abundant good things: Jared's mighty work ethic. His sense of humor. His faithfulness.

Wait—maybe don't just *focus* on the good stuff. Also be *grateful* for it:

I *give thanks* for Jared's mighty work ethic.

I *give thanks* for his sense of humor.

I *give thanks* for his faithfulness.

All of a sudden, I wondered: do gratitude and grace share the same root? I Googled it. They do—the Latin root, *gratus*.

We say grace for a meal.

We receive God's grace.

We give each other grace.

Say grace.

So it *is* more than just focusing on the positive. Giving *gratitude* for the positive is grace.

Unbeknownst to me, I was practicing advice I'd not yet read from Dr. Kerry Howells, who studies and writes about gratitude as a professor in Australia:

> Practising gratitude is itself crucial to the freedom of letting go of resentment, and not the other way round. In other words, the question, "How can I let go of my resentment in order to practise gratitude?" can also be phrased as "How can I practise gratitude in order to let go of my resentment?[49]

My old friend, gratitude, is the "something more" I'd been wondering about.

◆◆◆

When Jared came into the room this morning to say goodbye, I said, "Thank you for your love."

His voice was muffled in my shoulder as he hugged me. "I just have to continue to learn to show it." Pause. "It's in there."

Very good awareness, my dear.

◆◆◆

A laughter-filled Halloween eve at our place with Ben & Rebecca: salad, andouille sausages, savory squash galette.

I wore a little black dress with tan felt circles pinned to it (I decided I was a butterscotch-chip chocolate cookie). Onto one of Jared's turquoise T-shirts, I'd pinned crossed googly eyes and a half-circle smile in black-and-white felt—the classic Cookie Monster face.

But not a single trick-or-treater in the time of quarantine. Jared gets to keep all of his special-request Halloween candy.

Our first holiday season as a married couple has begun....

Kairos: Not What I Expected

Once upon a pre-pandemic time, I heard a famous writer say that when she looked back at her life, nothing had turned out the way she'd thought—and that wasn't bad. She said she could summarize what she'd learned about life with this simple statement: Not What I Expected.

I think that would make a great T-shirt.

:

This year certainly racked up more than its fair share of unexpected things—good and bad. I was scanning the calendar all the way back to the maskless days when I realized that so many big things I'd anticipated got cancelled, and yet even better things—things I could not have fathomed—happened in their stead.

Exhibit A: This spring, I was going to help lead a workshop in Paris and then stay on in the City of Light to begin the book tour for my poetry collection, *Hope of Stones*—continuing the tour in New York and San Francisco. It was kinda career-pinnacling stuff. And then, just a couple of weeks before my scheduled departure, the world shut down. But guess what? The day the workshop would have started, my now-husband proposed to me. And as grand as Paris is, even if I never return to the world's most romantic city, I have the chance to practice actual romance now.

Exhibit B: I had been invited to give a poetry reading and teach workshops at a college writing conference in Wyoming this fall.

One of those all-expenses-paid gigs poets dream of. The event managed to stay on the books all through the summer, but then…it was finally cancelled. The plan had been to drive out there with my husband, teach, and then continue our road trip. We wouldn't have had as much time to see all the places we hoped to visit, but we were going to make the best of it. Without the conference, we were able to take the entire time together— time that became so precious and relationship-building, I am grateful we did not have to give up a minute of it.

Exhibit C: Any moment now, I would have been boarding a plane to Sweden and then on to Latvia for a month-long writing residency. I would have spent all of November writing in a little village on the Baltic Sea. You guessed it: cancelled. But you know what? I'd almost forgotten that was going to happen. My life has taken such a different turn that many of the things I once wanted fiercely now seem like brief apparitions—like glimpsed prisms of light that all but fade by the time you focus on them.

I have no idea what November will bring instead of Latvia. And I'm not talking about elections or anything else one might expect. I'm actually glad to have no idea what specific goodness is on its way—I just know that something is. It *always* is; Goodness & Mercy are *always* at our heels. Maybe we just need to stop now and then, turn around, and acknowledge them. Something tells me those two are all the more thrilled to come closer with their surprising gifts when we're grateful for them. Even when they deliver stuff we never ordered.

Speaking of ordering, I'm seriously thinking about making that T-shirt. I haven't figured out what the back would say, but I might borrow a line from another famous Creator: "And it was good."

Chronos: November

November is here. My favorite month. I set out mini pumpkins and acorn squash and fall leaves and candles everywhere.

◆ ◆ ◆

An ethereal early morning—the full blue moon peering through the bamboo outside the bedroom window. Jared turned me to see it and said, "I'm so glad to be married to you."

I smiled, "Ditto."

The bamboo cast stripes of moonshadow across the room, across us.

I had known marriage would be hard, but I had also known it would be worth it. And somehow—in a way I don't think I'll be able to explain until we've been married at least a decade—I know it's worth roughing it out with this man I chose to marry. And I'm glad he's willing to rough it out with me, too. Strong man.

Aloud, I said, "I'm grateful for your strength."

I could see him smile in the semi-darkness, "Your brains, my brawn."

I laughed. "You've got brains, too—I just don't have any brawn!"

But I'm working on developing emotional brawn.

◆ ◆ ◆

We met the electrician at the new house to decide on light placement. Jared was mostly silent as we walked through. But later, at dinner, he kept saying firmly that when he was a bachelor, he only ever turned on one lamp in his house. Each time I mentioned a kind of lighting I enjoyed, he responded with "If it were just me…" or "When I was alone…" or "If I just had an apartment by myself…."

I interpreted this to mean that he was taking my lighting ideas as obstacles to his bachelorhood. And that he'd rather sit alone in the semi dark. This interpretation grew heavier in my heart the more I mulled over it.

◆ ◆ ◆

By dinner today, I was finally able to articulate a solution. I told Jared that lights are invitational to me—welcoming, hospitable. More importantly, I'd love to make decisions together as an "us"— not as if bachelorhood is the high standard.

Jared clarified that his single-lamp bachelorhood is no longer what he wants. He was just referencing what he was accustomed to, not his ideal. That, essentially, he wanted to be in the light with me.

Well that's lovely. And I was happy to be wrong. Yes: let's be in the light, together.

> and the sky as breath and the river
> as chant and the sun as aria
> aria for breathing and for loving
> aria for the dancing light & shadow
> light & shadow upon the dancing globes
>
> —from "Light & Shadow" by Anne Waldman[50]

I drove out to the land to bring Jared the house plans marked with the light-fixture placement we'd finally agreed on. The lot was humming with trucks and workers.

Jared stood beneath an oak tree, painting angle irons. He looked happy to see me when I approached, and he was excited to show me that he felt there would be plenty of room in the kitchen for a larger…let's call it "steak."

Except that, as when we'd last talked about it, I still wanted the "steak" a bit smaller.

This conversation did not go so well.

I tried to share that how a space *feels* is as important to artist-me as how builder-he wants a space to measure up in numbers.

I was clunkily trying to practice this advice:

> Developing the ability to experience the world through your partner's eyes, while holding on to your own perspective, may be the single most important skill in intimate relationships.[51]

But it wasn't working.

Neither of us understood each other's reasons, and for the sake of abbreviation, let's just say my reasons got mocked.

Finally, my eyes swimming with tears I did not want to shed on the busy construction site, I held out the plans to him and asked, "Can we do this later?"

He didn't say anything. In fact, it took a few seconds for him to reach for the plans. I left.

Many tears.

Many conversation replays in my head.

Verdict: that *sucked.*

That evening over dinner, we discussed the "steak," and I raised the issue behind it: *how* we speak to each other, not what we speak about.

We still had a lo-o-o-o-ong way to go to figure out that *how.* But a beautiful thing: after this hard conversation, Jared has tried to honor my love of beauty as I've been trying to honor his love of logic.

◆ ◆ ◆

Saturday. Jared left in a hurry this morning. I thought he was still miffed about our "steak" discussion.

Communication!

Only later did he say he'd awoken at 2 a.m., remembering he'd left his construction laser at the house. The laser is expensive, and he almost drove out in the middle of the night to get it.

But he had said nothing. Looked grim. The story in my head: he can't take it when I tell him the hard stuff.

Nope. Forgot a laser.

Lesson? Ask him to tell me things and don't assume the worst. Make that: expect the best. Maybe expecting the best is a healthy expectation—prophetic, even—if it's less about specific outcomes than how the outcomes can turn out best for all involved.

Later that day, I met Jared at the new house to look again at the "steak." I recalled this dialogue from *The Queen's Code:*

> "When someone is stating an opinion, catch yourself in
> the mode of agreeing and disagreeing. It will be there

because it is the human default. Then switch to thinking… 'What matters to this person?' Or 'What are they showing me is important to them?' Either question will do. Listen for their values, that expression of who they are."[52]

Before stepping over the threshold into the future kitchen together, I gave Jared a hug, and we agreed to have a do-over in kindness.

We still didn't agree about "steak" size, but we were respectful, and when we reached an impasse, we decided to wait to continue the conversation.

Better.

The game of marriage seems to require a lot of practice. And though practice might not make perfect, it makes *better*.

"Love is a practice."[53]

◆ ◆ ◆

Hiked Cathedral Hills with Christina and her dog, Guapo. I love these times together; our conversations stream through the trees. My two favorite revelations of the day:

1. When we remember that life's not about being happy, it's so much easier!
2. Men often don't feel enough and women often feel too much.

◆ ◆ ◆

No soul that seriously and constantly desires joy will ever miss it. Those who seek find. To those who knock it is opened.
—C. S. Lewis

I turn 44 today. Maybe the best birthday gift I could receive would be this advice I've always heard from Mom & Dad: don't take anything personally, and keep a sense of humor.

On my walk, I thought about joy—how I've been confusing it for happiness. Big mistake. Happiness is limited to what happens, but joy transcends what happens. The part of me that over-identifies with pain and longing forgot to knock on the door of joy.

To quote from one of my own books (funny how much we can forget!):

> Joy is an active choice we make. I like to distinguish happiness from joy. To me, happiness depends on a certain outcome or circumstance, but joy is independent of any externals—it's a heart-set. A choice.[54]

I had heard a version of this distinction decades ago but lost the source. Then, reading Brother David Steindl-Rast's book on gratitude recently, I found this perfect expression:

> Ordinary happiness depends on happenstance. Joy is that extraordinary happiness that is independent of what happens to us.... The root of joy is gratefulness. We tend to misunderstand the link between joy and gratefulness. We notice that joyful people are grateful and suppose that they are grateful for their joy. But the reverse is true: their joy springs from gratefulness.... For it is not joy that makes us grateful; it is gratitude that makes us joyful.[55]

I returned home in joy.

Birthday in the time of quarantine-closed restaurants has made me very glad I love to cook. I prepped salmon, asparagus, and mashed potatoes for dinner.

Jared said a lovely prayer—thanking God for me and musing how extra happy He was when He created me.

After dinner, we snuggled on the couch and ended up talking

about marriage and how we both dislike the ball-and-chain metaphor. Jared asked me to come up with something better.

What popped into my mind: marriage is like an expedition. You've packed all kinds of gear in preparation—things you think you need—but you only use a fraction of what you packed, and you leave a bunch of it along the way. The climb is hard some days, and at higher elevations, it can be a bit difficult to breathe. But each time you reach a point where the vistas open up, it's all worth it, and you're inspired to keep going.

Oh, yes: Jared's birthday gift to me: organic peach lip balm and a "Guns & Drugs" sweatshirt, both from our soon-to-be town's pharmacy—where one can apparently pick up Flonase and firearms. Rural one-stop shopping! My husband's sense of humor shined.

I don't know where I'll ever wear that sweatshirt, but I do know that "Expectations can be the true thief of joy when it comes to giving."[56]

Far better: Steindl-Rast's "gratitude that makes us joyful."

◆ ◆ ◆

When the author of *How to Be Married* climbed part of Kilimanjaro with her husband, their guide told them he'd seen more than twenty couples break up attempting to summit:

> "Climbing the mountain is actually a good metaphor for succeeding in marriage…. What you have to remember is that both the mountain and a marriage can be completely different in the afternoon from what it was like in the morning. You can't try to predict what any day will bring. Trying to predict it will only bring grief. You have to try to enjoy the parts that are wonderful."[57]

This was a marriage expedition day of good *and* grief. If I were to give it an emotional forecast it would be: sunny and still through the evening, then changing dramatically to dark skies and gale-force winds by night.

Good grief!

I was about to forget my recent reminder of joy—and about to answer these questions from a dialogue I'd not yet read:

> "When a great wind moves through the branches of a tree, making it sway and rock, left and right, has it come to knock down the tree? Or is that wind nature's way of secretly working to strengthen the roots of that tree?"[58]

Jared and I had a lovely morning before he left to work on the house. He said, "You are so beautiful, Anna."

I thanked him, adding, "And you are so handsome."

When he hugged me goodbye, I told him I felt cherished.

A pause.

As he turned to go, he said, "Can you check the bank account at noon to see if the transfer came in? Need to pay the builder."

His and hers minds!

Dinner at Hayley & Michael's was splendid—crostini with minced mushrooms from the Growers' Market. Italian meat stew, gorgonzola polenta, salad, glazed carrots with carrot-top pesto...and carrot cake with cream cheese frosting.

Jared was Friday-tired, and I meant to leave by 8:30, but there was no clock in sight. Eventually, I had the feeling it was getting late, so we said our goodbyes.

When we got in the truck, I asked a sincere question, and Jared responded with something I construed as mean. Let's call it "kale."

I told him what I felt, but he denied the "kale" was mean and said it shouldn't have bothered me.

And then I came unglued.

As the saying goes: "if it's hysterical, it's historical." I didn't realize my husband had unknowingly touched my old fear of being misunderstood and dismissed—at the time, I didn't even know I was afraid of those things.

I am embarrassed to say: we fought all the way home—a 45-minute drive.

As with The Cracker Incident, what was hardest for me was his refusal to acknowledge that the "kale" hurt. In my Anna-Paradigm, even if you unintentionally hurt someone, you apologize. Apparently, that's not in the Jared-Paradigm. And I was determined to cram it in there.

So I went full bore and brought up all the unacknowledged stuff that has hurt since the Alvord Desert. I know better. But I couldn't seem to get any reaction from him, and my inner four-year-old sure as heck wanted to.

I wasn't graceful, and he was defensive.

Eventually, I came up for air and apologized for my part. He did not apologize for his.

What I wish I'd known that evening:

> If you are on the receiving end of a hurtful communication, it is important to wonder about the other person's intention. Many people confuse intention and impact. Just because something your partner said (or did) landed poorly in your world, doesn't mean they intended it that way…. When you are hurt or offended, can you move to curiosity? Sometimes, your partner will have no idea why something upset you. Look within and

figure out what got stirred up in you. How are you interpreting what just happened?[59]

This is becoming a theme. May we both learn to be curious.

◆ ◆ ◆

Sorrow prepares you for joy. It violently sweeps everything out of your house so that new joy can find space to enter.
—Rumi

I made Jared a breakfast burrito, but he only took a few bites before leaving to work on the new house.

I spent all morning writing, trying to figure things out, trying to see from my husband's perspective, trying to get to the heart of my hurt. I eventually came up with the merry-go-round analogy. Say a little boy and girl are riding a merry-go-round, going faster and faster. The boy loses his grip and accidentally knocks the girl off. The girl goes flying and lands hard, hurting herself. The boy didn't mean it. Here are a few possible outcomes. One: he apologizes and the girl, still hurting, feels emotionally supported, so it's not as bad. Two: he doesn't apologize, and the girl's hurt increases. Three: not only does he not apologize, he tells the girl that her pain is her fault. She is then left with even more pain.

When I brought Jared a sandwich for lunch at the property, I told him the charcoal brick looks great. The main house is red brick, and he created a kind of stitching effect on the corners with the charcoal—also lining the lintels and sills with it. His work is beautiful.

We sat on the stoop, and I unpacked his lunch in silence, giving him space to say something if he wanted.

He took my hand—I thought to bless the food. But he quietly said, "I so appreciate you."

I looked down at his hands—cracked and calloused from the work on our house. I said, "I appreciate you, too."

When I glanced up, a tear was running down his face. He said, "Thank you for your grace."

I leaned toward him, and we held each other.

After lunch, Jared continued his work, and I returned home to continue mine. My spirit felt lighter, though I know we both still have some False-Self-baggage weighing down our marriage.

> And the self
> is the darling's darling
> (I=darling2).

—from "I could name some names" by Lucia Perillo[60]

Perillo's lines remind me of the writing advice to "murder your darlings"—those too-precious parts that don't serve the whole. I think that advice might also apply to the False Self. In fact, thinking of "darlings," plural, I wouldn't be surprised if our False Self spawns litters of Mini-Mes over the course of our lives. I say murder 'em all!

Some theologians suggest just letting the False Self fade away, but since I'm pretty sure my False Self needs to be slayed, I'm more inclined to go with Tozer:

> The tough old miser within us will not lie down and die obedient to our command. He must be torn out of our heart like a plant from the soil. He must be extracted in agony and blood like a tooth from the jaw.[61]

Tozer wrote that in the context of the scriptural story of Abraham: God had asked Abraham to be willing to sacrifice his long-awaited, God-promised son, Isaac. That story has always been difficult for me. Why would God want to take away the very thing He'd promised? But now I wonder....

What if God never intended to kill Isaac but to help Abraham kill his False Self's *idolization* of him?

What if I were willing to sacrifice the idol I'd made of my long-awaited, God-promised husband?

And what if doing so would help me love the husband God gave me without idolization…but with His limitless love?

◆◆◆

The next morning, Jared said, "Marriage is weird."

Truth.

He finally did decide to go kayaking on the Smith. I am *so* thankful. He needed to get away with his friends on the water. He has spent so many weekends working on the new house.

Go play!

◆◆◆

I listened again to *The Zimzum of Love*. So much goodness in there, including an "aha" interpretation of the Scripture about God giving grace to the humble. To apologize is to humble ourselves. Humbling ourselves opens us up to grace. When we don't apologize, we're essentially blocking ourselves from receiving grace.

In her book, *Why Won't You Apologize?* Harriet Lerner* writes:

> I believe that tendering an apology, one that is authentic
> and genuinely felt, helps the other person to feel
> validated, soothed, and cared for and can restore a sense
> of well-being and integrity to the one who sincerely feels

---

* Though my views on forgiveness differ from Lerner's, I do share her views on apologies.

she or he did something wrong. Without the possibility of apology and repair, the inherently flawed experience of being human would feel impossibly tragic.[62]

When Jared came home, he mentioned he'd be working in Coquille near the coast for the rest of the week. And for the three days before Thanksgiving. Which our Governor has said we're not allowed to celebrate; she just announced no gatherings of more than six people from no more than two households. My favorite meme in social media land right now: a photo of the Kramer-turkey, with the text:

> No more than six people can gather for Thanksgiving, but thirty people can gather for a funeral. So we're having a funeral for our turkey.

Pastor Dad added, "And I'm officiating!"

Not related to the upcoming holiday, Jared and I hung ropes across the garage, laundry-line style, so I can dip the cedar shingles in stain and hang them to drip-dry. Which audiobook on marriage to listen to while doing that?

(Future Me sees that I had an advantage: much more time to study relationships. Jared runs work crews all day long. I can do my non-writing work while listening to all kinds of resources, and since I haven't been on a construction site all day, I also have the energy to read in the evenings, whereas Jared comes home bone tired. Bonus: I can share highlights with him now and then. By the time I finished writing this book, I'd become a walking CliffsNotes for marriage books.)

◆ ◆ ◆

After dipping shingles in stain and praying and thinking about forgiveness all day, I scrubbed up, donned a nice dress, made spaghetti and meatballs, and set out communion: the Tullamore D.E.W. Mom & Dad had given me for my birthday last week and a RITZ cracker.

Jared and I shared dinner and then sat in front of the fire, which was surrounded by his dripping-wet work clothes (Twice, now, I've rescued a lamp shade from a soggy jacket, though some dents and discoloration predate me!)

Before communion, I shared a Very Long Speech, detailing what I'd been trying to clarify in my heart since the fight-drive home the other night. I tried not to be in teacher-mode, though I'm pretty sure I was.

Have I mentioned that Jared is a good listener? He was a trooper this evening. The summary:

I told him I'd been thinking about how God gives grace to the humble. How apologies humble us and open us up to grace.

"We experienced that first hand in the Alvord Desert. After I lost my temper, I apologized and asked you to forgive me—through gritted teeth and tears and not feeling like I was wrong, but I had angered you—and anger is usually some kind of pain. And then you asked me to forgive you. That changed everything for me. For us. It broke open a new level of trust. And it provided emotional safety: very important to me. I can feel safe when things I bring up are acknowledged.

"You thanked me for my grace after our last fight. And that was beautiful. But I still think apologies are important on both sides. What if *not* apologizing blocks us from receiving each other's grace? Even when we don't feel like it—and even when we don't mean to hurt each other—I think apologizing keeps the grace channels open."

We usually take 10-20 minutes for communion. This one lasted almost an hour and a half. Not with words, but Jared's long, listening silences. Talking-with-God silences.

After communion, I looked up. Jared was watching me, softly. He said, "I love you."

I had the feeling those words were his way of saying, "I'm sorry."

I said, "I love you, too. You're my favorite person on the planet."

He smiled, "Except when you want to punch me in the nose."

I laughed and hugged him. "Even then."

◆ ◆ ◆

After I prayed for our marriage this morning, I remembered advice Mom had once given me: when someone says something that hurts, take it to God first. Ask Him why it hurts. See if there's anyone you need to forgive. Usually, it's someone in your family of origin. She had smiled and added, "So it's me, your Dad, or your brother."

Something surfaced in my spirit. As kids, my younger brother, David, and I got along pretty well. Except when we didn't—which usually started when he did or said something I perceived as an offense. We'd argue. I'd wait for him to apologize, since I felt that he had initiated whatever Armageddon we found ourselves in (I hadn't learned that it takes two to fight). I would sit on my high horse, waiting for his apology. Meanwhile, the rift between us grew. My dear brother and I were both stubborn in different ways, but if I wanted the relationship repaired, I would have to apologize first. After I did, he finally would. Chelsea Wakefield writes:

> Intimate relationships stir things up in our psyches that have been resting undisturbed for a long time. We often need to circle back and revisit formative experiences that have created narratives and worldviews, insecurities and defenses that will only present themselves when an intimate "other" starts to really matter.[63]

I also remembered Mom's concept of "the exchange."* My boiled-down version: when something triggers me to behave or feel badly,

---

* You can find more about this in Resource 2.

I can stop and ask myself, "Am I believing a lie?" And if so, I can ask God, "What truth do you have for me in exchange?" Often, God also reveals the original source of the lie I hadn't even realized I've been believing—and the thing I need to forgive or ask forgiveness for.

Jared didn't call from Coquille this evening. He's probably sound asleep—well deserved after a hard day's work. I didn't want to wake him with a call. Still…. When I started to feel hurt that I didn't hear from him, I took the hurt to God and asked what He had for me in exchange.

Peace.

And this memory: when I was in my late teens, I traveled to Ireland with my friend, Abby. I didn't call my parents at any point during the trip—until the day before we were going to fly home, and I wanted to confirm that someone would be at the airport to pick us up. Teenage priorities. I'll never forget the sound of worry and relief in Mom's voice on the other end of the phone. It hadn't even occurred to me to let anyone know that we'd arrived safely.

So sorry, Mom!

◆◆◆

While staining shingles, I've been listening to the *I Do Podcast*. Such a wonderful resource. The hosts interview relationship experts, and many of them are authors. My reading list is growing. After listening to an interview with Guy Finley, I ordered his book, *Relationship Magic*. It came with an audio version I could start listening to right away.

His material is transforming the way I think about love—the way I think I need it to be. I'd take notes if my hands weren't covered in industrial-strength gloves and dripping with coffee-brown stain.

I am trying to apply Finley's wisdom to the contradictions. Even when my husband agrees with me, he'll start with, "No…"

Me: "So you got off work early?

He: "No. At 3:30"

3:30 *is* early.

Curious.

So I decided to ask myself, "What in *me* is contradictory?" Probably plenty. And that's probably why contradictions bother me so much.

I feel a shifting in my soul—as if I'm on the brink of figuring something out.

In his delicious book on cooking and theology, Robert Farrar Capon writes about our inability to deal with mystery, how humankind "cuts the wine of paradox with the water of consistency."[64] Though his context is God and mystery, I might be forgiven for thinking of Capon's observation in the context of *marriage* and mystery. Both God and marriage can be ineffable.

When Jared came home, I made us hot toddies and suggested a funny movie. He chose *Tommy Boy!*

In all my years of art-house film viewing, I had missed this epitome of all things "boyz," which is my word for men acting like boys—in a cringe-silly but good way. Though I definitely cringed, I confess I also laughed.

Afterward, we sat by the fire. Jared mentioned a friend recovering from cancer after a divorce. He wondered if some illnesses develop because of emotional things. I said I believed so: emotions very much affect the physical body. Another reason forgiveness is vital. Unforgiveness breeds bitterness. And as the saying goes: bitterness is like drinking poison and hoping the other person will die. You know bitterness when you see it in people. In fact, you can almost *smell* it—like rancid patchouli oil. It leaves a spirit reek in its wake.

Earlier that day, I'd tossed some old notes into the fire-starter box after transcribing them into my journal. I remembered one, fished around for it in the pile, and read aloud the Anne Lamott quote I'd jotted down: "Earth is forgiveness school."

And I don't think we graduate in this lifetime.

As we got ready for bed, I asked Jared his thoughts for Thanksgiving weekend. He said he wanted to work on the house and go kayaking. When I mentioned his family's invitation to join their annual tree hunt over the holiday weekend, he said he wanted to keep time open for his "usual" holiday kayaking.

But aren't we building a *new* usual? For the both of us?

I tried to focus on sharing a solution—not the problem of feeling like we don't get to spend much free time together. So I said, "I'd love to go away, just the two of us, for a night or two sometime this winter—not camping." I smiled and added, "I'm not a subzero camper."

He smiled back. "You don't have to worry about that in Oregon."

"Well, Celsius then. Freezing point. *Actual* point is: I'd like to go somewhere where there's nothing to do but just *be* together."

◆◆◆

Jared returned from his Dad's land with a dump truck full of firewood. There is now a massive pile of wood in the side drive. Good thing I love the functional exercise of wood stacking; I'll have plenty of it over the next few days.

Jared and I shared a mid-morning work break of coffee and cookies. He had some stuff to do at the shop then suggested...a hike! I thought he would just ride his bike like he often does, but he made time for both. And: he suggested we go to Bandon for a winter-weekend getaway after the holidays. He really is a good listener.

Before bed, Jared packed for the week's work in Coquille by upending his travel bag in front of the fire and patching the ripped crotch of a pair of work pants with a piece of flannel and Shoe Goo.

Ah, differences.

> Love for one's mate
> is a wild brook
> hurtling from rock to rock,
> pouring into deep pools.

— from "Differentia" by Emily Porter St. John[65]

◆ ◆ ◆

Remembering the insight my friend Bobbi had shared: marriage is a daily dying to the False Self.

◆ ◆ ◆

Listening to Guy Finley's *Relationship Magic* while staining shingles makes the messy work fly by. His words are worth peeling off my gloves to hit pause and scrawl notes because I need to embody this stuff at a cellular level. Things like: don't bring up the past. Don't blame. Focus on creating the positive you want. Stuff I thought I knew but which falls out of my brain in tense moments.

Another golden bit of Finley's I needed to embody:

> The instant we become aware of any opposing force at work in us—some negative thought or feeling wanting us to embrace its agitation—not only must we drop it on the spot, but *we must also drop any familiar sense of self that has appeared with it in that same moment.*[66]

I'm pretty sure I have plenty of False Selves that need to get dropped. As in, hitman-lingo for "taken out."

◆ ◆ ◆

I had guessed that the Wednesday before Thanksgiving would not be a date night because Jared would be driving back from Coquille. I made elk burgers and sweet potato fries for dinner, but I had no idea when he'd be home, and he didn't text to let me know, so I ate on my own.

When he did come home later that evening, I was shocked to hear he planned to work on the new house tomorrow: on Thanksgiving Day. I knew he wanted to work on it this weekend, but it hadn't even occurred to me that he'd want to work on the holiday itself.

I said, "I'd hoped we could spend time together."

He asked, "What are we doing now?"

I said, "It's the end of your long work day, when you're exhausted and just drove home from the coast. I meant some time when we're fresh, the two of us. Is there *any* time this weekend for that?"

He looked at me blankly. "No."

◆ ◆ ◆

We can complain because rose bushes have thorns, or rejoice because thorns have roses.
—Alphonse Karr

I cried so much last night that my eyelids and cheeks are swollen. I hadn't wanted to wake Jared, so I went upstairs for my Lament & Rumination.

After I came back to bed and tried not to sniffle, he awoke. He reached out and asked, "What's going on?"

I turned toward him and shared what I'd pieced together over the last couple of hours: "I'm sad. I had no idea you planned to work on Thanksgiving. I was looking forward to spending time with you, but I didn't communicate that. And you didn't tell me your plans. I figured tonight wouldn't be date night because you had a long work day plus the long drive, so I was looking forward spending our first big holiday together. And the story in my head is that you don't want to spend time with me."

He held me, but said nothing. Eventually, I heard the rhythmic breathing of his sleep.

I lay awake a long time.

Me: *Dear God: here's my messy sadness. What do you have for me in exchange?*

Him: *Joy.*

Me: *How?*

Oh, that I had read Rick Johnson's opening line in *How to Become Your Spouse's Better Half*. He tells it straight: "Marriage is tough. Anyone who says it isn't is either a liar or a fool."[67]

And in the last pages of the book, he writes:

> If you believe that the right person will come along and make you happy, you are deluded. You, not other people, are responsible for your own happiness. Every relationship, especially one of love, is painful and often difficult. That's why it is worthwhile. With the beauty and fragrance of a rose come the thorns that scratch and sometimes draw blood. Going through the struggles of life together brings you closer and bonds you deeper. Those relationships without conflict and pain are dead, cold, and passionless. I say rejoice in your conflicts because it means your marriage is alive and growing![68]

I didn't know how much we *were* growing! Long after our first anniversary, we went to dinner with friends. When they asked what we'd learned so far in marriage, Jared was the first to answer. He told of starting to work construction as a teenager and how he was quickly mocked out of any tenderness. He learned to talk tough on the job to survive. But when he married me decades later, he was completely surprised when he would say something and see my reaction—how I looked as if I'd been chopped in two and was bleeding out (which is often how it felt!). Hearing him acknowledge that—and adding that I'd learned to not take things so personally—showed us how far we came in just a year.

But we had a few more communication fails to go before we began to figure that out.

In fact, at this *chronos* point in our story, I realize that to contemporary culture, this marriage might look like it wasn't working out. But my husband and I were *working* it out. In the Christian tradition, you don't give up when things get hard. I hope it's obvious I'm not suggesting people stay in abusive situations; I *am* suggesting that sorrows and rough seasons are worth pressing through with God,

> who by his mighty power at work within us is able to do far more than we would ever dare to ask or even dream of—infinitely beyond our highest prayers, desires, thoughts, or hopes.[69]

I wouldn't even try wading through hardships without God. And I probably wouldn't have survived my first year of matrimony without Him—especially not in an era long-saturated with the myth of individualism. A myth so pervasive, we forget it's only been around a matter of centuries. What once was "we" is now all about "me." Which is conducive to the False Self's image but not to marriage.

When things get rough, we don't have to jump ship in a solo, self-righteous fury. Neither do we have to stick around in a way that sinks us, taking emotional hits in isolated, misguided martyrdom.

There is a third way, a Third Thing. Actually, it's three things: grace, faith, and forgiveness. Grace to live in gratitude instead of resentment, faith to trust in a union bigger than our individuality, and forgiveness to love amid all the flaws and failings. These practices are not "one and done" but daily. Even moment by moment.

Maybe you've heard the saying: "I've been married five times...all to the same person." A marriage grows and changes. *Chronos* and *kairos* will continue to work in us over decades. Heck, they have already begun to work: our marriage is completely different today than it was the first morning we awoke as man and wife.

Speaking of waking, we were just about to make it to the counselor-classic milestone of matrimony: the day you wake up next to your spouse and think you've made a terrible mistake is the day your real marriage begins.

◆◆◆

Thanksgiving Day. This morning when we woke up, Jared asked, "You want me to stick around today?"

(Our marriage has begun!)

To myself, I said, *I want you to want to.* But aloud, I just said with a wobbly smile, "Go."

I had thought we were hosting Thanksgiving together. I had thought he'd be here to cook the prime rib he had suggested.

But perhaps "I had thought" is just another way to say "I expected." I would add a word to the start of the maxim Mindy shared: *Unspoken* expectations are premeditated resentments.

After Jared left, I indulged in a bit of melodrama. I cried in a heap on the couch and then slunk down onto the floor. After I peeled myself off of the carpet, I texted my friend, Janis, for prayers of peace. I went on a morning walk in Cathedral Hills—a walk I had hoped Jared and I would do together.

By the time I came home, I felt the brink of peace. I decided to get myself ready long before anyone planned to arrive. I had just finished pulling on my dress when I heard the back door click as Jared entered—early! I was relieved to *not* be a tear-stained puddle on the floor.

He stacked firewood while I whipped cream. When the cream was fluffy, I stuck a finger in it and opened the back door, leaning out to offer it. He sucked it off. I said, "Mom's bringing two pumpkin pies to slather it on."

He said something I didn't quite catch. I'm glad I asked "What?" instead of assuming it had to do with the pies.

He repeated, "You look great."

"Thank you." I hugged him. "And you look handsome."

Incredibly, the sun came out, and it was balmy enough to sit out on the front stoop. We brought our coffees outside and ended up sharing a beautiful time of prayer for the family gathering.

Then I brought up my tears from last night without shedding any more of them. I shared the story in my head again: that he didn't want to spend time with me.

He said he hadn't spoken last night because, in his mind, the idea of extended time together was at the expense of friend time. It seems he'd thought my desire to be with him excluded seeing his friends.

Oh, pesky assumptions on both sides!

I pointed out that he has been working mightily on the house every day until dark, and then the time changed, shortening daylight hours for his outdoor actives after work, then he'd been away in

Coquille—and all of this in the time of Covid shut-downs, so *everyone's* social life has been tweaked.

He then said that he doesn't like spending time with stuff like "sea salt."

I asked why.

"It isn't dangerous," he said with a maybe-I'm-joking smile.

"Like kayaking. What about danger appeals to you?"

"The challenge."

What I wished we'd known was…most everything in the book *101 Things I Wish I Knew When I Got Married*—written by long-married couple Linda & Charlie Bloom. But specifically, this part of their introduction:

> Stephen Levine…called marriage the "ultimate danger sport." People can, he said, learn more about themselves in a week in a relationship than by sitting in meditation in a cave for a year. Having tried both marriage and mediation, we'd have to agree.[70]

I asked Jared, "What if you saw 'sea salt' as an adventure, a challenge?"

Just then, my parents pulled up. It was probably best to leave that question in the air.

The holiday pivoted to be grand. Everyone self-staggered their arrivals, and our neighbors didn't bust us for having nine extra people in the house during shutdowns. We enjoyed a family potluck of prime rib and herbs-de-Provence-crusted turkey and stuffing, pumpkin pies, fresh cranberry sauce and the requisite sides: green beans, mashed potatoes, salad, stuffing. And a full mule-and-wine bar.

Over pie, I clinked my glass and asked if everyone would share something they were grateful for.

Joy wove all the answers together.

Thanksgiving on Thanksgiving Day.

◆◆◆

Shingle bells, shingle bells…. Then delivering turkey leftovers for Jared and his employee, Robert, who is helping him work on the new house—gratitude! Then staining more shingles.

◆◆◆

Jared decided to join the Christmas tree hunting instead of kayaking after all (I'd told him *I* was going with his family even if he wasn't.)

We met Alex, Rachael, and the kids and drove the big, white work trucks up toward Onion Mountain. We passed through previous years' burns—skeletal forests that could be sets for an animated Tim Burton film—to find a dense, green knoll covered in evergreen trees and surrounded with logging roads still deep in snow. We enjoyed the sunny side of an inversion while the valley lay beneath a cold fog.

After we found our trees, Alex made a fire, and we ate leftover turkey sandwiches. At which point we realized we should have brought camp chairs. And s'mores makings. Natalie made a snow marshmallow and "roasted" it until it melted, and then she and her brother and their uncle zoomed down the logging road's packed snow on sleds.

On the drive down the mountain, we stopped to marvel at the valley below; it had turned into a lake of fog, the tops of mountains rising above the inversion like little islands. And then, we continued on, slowly driving back into the clouds and cold.

❖ ❖ ❖

LAST DAY OF STAINING SHINGLES! And yes, that deserves shouty caps. I started early this morning, determined to finish the things. And I did. After dinner, I rewarded myself by trimming the tree while Jared caught up on his digital work.

I hadn't opened my box of Christmas ornaments in over a decade. So many memories. Mom & Dad gave my brother and me each an ornament every holiday from childhood through college. I hung up the very first one I'd received: a ceramic angel from the year I was born.

When the box was empty, I sat on the floor and looked at the years of my life represented by each ornament. I could never have mapped a single one of them.

Even last month, I could never have guessed that the "unexpected goodness" of November would come from unexpected badness: a massive fight, which led me to listening to a relationship podcast while staining shingles, which opened up so many helpful resources. I guess you could say the unexpected thing November brought me was emotional shingles! If all of that hadn't happened, I might not have so earnestly looked for a way out of my own head and into my True Self. I might not have seen how I was spinning 'round and 'round in my own negative patterns, looking at all that I *didn't* want.

I remembered Pastor Kris Vallotton teaching that not all things are good, but God *works* them for good. And then he added something that made me laugh until I cried: "God takes your crap and uses it to fertilize your promises."

Truth. But believing it requires faith.

"Faith is not a once-done act but a continuous gaze of the heart."[71]

Faith is a gaze.

125

Faith is sight.

May I have the eyes of faith.

Kairos: Above the Fog, Above the Fray

Last weekend, I went Christmas tree hunting with my new extended family. We drove out of the foggy valley in trucks, careening up old logging roads into the mountains until we hit sunshine—and snow.

The day was an overdue catalog of goodness: leftover turkey sandwiches by the fire (and roasting of "snow marshmallows"). Gentle, sunny walks for some, sledding (and wiping out) for others. Hot cocoa with whipped cream, optionally spiked with peppermint schnapps (yes, please).

It was a very good day for Jared to get away from bricking the new house and me from staining its shingles. Tree hunting and snow playing were welcome respites.

When the sun and fire got low, we all piled back into the trucks and started for home. Through the forest, we kept glimpsing the fog still covering the valley. And then, before descending back down the mountain toward home, we came to a clearing and saw what looked like a massive lake spread out below us, framed by the valley's mountains. It was the fog.

Up on that sunny rise, we felt warmth and had perspective. Back beneath the fog, we'd feel the cold and have limited visibility.

Oh to remember that beyond what we can feel and see in our valleys—geographical or emotional—a higher elevation rises above us.

Whole days of marriage can feel like they look: heavy and damp and dark.

But.

Standing above the fog, I saw that even when we can't always get to a higher vantage with our physical bodies, we always can with our hearts and minds.

I took a photo of that "lake" to look at on days when I feel stuck below the fog and fray. It's a reminder that—above what seems oppressive and heavy—there stretches a bright, wide scope of possibility for love.

While we wait for the sun to burn away the fog, we can choose to enjoy the lights on the tree and the warmth of the wood stove. And perhaps a bit of peppermint schnapps in our cocoa.

Chronos: December

First day of Advent. Done with shingle-staining, I am delighted to spend a long morning writing in front of the lovely Christmas tree we found in the forest.

Other than a few highlights, last month was *hard* for me. But instead of a writing residency in Latvia (which I had almost forgotten I was once scheduled to do), I got a bit more freedom from my False Self:

> This is what the poet knows and what every wisdom tradition teaches: there is a great gulf between the way my ego wants to identify me, with its protective masks and self-serving fictions, and my true self.[72]

Date night tonight. I made meatballs and brought out Niesje's pinot noir, the one she'd given me for my birthday. She'd left the bottle bare and included a blank, watercolor sticker label. She suggested Jared and I choose a word I could paint—something we wanted for our marriage.

Jared left the choice to me, and I chose *zimzum:* the divine space between. I painted the word in a field of gold and violet. And so, we had communion with *zimzum* wine.

Earlier in the day, I'd texted Jared Matthew 6:21: "For where your treasure is, there your heart will be also." I added: "You and God are my treasures."

A while later, he texted back: "I treasure you."

◆◆◆

Friday. I took the car to the tire shop for new tires and walked downtown to pick up Jared's work truck from the service department. Yesterday, I'd picked up the van from its service in Medford. In dream interpretation, vehicles can represent our spirit. Maybe our marriage is getting spirit alignment!

When Jared came home, he suggested we watch a Cary Grant movie—miracle! And so we watched one of my favorites, *To Catch a Thief.*

◆◆◆

Gahhhhhhhhhh!

◆◆◆

I woke up still thinking about what triggered the "gah" of Saturday but tried to keep my balance and not let emotions highjack the day. And I tried to remember how lovely our Friday eve had been.

This morning, Jared asked if I wanted to go for a hike. With pleasure. After lunch we drove up to the "B" Street trails he'd been looking for. He was delighted to find them. As we walked, he narrated the jumps and landings, illustrating with his hands how a bike would fly off of berms. It was fun to see his happiness, and so I didn't bring up what he'd said last night.

During pre-dinner drinks with friends, Jared had looked at me and said, "Oh, yeah, I haven't told you yet. I decided to keep the 'bacon.'"

My heart went *clunk*. I said the only true *and* kind thing I could think of: "Well that's a surprise." Especially to hear about it for the first time in front of others. And to not have been invited to help make the big decision in the first place.

Today, in the trail-braided forest above "B" Street, I made a correlation. We came across an old car that had been driven into a ravine. It had seen decades of spray paint, rocks, a few bullets. Jared started tossing rocks at it. I asked why, genuinely curious. He said something about hearing the sound of contact, of seeing what happens. I realized he often says things for the same reason: to see what happens.

On the way home, he asked brightly, "Oh, what do you think about my decision to keep the 'bacon'?"

I echoed my reply from the night before, "I was surprised."

I wish I'd also been brave enough to say that I'd felt hurt that he had announced it without asking what I thought. It was a decision that would greatly affect me. But I didn't want to be a killjoy after a pleasant afternoon. And I needed some time to figure out how to respond well.

I tried not to think about all the ramifications of keeping the "bacon."

◆◆◆

The "bacon!"

Say grace.

I give thanks that Jared makes good decisions. Now I just have to figure out a way to work with this one.

So tonight, I answered his question about the "bacon" with what I hoped for: that we can figure it out together. And since we're not in a rush, maybe we can wait until after the New Year to talk about everything that would be involved in keeping it? (Which would be a *lot*.)

◆◆◆

Rediscovered Philippians 4:6-9 in *The Message:*

> Don't fret or worry. Instead of worrying, pray. Let petitions and praises shape your worries into prayers, letting God know your concerns. Before you know it, a sense of God's wholeness, everything coming together for good, will come and settle you down. It's wonderful what happens when Christ displaces worry at the center of your life.

> Summing it all up, friends, I'd say you'll do best by filling your minds and meditating on things true, noble, reputable, authentic, compelling, gracious—the best, not the worst; the beautiful, not the ugly; things to praise, not things to curse. Put into practice what you learned from me, what you heard and saw and realized. Do that, and God, who makes everything work together, will work you into his most excellent harmonies.

Where were those verses last month? I should have them tattooed in my mind and on my heart.

Jared's grace for dinner tonight included being excited about what God is doing in us individually and together in our marriage. I like how he framed that.

After dinner, I cut slices of galette to enjoy by the fire. It was balmy at 72 degrees—a bit too toasty for him. I'm trying to figure out how to load the wood stove so that it doesn't get too hot. I told him the inside temperature is usually in the mid-sixties most of the day, but by late afternoon, it often rises to 72.

He mentioned, not for the first time, that most people get too used to being comfortable. I decided not to take this as an indictment against my love of comfort—especially the comforts of home in an uncomfortable world. Instead, watching the andiron shadows dance in the stove, I asked what he hoped for in the coming year. He said he doesn't tend to think far ahead.

Years ago, he took me to Takelma gorge. As we walked through the forest, I asked him something about the future. He had replied, "I try not to walk too far ahead of my own life." Poetry.

Here and now, I said I admire his ability to be fully in the present.

He said, "But I need to think about the future, especially with relationships." (Hey! A good contradiction!)

The fire shadows danced in silence for a long while.

Eventually, I turned to him, "What planet are you on?"

He smiled. "Lots of them."

I leaned over to kiss him. "Maybe you could finish your orbits? You're good about being in the present."

Another smile. Some kissing. I pulled him to the floor where the blanket had fallen.

He said, "The loveseat is more comfortable."

With a laugh, I said, "Oh, but you don't want to be comfortable, do you? So the floor is perfect!"

◆ ◆ ◆

I remembered a time my parents described their early marriage and how they'd worked through a similar dynamic regarding contradictions.

Mom looked at Dad with a twinkle in her eye, "I learned to say with a smile, 'Go fight with someone else.'"

Dad laughed.

And when it comes to different opinions, Mom also learned to say: "I appreciate that you see things that way. It would help if you could also appreciate the way *I* see things."

◆ ◆ ◆

Tonight, Jared and I watched *Starsky & Hutch* and laughed. Snoop Dogg quoted Shakespeare: "To err is human, to forgive divine."

I've held that line in my heart ever since I first read it in high school.

◆ ◆ ◆

This morning, Jared said, "I love you, Anna."

I replied, "I love you, Jared. And I love watching our love grow."

Then he mentioned the line: "to forgive, divine."

We agreed that forgiveness makes it possible for love to grow.

After he left to work on the new house, my niece Noel and her friend, Bre, came to bake gingerbread cookies. They created an impressive nativity, complete with misshapen-star-turned-baby-Jesus. Cute and clever.

I brought a batch of cookies to Jared that afternoon, and that evening, we shared a delightful dinner at Dan & Janna's. When we arrived, Jared joined Dan outside at the patio grill while Janna and the sweet trio of kids—Ender, Jude, and Evie—showed me all of their Christmas decorations, from the Elf on the Shelf to the legit-antler'd Rudolph.

Near the end of grilling, Jared popped his head inside the patio door and asked me to quote Snoop Dogg's line on forgiveness. I laughed, "You mean Shakespeare's?" Apparently, he and Dan had been talking about forgiveness. As Jared turned to go back outside he said, "I love that I got you to quote Snoop Dogg!"

I shook my head and called after him, laughing, "Shakespeare!"

The evening was deliciously holiday-family-homey. We ended up having a "late-over," what Janna calls weekend nights with close friends, when you all but sleep over. So thankful for good friends with strong marriages.

◆ ◆ ◆

Bobbi is a sweetheart. She sends me bits of encouragement all the time. Today, it was *The Passion Translation* of Philippians 4:6-9:

> Don't be pulled in different directions or worried about a thing. Be saturated in prayer throughout the day, offering your faith-filled requests before God with overflowing gratitude. Tell him every detail of your life, then God's wonderful peace that transcends human understanding will make the answers known to you though Jesus Christ.
>
> Keep your thoughts continually fixed on all that is authentic and real, honorable and admirable, beautiful and respectful, pure and holy, merciful and kind. And fasten your thoughts on every glorious work of God, praising him always. Put into practice the example of all that you have heard from me or seen in my life and the God of peace will be with you in all things.

Yes & amen.

◆ ◆ ◆

I served Jared corn dogs for dinner. He had three. Before he took his last bite, he said with a sigh of appreciation, "There will be corn dogs in heaven."

He can be adorable.

◆ ◆ ◆

Jared walked in just after four this afternoon—a nice surprise. I was sitting on the floor by the tree, scouring around online for light fixtures for the new house. It was pouring rain, so he had come home to go over job-site plans by the fire instead of sitting in his truck. I made him coffee with steamed milk and set out cookies. He sat near the fire with the rolled-out plans—the warmth apparently a good thing today.

At five, he came to sit behind me and hold me. He said, "I love you."

I smiled and reached up for his arms. "I love you back."

We ordered sushi takeout and brought it home to eat in front of a movie. I had picked out a couple of holiday options for him to choose from. The winner: *It's a Wonderful Life.*

It is.

In all its messy imperfection, it is—some-insane-how—a wonderful life.

◆ ◆ ◆

In his book, *Change Your Brain, Change Your Life,* Dr. Daniel Amen suggests that, before going to sleep, you think about good things that happened that day.

And I'd add: give thanks for them.

Say grace.

◆ ◆ ◆

I started breakfast while Jared started a fire. I formed a too-thick sausage patty, so he flattened it between his hands and returned it to the plate. He then turned to the sink, saying, "Umm…"

I had swapped out the plastic pump of liquid soap for a tin of solid soap. I demonstrated. He looked at me, bemused—then at his sausage-covered hands.

I smiled. "Good thing I kept the liquid soap for especially greasy things." I pulled it out from under the sink and squirted some onto his hands with a laugh, "Like you!"

Not long after, he pulled on his sweatshirt and noticed a hole in the arm. "That's gonna drive me crazy." He went out to the garage to get a piece of fabric from his "pile" and then came in and started rummaging in the cupboard of sliding drawers at the edge of the kitchen. I didn't ask what he was looking for. I waited until, still bent over and peering in, he turned his head and gave me another bemused look of question.

I smiled, trying not to laugh: "I was waiting for you to ask."

"Scissors."

"Top middle drawer on the island." Which I knew because I'd brought them from my old place, finding only a single pair of haircutting scissors in the bathroom before I moved in.

When he finished his Shoe Goo patch and went to leave, we kissed goodbye. I thanked him for sharing his home with me—and for his patience.

He replied, "Thanks for giving my brain a work out."

I smiled, "Hey, you won't need to do crossword puzzles in your old age. You have a wife!"

◆ ◆ ◆

While listening to a podcast, I discovered that my mode of operation flows like this: *Feel, Think, Do.* I feel and think through a thing before doing or saying it. Which is why I can get stuck in feeling or thinking and not move toward action.

Jared's mode is the complete reverse: *Do, Think, Feel.* Which is why he can say something and then think, "Oops, I shouldn't have said that." And then feel bad.

Recognizing these opposite patterns has just this minute revolutionized how I understand our communication. And it will help me take things less personally.

Of course, there are exceptions to both modes; I can move quickly to action and Jared can think through things he wants to say. We just tend to default into our "factory settings," especially when we're tired or overwhelmed. This knowledge can help us give each other grace.

After dinner, Jared had the sweet idea to walk around downtown and look at Christmas lights, so we drove to the Presbyterian church. Five years ago, I told a story there for a regional storytelling series, The Hearth.

That was back in my former life of helping Christina lead Deep Travel Workshops. One year, we created a workshop to be held with the last of the Marrakech storytellers, and we would be telling stories in Morocco and Paris.

Before we left, I spent weeks practicing to tell the story of a "gold" ring a Gypsy had "found" at my feet while I was walking alone in Paris. How she'd told me it would bring me good luck in love. I'd first shared that story at this very church as practice for the trip.

And tonight, Jared and I parked in front of the same building. All those years ago, I would not have guessed, as I told a story about a wedding ring I never thought I'd wear, that one day I'd be here again—this time holding a ringed hand with the man I married, walking up the road together.

> And if only a single
> miracle remains
> perhaps it will be that one
> won by the soul's sweat
> plucked like a rose
> lost in a minefield
>
> —from "Just Love" by Abdellatif Lâabi[73]

♦♦♦

I made beef and broccoli stir-fry with jasmine rice for dinner, and it was a hit. We shared a quiet eve by the fire.

He: sketching the hearth he'll build in the new house.

Me: researching cabinet hardware.

We: reading *Winnie-the-Pooh*. Pooh got stuck in Rabbit's hole, and Jared laughed.

♦♦♦

I walked another section of town today in an effort to get to know Grants Pass before we move. I found myself in the neighborhood of Jared's first house—the one he owned when we first met. The one on which he had practiced bricklaying.

Standing across the street, I saw that I never would have fit into that house—that life—with him. We each had so much more growing to do.

In the almost-decade between our meeting and marrying, I wrote books, held art shows, and helped lead workshops around the world—freelancing through it all. I'm glad I did. Glad I made it to six continents. Glad I kissed a Dutch filmmaker in Paris after a literary salon.

And I'm glad Jared lived his life, too—built his work, saw the continents, kissed the girls.

We each did most everything we could and everything we dreamed.

And, after decades of cobbling together a living as a poet-painter, I have no illusions about how hard the hustle is. I'm glad to have done it…and glad to no longer need to do it that way. Now I get to write and paint full time.

Thank you again, dear husband, for making that possible by being a mighty provider.

◆ ◆ ◆

A lovely, lingering Christmas morning. Woke still full from the Christmas Eve family gathering at Andy & Linda's last night. And today we'll share Christmas Day lunch with my parents.

Before we rolled out of bed, I said to Jared, "I love that Song of Songs line, 'I am my Beloved's and my Beloved is mine.' I love being yours, and I love that you're mine."

He added, "And I'm proud to be yours. And proud that you're mine."

Mmmm. I like that.

We warmed Mom's cinnamon rolls on the wood stove and cooked eggs to go with them. Also, mmmm.

And I pulled out the oranges I'd symbolically put in the "marriage stocking" for both of us. In our family, the stocking toe always holds an orange: a reminder of my Dad's Dad, who grew up on a "dirt farm" in Oklahoma during the Great Depression. For him, a good Christmas was getting an orange. What plenty we now enjoy!

After breakfast, Jared and I opened each other's gifts. The gifts were Jared's fun idea—to give each other children's books we can read together.

The results:

From her to him: a hardback copy of *Stuart Little*, wrapped in creamy white paper, and decorated with a slip of eucalyptus and a card made from one of our wedding photos. It had been sitting under the tree for a month.

From him to her: a package had come for Jared from Thrift Books a few days ago. He hadn't touched it, and this morning, he grabbed the package and sat cross-legged in front of the fire to wrap it— still in its mailer—in a page of comics from the fire-starter box, the ends of which he twisted closed. He had ordered four books: *Mathilda, Harris and Me, The Giver,* and *Black Beauty.* (Thank you, Janna, for giving him the great recommendations!)

The difference in our gift giving—or maybe gift wrapping—pretty much sums us each up. I was laughing.

We drove to Jacksonville, bacon-walnut Brussel sprouts in tow. I took Jared's hand and said, "I love being your wife." He turned to me and said, "I love that you're my wife, too."

He acknowledged the hard parts of marriage but added, "I can't imagine it working with anyone else. I'm glad you're in it with me, and I'm glad you desire to connect and press through."

Hearing that is the best Christmas gift I could receive, and I said so. I also said that I'm learning to let go of my old, False Self and to release the negativity it aligns with—creates even. My mind still can't articulate it so well. But my spirit is learning it.

We arrived early enough to walk through Jacksonville's lovely historic buildings. Jared wished everyone we saw a Merry Christmas. Dinner with my parents and brother was lovely, and it was great to feel in love. Dad's prime rib. Mom's pies.

Our first holiday season, mostly enjoyed. I realize there is a burden of firsts this initial year of marriage. It might sound strange, but it's a relief to have made it through so many of them.

◆ ◆ ◆

This morning, I said to Jared, "I enjoy feeling how our marriage grows us together. It's like…I can't think of the right word."

141

"Cohesion," he suggested.

"Yes! That's even better than Shoe Goo. Cohesion is a good word for it."

I looked it up later: cohesion is the action or fact of forming a united whole.

May we be the act & the fact.

> we met   and found
> ourselves in flight
> and now I'd say
> the wings were love.

—from *Meaning A Life* by Mary Oppen[74]

◆◆◆

I brought Jared dinner at the land. It was my first time approaching the new house in the dark and seeing a light on inside. The lights haven't been installed yet, but he had set up his shop lamp to brick the hearth, the back of which extends all the way up to the high ceiling. When I entered the living room, he was far up the scaffolding.

After chicken stir-fry, I read three chapters of *Winnie-the-Pooh*—including Pooh's expedition to the North Pole—while Jared finished the expedition to the North Pole of the brick fireplace.

◆◆◆

I spent today going through The Box.

The Box is an open-faced, three-foot square thing, living in the garage, into which Jared has dumped every financial record he's received since moving into this house. (I thought it was the burn pile when I first moved in.)

Now? Everything necessary lives in nicely labeled manila folders in the filing cabinet.

Everything unnecessary…is in the *actual* burn pile.

◆ ◆ ◆

Jared and I shared dinner by the fire, talking. About kindness. About different ways of communicating. How he doesn't care about some things and I care too much about them. How we're balancing each other out.

I missed a few bits I wish I remembered. It was a rare chunk of time talking easily about our relationship. But, as with dreams, the residual feeling is more important than what was said, and it was a feeling of building peace and joy together. Of being glad I get to learn to let go of pain and build up love.

Kairos: Love for the Win

I used to take the week between Christmas and New Year's to review the previous year, evaluate it, and then set goals for the next twelve months. (How a plan-loving introvert likes to spend her holidays!)

Some years, those goals were bullet-point specific. Like when I resolved to go on an archaeological dig, learn salsa dancing, and take up archery: check, check, check. I discovered that I hated the heat and dirt of the dig, I wasn't a fan of prescribed dance steps, but I *was* a decent aim with a bow and arrow.

Other years, I was more open-ended, listing several feelings I wanted to cultivate. Once, I painted a four-point compass with harmony at its center and joy, peace, prosperity, and grace as its points.

At the end of last year, while housesitting a lovely home in the country, I sat in front of the fireplace and started my review and projection.

Or I tried to.

I even had a fancy calendar that led you through all the steps with lots of questions to answer and blanks to fill in. (I am very good about answering all the questions and filling in all the blanks.) And yet, as I flipped through the pages I usually looked forward to filling, I found myself completely uninspired by all the specificity.

For once, I didn't want to grip the steering wheel of my life and beeline for the next goal. And I can beeline! From putting myself through undergraduate and graduate school on scholarships to getting a Fulbright Fellowship to write poetry in Germany for a year to all manner of less scholastic but equally daunting goals since: I. Get. It. Done.

But those last days of last year, I didn't *want* to get it all done. I had a hunch that there would be things coming I could not control...and things waiting to happen if I were willing to let go of my limited ideas of what I could achieve and maintain in my own strength. And so, to my surprise, I found myself writing the word "Love" in big, loose cursive across all those blanks I was supposed to fill in.

Then, not long into the New Year, Jared and I started dating. Then came the global bizarreness of The Time of Quarantine. Then Jared proposed. Then we got married during a miraculous summer gap in outdoor gathering restrictions. And then we spent the rest of the year learning the intricacies of love. None of which I could have forecast.

I have given up on the fancy, fill-in-the-blank calendars. I'm keeping it simple. And I'm metaphorically writing "Love" across every month this coming year.

I believe one of marriage's purposes is to teach us how to forgive.
—Gary Thomas
Sacred Marriage

Between stimulus and response, there is a space. In the space there is the power to choose our response. In our response lies our growth and our freedom.
—Viktor Frankl

Before you know kindness as the deepest thing inside,
You must know sorrow as the other deepest thing.
—Naomi Shihab Nye
From "Kindness"

Part III: Comm(union)

[As] our relationship to God becomes closer, the joy of this communion sustains us.

—M. Scott Peck

In my early thirties, I taught high-school English and art on a tiny island in Micronesia. After many seasons there without a spiritual community, I craved God. I started looking into doctoral programs in divinity, but I ended up returning to the mainland to attend an unaccredited school of supernatural ministry. My three-year stint there was a wild ride. By the time I left, I saw that I'd already had what I'd gone there to get: union. God with us—*within* us. Within *me*.

A decade later, right before Jared reconnected with me, I had once again felt the pull to get my doctorate. This time, I had gone so far as to initiate the equivalency process with a well-respected university. But my master's degree is in poetry, and a master's of divinity was the prerequisite for the doctorate I desired. I spent days and days gathering materials, including all of my post-graduate studies of spirit, books of theology I'd edited, my own writings, the prophetic workshops I'd created, etc., etc.

Marvelous thing: the university accepted my decades of self-guided work. I would only need to take two Bible history classes, and then—doctorate-bound!

But a strange thing happened when I heard back from the university. I saw that all those years of learning and growing with God had occurred without the academic version of a priestly blessing. My actual equivalency process was seeing that I needed no degree, no mediary to know Him. As I had, years ago on a far-away island, I simply craved straight-up union with God, One-on-one. And I already had it.

It is so easy to forget.

And then Jared reconnected with me, and a new kind of union began.

I mention often in these pages that Jared and I receive communion together. We share the elements; the bread is the broken body of Jesus, the wine is His blood. These represent His sacrifice on the Cross, which made possible the forgiveness we receive from Him.[75]

During what later came to be called the Last Supper or the Lord's Supper, Jesus gave thanks before each of the elements, modeling how to receive the bread and wine in remembrance. By giving thanks, He also modeled a key to the remembrance of forgiveness: gratitude.

Interestingly, the early Christian church did not have a dedicated marriage ceremony. Marriage was fulfilled when two people shared communion, or Eucharist, together.[76] And Eucharist stems from a Greek word for thanksgiving.

Ah, marriage: forged in forgiveness and gratitude. Oh, to remember that!

To remember that we are already in comm(union) with God.

To remember that we already play on the Unified Field, which is "our complex and inexplicable caring for each other, and for our life together here."[77]

To remember that "We are all drawing upon a larger source: the unified field. The shared spirit."[78]

The great, romantic union I've longed for? I've had it all my life. It took marriage for me to truly know that. To *yada* that.

To *yada* the union in communion.

Chronos: January

I spent the first day of the new year happily prepping for Rebecca's birthday dinner. Cleaning: too boring to list the details. Decorating: linen runner on the coffee table with mandarins and pinecones entwined with twinkly lights. Cooking: Chicken Marbella, kale salad so green it made you look twice, loaf of nine-grain sourdough.

Christina & Conrad brought a sweet-potato dish, Chris & Shannon brought kombucha. I had several bottles of prosecco chilling on ice, and they were all empty by night's end.

Rebecca doesn't eat sweets, so instead of a birthday cake, I baked a huge wheel of brie that filled a pie dish. We sang happy birthday, handing her a separate, Covid-friendly candle to blow out.

At one point, Christina and Rebecca were trying to convince each other to sing "Don't Cry for Me Argentina" from the Juliet balcony above the living room.

At another point, the eight of us paired off into different conversations, and I talked Enneagram with Shannon. We realized her personality is similar to Jared's and mine to Chris's—so we can give each other relationship tips. Brilliant.

A fine way to start the new year.

◆ ◆ ◆

A not-so-fine way to start the new year: bringing up the "bacon." Last month, I'd suggested we figure out what to do about it after the New Year. And so, on a fresh Sunday morning over breakfast, I brought it up, along with several details I'd researched for my logic-loving husband.

Somehow, that did not go well.

The nutshell: I shared my research and presented some options for the "bacon." Jared did not like these options. When I suggested my research would save him time regarding the bacon, he told me I was being coercive.

I clarified: I wasn't coercive. I was responding to his pronouncement about the "bacon"—a decision that he had made without asking me, that would greatly affect me. I reminded him that he had asked me what I thought about it, so I had studied ways to best move forward because he liked concrete facts.

But more important than what we *do* with the "bacon" is how we *decide together* what to do about it—or anything we disagree about.

There was a lo-o-o-o-ong silence.

Like the greasy miasma that rises from pan-frying *actual* bacon in a closed house, we sat in the unventilated heaviness of our conversation.

I reminded myself that Jared's silences are often times of processing.

Finally, I took a deep breath and offered to bring him a sandwich at the new house for lunch, but he said he wanted chicken strips. I took this to mean he did not want me to come out to the land, and he would be going to Lil' Pantry solo. Fine by me.

After he left, I spent the rest of the day cleaning the second quarter of the garage, from the door to the moldy gold chair, unearthing more spiderwebs than I'd like to think about. I found a box of jumbled bathroom toiletries that looked like they had just been upended from his last house's bathroom and had sat on the shelf for half-a-dozen years. I inspected the contents of the containers. Whatever had been solid had liquified, and whatever had been liquid had solidified. I chucked the whole box.

This evening, we started reading *Matilda*. One thing I'm grateful for today: Jared's desire to read light books together at night. They help lighten things.

◆◆◆

In social-media-land, I saw a word-search puzzle—one of those squares of letters that hide words. The caption said that the first four words you spot would be your words for the year. I found connection, love, alignment, and breakthrough. I'll take 'em all for our marriage in this new year.

> I would like to describe a light
> which is being born in me
>
> —from "I Would Like to Describe" by Zbigniew Herbert[79]

◆◆◆

I still practice the three-fold advice I read decades ago for mitigating minor depression: plan something, clean something, do something for someone.

And so, I did all three today: made plans to meet up with a friend, cleaned out more of the garage, and made a chocolate cake with red-wine-chocolate glaze for Mom & Dad's annual, shared birthday meal. Their birthdays are within a week of each other, and we always pick a day in between to celebrate. They've been married for almost half a century. I have no idea how in heaven they did it, though they've always told me their marriage was a miracle of God's mercy and grace. Seems the only possible way!

Dr. Daniel Amen's book *Change Your Brain, Change Your Life* is—not to be punny—life-changing. Oh, my limbic system! Overactivity in that region causes depression and endless focus on negative things. I took a quiz: a score of five or more indicates limbic system issues. I scored a seven.

One prescription for limbic system health: omega-3 fatty acids. I need to start taking those. And I need to remember this:

> Your habits and emotions can impact your biology so deeply that it causes changes in the genes that are transmitted to the next several generations.[80]

Going to up my habits of gratitude.

◆ ◆ ◆

Today was the day of Epiphany. Little did I know.

For date-night dinner, I warmed up a Pennington chicken pot pie and made a salad. And then…the topic of "bacon" arose. (I did *not* raise it.)

Long discussion short: Jared didn't remember announcing to me his decision about "bacon" in front of dinner guests in December.

I took a deep breath and said, "You announced it to me for the first time in front of other people. But *I* got accused of being coercive for trying to find a solution that would work for both of us after a decision had been handed to me that I didn't have a voice in. I could have called *you* coercive for telling me what we were going to do without asking me. But I didn't."

I might have been a teensy bit self-righteous.

We tried to figure out our doomed communication loops, which usually go like this: I hear something from him, I respond in the best way I can—which is not always the best, he contradicts my response in a way that I perceive as hurtful, I say so, and then he denies that his words should hurt me. I added that my response is often to ask clarifying questions, but that seems to be coming across as criticism instead of curiosity. And then he locks down.

I continued, "When you do that, I try really hard to remember it's not me you're fighting in that moment. It's the ghost of whomever once said what you assume *I'm* saying. In this case, you somehow hear me saying that you make bad decisions or that you don't have good ideas. But I've never said—or even implied—either.

"In fact, I often tell you make *good* decisions. Which is why I know that someone *else* once told you otherwise. Please forgive them, whoever they are! I can't bear the weight of that judgement anymore."

And so, in a way, tonight was indeed our day of Epiphany. Jared finally saw that I actually *did* have his best interests in mind. That my "bacon" suggestion was made from a place of thinking about both of our best interests. But it took a while. A long while.

After I got up to do the dishes.

After he got up to shower.

After he came back to sit on the couch.

After I came back to sit next to him.

After I reminded myself to *say grace*.

I give thanks for this really annoying problem because we're learning to figure it out together.

I give thanks that we're figuring it out mostly civilly.

I give thanks that my husband is extra handsome when he's concentrating.

We sat side by side and took each other's hands. Eventually we saw that we are learning to trust each other—to have faith in each other. And since we speak different trust languages, we've been misunderstanding each other. We're learning to trust God's best for both of us and to pull that into our marriage-trust instead of trusting with our brokenness and with broken trust from our past.

Maybe marriage offers us an opportunity to reshape our faith—to see what we really believe. It certainly offers us an opportunity to hold on to our True Selves:

> Holding onto yourself—maintaining a relationship with yourself—is not easy. However, the benefits to you and your marriage are incalculable. Your ability to hold onto yourself allows you to pull out of negative interactions and conduct yourself in ways that lead to positive ones. It lets you break the "set" of your communications— habitual topics, patterns, intensity, and tone.[81]

I said, "I love you, Jared."

"I love you too, Anna."

I added, "I'm still trying to figure out *how* to love you."

After a pause, he said, "The thing about trust…is grasping that the person has your best in mind."

I took a deep breath. He hadn't believed I had his best in mind? Only much later did I see that I hadn't yet believed he had my best in mind, either. So much trust to learn.

But at that moment, I just said, "Always remember that I'm your advocate."

After a while he said, "I'm sorry I misread you. I'll try to do better."

At his apology, my entire being softened, and I said quietly, "You are wholeheartedly forgiven and wholeheartedly loved. And thank you for forgiving and loving me back."

The theme song of the evening could have been, "Have a Little Faith in Me." We are each learning to trust that the one we love loves us. That what they do and say is from a place of love—even if it looks and sounds totally different from what we would do and say.

◆ ◆ ◆

Jared mentioned that Chris had stopped by the new house to help him this afternoon. Chris asked what we'd decided about the "bacon." Jared told him we aren't sure what *we* are doing about it—as he narrated, he gently and kindly emphasized the "we" and looked at me.

Progress. I smiled big. Then I read him a little gratitude piece I'd composed before he came home. I prefaced it by saying, with a wink, "I know you told me you don't need me to thank you for things, but I'm going to anyway."

The Gracias List
For my love

Thank you for your generous heart.
    For sharing this home
    & the one we're building.
    For all the hours of building—
    in heat, in cold, in exhaustion.
    For all the hours of *all* the buildings, over *all*
    the years that made what we'll share possible.

Thank you for the work of your hands but also the work
of your heart.
    For the brick you lay
    & for learning to love with me—
    for listening to my heart
    with its different rhythm.

Thank you for nighttime spoons & morning snuggles.
　　For rivers & mountains, sausage & sauerkraut.
　　For liking whiskey but trying wine.

Thank you for loving family of blood & family of gift—
　　from nieces & nephew
　　to stepmother & mother-in-law.

Thank you for seeing behind the visible—
　　to core & quality,
　　to what is coming.

Thank you for holding me,
　　for holding fast to your beliefs,
　　for holding space for Holy Spirit.

Thank you for the work of your hands & heart
　　& for resting in God's heart & hands.

(And a happy conclusion to the "bacon": we later decided not to keep it after all.)

◆ ◆ ◆

After my morning writing, the afternoon's work was cleaning all the soggy autumn leaves off the patio, hosing it down, and pulling out the winter-dead weeds, which had been somehow beautiful right up until I looked out the window at them this morning, at which point they suddenly seemed dismal and dank.

When Jared came home, he said, "Wow. I haven't seen the back yard so clean, ever."

I silently celebrated the compliment.

We had a kinda date-night do-over. We watched a silly movie, and we laughed, and we ate leftover chicken pot pie and fresh salad.

Jared mentioned that Chris had also asked yesterday how married life was going. Jared had replied along the lines of "good but hard."

He said "hard," with an endearing look of bemused confusion.

I laughed in understanding. I reached for him and said, "I love you."

My "I love you" also meant, "Same here!"

◆◆◆

Today I cleaned another quarter of the garage. The entire, south-facing wall of shelves is now *wow*. Another discovery: a forgotten box of what I guessed to be camp-kitchen stuff. It was filled with dusty plastic bowls, long-ago expired condiment packets, and a non-stick frying pan scratched into rusty hieroglyphics.

I transferred three box contents from their moldy cardboard to fresh boxes and ripped the moldy ones up. I can't wait for a burn day.

Almost done cleaning the garage. Just the shop corner and external windows to go. Saving those for another week. Inch by inch, and I'll have gone through every single drawer and shelf before moving day, which I hope will help prevent last-minute overwhelm. I've been careful to leave everything necessary right where it was—just cleaner.

And I've been sure to cross-check everything unnecessary with Jared before tossing or donating it...except for the coagulated toiletries box—that needed no consultation. It is such a purge-pleasure to make massive piles for donation and the dumpster: a grimy AC unit, a box of defunct electrical cords, high-school posters, a faded pink pool noodle. I am thankful Jared is willing to let most of it go.

When he came home, I had dinner waiting. Afterward, we took communion with a RITZ and the Saint Lucia rum Alex & Rachael had given us. Jared's prayers were full of sweetness and gratitude for forgiveness.

Yes, "Marriages survive on waves of forgiveness."[82]

◆◆◆

When Jared came back into the bedroom to say goodbye this morning, he said, "Thank you for all your support."

"You are most welcome. And thank you for all your work."

He added, "I couldn't do it without you."

I soaked in the kindness. We exchanged the happily now-ritual "I love yous," and he headed out into the cold. I slept for another hour, until my usual 5:30 alarm signaled time for Coffee & God & Writing.

That afternoon, when a negative script about past hurts began scrolling through my head, I noticed it happening and stopped it. I spoke gratitude for the morning goodbyes—for the nighttime spoons and snuggles, for all the now and good things. And I finished the rest of the day's work with joy.

> Fire, light, again
> beginning to dry tears: awaken, illumine.
>
> —from "Dialogue" by Denise Levertov[83]

◆◆◆

The January day turned out to be practically balmy. Green shoots in Cathedral Hills. Glisten-y trees from the downpour.

I decided to drive out to Pennington Farms. Jared had mentioned wanting their strawberry-rhubarb jam for his lunch PB&Js.

By the time I arrived that afternoon, only a few baked goods remained. I snagged a mini apple pie for date-night desserts and molasses cookies to pad out the Cookie Monster bag I keep in the freezer, ever-stocked for my cookie-loving husband.

Only when I returned to the house did I realize: I'd forgotten jam. The reason I went to the farm. I don't usually forget my list, so I wondered.

Then I remembered: our first month of marriage, I'd bought a nice jar of Pennington jam for Jared's sandwiches. He had said just to get a generic brand for his work lunches and save the good stuff for home. So I did.

Then, the other day, he mentioned wanting Pennington jam for his lunch sandwiches....

But when I went to the farm, expressly to get it, I forgot. It didn't take me long to figure out that I have been holding on to a grudge against my husband for all of the contradictions—including which jam to buy.

So I forgave the contradictions.

Then I prepped salmon and jojos and salad for dinner. And allspice simple syrup to make whiskey sours.

But dinner felt awkward. Jared's one comment on the meal: "I think it's funny you try to make jojos."

Not taking the bait, I said with a big, forced smile: "I'll call them potato wedges then." What I *wanted* to say: "The receiving office for criticism is closed for the day."

This was a golden moment to practice advice from Winifred Reilly's book: *It Takes One to Tango: How I Rescued My Marriage with (Almost) No Help from My Spouse—and How You Can, Too:*

> It helps to keep the long view in mind: though your partner may or may not admit it...he or she is likely to be grateful (and perhaps even impressed) that you had the wherewithal to raise your own standards and not take the bait.[84]

Since I usually *do* take the bait, I was kinda proud of myself for *not* taking it.

◆ ◆ ◆

Today was a killing field for many of my old, False Selves, some of whom apparently needed compliments for homemade dinners and none of whom could stand to be criticized or contradicted. Richard Rohr writes:

> The True Self has knocked on both the hard bottom and the high ceiling of reality and has less and less need for mere verbal certitudes or answers that always fit. It has found its certainty elsewhere and now lives inside a YES that is so big that it can absorb most of the little noes. The False Self fears and denies all seeming contradictions, probably because it unconsciously knows that it is itself a mass of contradictions and is searching for some external order or control.[85]

Rohr goes on to say that the False Self is "passing and not substantial, a largely mental and cultural construct."[86] The False Self is like the silver-screen heroine of romantic comedies. The Self that gets peeved when her partner pushes her buttons. The Self that reacts in pain instead of curiosity and wants to find someone to pay—not realizing *all* has already been paid for by grace. Which we receive from God and then extend to others. Like forgiveness. Like love.

This all sounds nice and tidy in the retrospect of revision, but while I was wrestling with it all, it felt like a goopy liquefaction phase—no butterfly wings in sight.

I sensed I was holding a funeral for a core False Self—the part of me that had focused on the negative and had looked for evidence to support its judgment that the world was a hard, cold place. The part I hadn't even realized was in me until I married—and which would have arisen with *whomever* I married because it was sourced in all my own stuff. Suzanne Stabile suggests:

There is a big difference between change and transform-ation. *Change* is when we take on something new. *Transformation* is when something old falls away.[87]

For two to become—change into—one, we must transform all that is false in us. My husband and I each have plenty more that needs to fall away. We are certainly practicing the truth of this passage I underlined in the hardcopy of *Relationship Magic:*

> *This* is the real magic, the real power, and perhaps—in the end—the true purpose of all our relationships in life: *to help us and to help each other outgrow whatever stands in the way of perfecting our love for one another.*[88]

Whew. Perfecting is painful.

When Jared came home, he was tired but kind. Grateful for the elk burgers. Even said he'd been craving a burger. He asked how my day was. I didn't trust myself to say anything other than, "I'm just excited to wake up tomorrow."

As I started to clean up, he came around the counter, looked me in the eyes, and then held me, saying, "I'm so glad I get to come home to you."

I squeezed him and then whispered, "Thank you for saying so."

Something told me it was no coincidence that the day I let go of old resentments was the first time he ever said that—and that I ever felt it to be true.

◆ ◆ ◆

On my walk, I realized that when we start to demand all of our rights and feel wronged all of the time—in family, friendship, marriage—or in *any* relationship with *any* human being—another False Self is dying away. It's easier to let that False Self die—or to slay it—when I remember that my True Self is tender and strong and wise and waiting.

In *Begin Again,* Leeana Tankersley writes:

> One of the most genuinely inconvenient truths I know is
> that often something has to die in order for something
> new to live. And so when we know—deep down—that
> something isn't working, there's also a part of us that
> knows what it's going to take to make the thing work
> again. Likely, it's going to take a death.[89]

And later in the book, she muses:

> Why are the things that matter most in life so hard? Such
> beautiful burdens? With every beginning comes some
> kind of ending, and endings often hurt.[90]

I would add: after the pain subsides, and after the time of
mourning, it's time to celebrate what lives!

I saw that I've been hoarding resentment for all of Jared's
contradictions and criticisms, using them as justification for my
anger. I need to ask him to forgive me. I don't want to carry
around cadavers of the past.

This morning Jared texted to suggest we see if any downtown
restaurants have outdoor seating for dinner. Indoor dining is still
banned due to Covid.

When he came home, we drove to The Haul. It was a chaos of
"contactless" ordering—QR codes via smart phone and glitchy
payment software—and the orders we'd entered into my phone
weren't going through. Knowing Jared was Friday tired, I said I'd
take care of it. On my first trip inside, I waited a long while. There
were so many take-out orders and so few servers that the staff were
reasonably overwhelmed. By the time someone came to the
counter, our order had gone missing from my phone, so I went
back outside to check what Jared had entered (sausage pizza), then
returned inside to wait even longer; there was now a line of other
befuddled customers. When it was finally my turn, the frazzled
server didn't know what I meant by Jared's "sausage pizza."

So I smiled and said, "A pizza with lots of sausage." And then I remembered Jared had once told me his favorite pizza combo, so I added, "with green bell peppers and black olives."

When I made it back to the table, grateful to be out of the overheated restaurant (I'd dressed for January outdoor seating), I told Jared what I'd ordered for him. He glared at me and said, "You shouldn't have done that. I just wanted sausage."

I blinked. I thought he was joking. He wasn't.

Our food came fast—because it was the wrong order. His: a pepperoni pizza with olives. Mine: a beet salad with no beets. But that's what the kitchen made, and the kind server apologized— they were swamped—so that's what we kept.

Jared ate a slice of his pizza before he said, "So you know when you see a friend every month or so, and you ask how they're doing? It's weird in marriage, since you see each other all the time, but...how are you doing?"

I thanked him for asking. Said it was interesting timing after yesterday. I started by thanking him for the sweet thing he'd said last night—how glad he is to come home to me. And I said, "I hope this makes sense—know that it's all good." And I explained that yesterday it was as if I'd been attending a funeral for my old, False Self. The one who needed to be right, to be acknowledged, etc. The goal: to be my True Self. I added, "This might sound odd, but I want to ask you to forgive me." And I explained the jam thing. How I had held onto bitterness about criticism and contradictions.

But he only seemed to hear that he'd been critical. He asked for an example, so I used the most recent instance: what he said just moments ago when I told him the pizza order.

And the conversation devolved from there. We both got defensive. It wasn't ugly, but it wasn't pretty, either.

I mentioned John Gottman's study of the ratio of appreciation to criticism in marriage. How he could predict with 90% accuracy which couples would make it based on this. How the healthy ratio was five appreciations for every criticism.[91] How that scared me.

I added, "Last fall, when you said you don't need me to thank you for things…."

He interjected, "Because I don't need it!"

"We *all* do! So I'm going to continue thanking you anyway. Gratitude is found all throughout Scripture. And apparently, it saves marriages, too."

We finished our meal in silence and then drove home.

Please, God, may we learn that "the purpose of disagreeing is to get closer rather than to win."[92]

I can't believe we got into a jam over *jam*.

[At this point, Jared would like to remind the reader that this book is written from my perspective. He is entirely correct; this is a one-author memoir. I told him I would love more of his perspective—for this scene and any scene—but baring that, let's just say I'm quite impressed he's game for me to write about our relationship. Though I often want more of a reaction from him, I'm learning to be grateful for how little bothers him. It's kind of remarkable, considering how much I let bother me!]

◆ ◆ ◆

Whether to wake him and say words and feel the year
clot
What should the poem do?
What can still be
Saved?

—from "The Marriage" by Jorie Graham[93]

I brought Jared a BAT and chips and salsa for lunch while he worked on the new house. He was grateful!

I shared what I'd felt while praying this morning: that God had set us up last night. From Jared's idea to go out to eat (we haven't dined out in months due to shut-downs), to Gottman's appreciation-to-criticism ratio. As painful as it was, we had a good relationship reset.

And we were starting to figure out what our friend Doug later noted: Jared's dial is set to action and mine is set to emotion.

◆ ◆ ◆

This evening, we started reading *The Giver*. After two chapters, I closed the book and said, "I didn't get a chance to ask—how are *you* doing."

Jared opened up easily. Said he was doing well even though he was too busy. He mentioned trying to keep me, friends, and work in order. He reflected; with all his extra work at the moment, he didn't feel like he was able to keep them in that order—though he wanted to. And that my gratitude for his work—both the job and the house—helped him know that I could see he was doing it for me. That *I* was his priority, not the work.

How about that?

From The Jam Fiasco insistence that he didn't need or want my gratitude, to this. I was impressed.

I smiled, "When I bring lunch to you at the land on the weekends—when you would ordinarily be out playing—I am so, so grateful for all of your work."

He said he'd been looking forward to going out with me on Friday, but he had been a bit blindsided.

I wanted to say that I, too, had been blindsided, but I could feel my defenses rising, so I said nothing.

He referenced my hunch that God had set us up. That each of us could see a new depth of the way the other is trying to love. He hoped that our new house could be a place of healing.

I hugged him, "I agree."

We are figuring out that "Being in war together is what keeps us from being at war with each other."[94]

And as Mom says: you learn to have peace *in* the war.

◆◆◆

Pete & Niesje came for dinner. Delight. They ask good questions and listen well. One of their questions while I was setting out appetizers: how are the first months of marriage?

Jared answered, "Well, I'm learning not to be an asshole when I come home from work."

I almost dropped the cheese plate in laughter. I walked over and gave him a hug. "You're getting so much kinder."

And later, sitting at the table, Pete asked, "What is the best and hardest part of building a house together?"

Jared's answer focused on the best: being outside working on the house, seeing the seasons change, watching the light. I noticed he didn't mention the hardest.

So I decided to answer the hardest as a joke: the "Champagne problem" of lumber prices having more than doubled during Covid, so we have MDF shelves in the closets and pantry instead of real wood.

Then talk of the Enneagram and learning to love others well. The topic of forgiveness arose, and I told the story of being bullied in first grade. How Mom taught me to forgive and then bless. How Dad always asked for forgiveness after moments of anger. Between them—theory and practice—they gave me a gorgeous gift.

◆ ◆ ◆

This evening, Jared mentioned that the bathroom tile wainscoting and baseboards for the new house would cost extra—important features to a woman who used to clean houses professionally. He joked, "That means I can get a new bike!"

I smiled in all seriousness, "Of course."

The happiness a bike would bring him—the happiness tiled bathroom surfaces would bring me. Easy.

While we ate grilled lamb chops and scalloped potatoes in the dining room, Jared leaned back and looked up at the ceiling and said, "I'll be glad not to have meals in this dining room soon."

"Oh?"

"I'm looking forward to the new house."

"Me too."

He thanked me for how I care for this house. I said it's an honor to steward places well. And I looked forward to our new home—getting to start fresh together.

◆ ◆ ◆

Jared has shifted from giving me criticism to giving me gratitude. I want to be sure and do the same internally. Interesting: I did externally, but inside, I was always harping on the wrong. And just simply focusing on the positive isn't enough: it's the gratitude for those positive things that changes us—that repositions our hearts.

This past autumn, I'd wondered if focusing on the positive in our partners is a way of giving them grace. I think it is—when we're grateful.

When we *say grace.*

And so....

I give thanks for my husband's constancy and dependability.

I give thanks for his mighty work ethic.

I give thanks for his washboard abs.

I give thanks that he doesn't dwell on the past like I do.

I give thanks for his wonderful, wild hair—and that he doesn't care about it.

I give thanks that he can be fully present.

I give thanks for the way he loves and listens to God.

The man has earned corn dogs. I defrosted the last four from the box I'd bought for him before our wedding. He ate 'em all—as happy as if I'd served him a ribeye steak.

◆ ◆ ◆

Such a marked difference in communication since The Jam Fiasco last week. When Jared says something that could be hard to interpret as serious or funny, he'll look at me, wait a beat, then smile. Offers plenty of thank yous. Zero complaints.

It was a full day. I met Mom & Dad for lunch, and they told me they'd driven out to the land this weekend. Jared hadn't mentioned their visit to me, but apparently he had told them: "My garage has never been so clean."

Reminder to self: more is going on in my husband's head and heart than he tells me.

> To see her leaves turning look up
> through the mind's perches. Quivering net
> of sparkles, chirps, twitters.
> Notes sprinkled across a page
> as she watches,
> listens to the undersides of thought.

—from "Compose Yourself" by Patricia Goedicke[95]

◆ ◆ ◆

Dan & Janna's for dinner. Such fun. And this time, all four adults ended up talking together—both before and after dinner. Usually, Dan and Jared go off and talk shop (literally: they both run businesses) and Janna and I talk shop (metaphorically: relationships).

While the kids watched a movie, the topic of early marriage came up. Dan said it had been hard learning how to come home from work. Janna translated: "Yeah, when we were first married, he was an asshole when he came home."

We all laughed. Seems to be a thing!

I paraphrased Laurie Mintz's concept of "communication about communication":

> Psychologists call this meta-communication. It's especially useful when starting conversations you're worried about having. As an example, you might say something like… "There's something I want to talk about, and I'm afraid you're going to feel criticized and get defensive rather than realize that I'm bringing this up because I care about you and our relationship." Starting a conversation with meta-communication allows you to put your fears out there, and it also generally helps the other person monitor his or her reactions—as well as

take loving care to avoid the reaction that you feared in the first place.[96]

Mintz also calls this "the preface"—a way of gently introducing a hard topic.

The guys said that when they get home from work, they're so tired, they just don't have energy for many words if they have something hard to say. So the fewer the better.

Jared agreed, "Like three or less."

Dan added, "But it doesn't really work to lead with 'No offense, but...'"

Jared said "Exactly."

Although really, a preface of "no offense" is better than nothing!

◆ ◆ ◆

I awoke thinking about another part of last night's conversation. How we can become aware of God's goodness in our partners—despite differences.

Jared said he had been thinking about that conversation, too—especially the idea of responding in judgement versus curiosity. How one response closes us off and one opens us up.

May we move forward in curiosity....

◆ ◆ ◆

Seek to understand—not necessarily to agree.

Say, "tell me more."

Be curious, not accusatory.

Wisdom garnered from podcasts while touching up the old, streaked paint job in the kitchen, courtesy of the previous owners. Now, it's all creamy.

I took longer than I planned and must have been getting out of the bath as Jared pulled up and so didn't hear him arrive. I was dressing when I heard the bedroom door open. I jumped and turned to see him standing there with a look of mild exasperation. He said, "I need coffee. And I can't find the coffee press."

I followed him to the kitchen where *every* single cupboard door was open. I smiled, "It's in the dishwasher. Just ask me next time." I started closing doors. "Though I love the drama of all the open cupboards."

> What matters is if we can repair tiny moments of misattunement and come back into harmony…. Relationship stability depends not on healing huge rifts but on mending the constant small tears.[97]

Jared said, "Why don't you just hand wash the coffee press?" Then he caught himself and added with a smile. "Just kidding."

I smiled, "Oh, I do. But once a week, I pop it in the dishwasher to get it sparkly."

I remembered something I'd heard decades before: if it can be funny later, it can be funny now. I was able to keep my humor on, and so was he. I was proud of us.

Still, I decided to change the subject while we were ahead: "The grocery store was out of the chocolate bars with nuts you like. But I'll keep an eye out."

"No problem. Just for the future." And he started to laugh, "I hesitate to say it, but…I like the ones with fruit, too. Just not fresh fruit and chocolate! I know, it's crazy."

I smiled big, "See! The preface totally works."

He made a face—but a funny one.

We went to Alex & Rachael's for tri-tip dinner. Good conversation. I feel like part of the family. At some point, the oddness of English grammar rules came up—how things that are right can sound wrong. I gave the example, "We say 'It's me!' though it should be 'It is I!' But these days, people sound silly if they say that, so we've come to accept the wrong grammar as right."

The kids grabbed the grammar and ran with it. Natalie decided she would henceforth announce her arrival with, "It is I!"

Before bed, I thanked Jared for sharing his family with me.

He didn't reply. I'm trying not to need one.

◆ ◆ ◆

Give thanks, take joy.

◆ ◆ ◆

Beautiful delivery today: a wooden bench from the Penningtons with a brass plaque that reads:

Jared & Anna
"Come grow old with me,
the best is yet to be"
Robert Browning

I sat on the bench a moment in the cold, excited to show Jared the gift.

When he came home, he was soaked from the rain and silent. I waited until he had finished dinner before saying, "I have something fun to show you."

I took him out to the porch and showed him the bench. He smiled.

I read the inscription aloud and sat down. He stayed standing, silent. I patted the space next to me and said, "Let's inaugurate it with a kiss."

He sat. We kissed. He took my hand and said, "I love you."

He kept quiet the rest of the night, and I silently blessed whatever worries he was carrying.

◆ ◆ ◆

Over date-night dinner in the dining room, Jared smiled and said he'd made an executive decision.

"Oh? Do tell."

"Picture the 'brownies' at the new house as they are."

"Okay…."

Within minutes, I felt like we'd been caught in conversational crossfire. I asked, "Can we pause? I feel like we're not getting anywhere."

We had gotten stuck:

> The natural compassion that couples have for each other gives way to a defensive resentment as they begin to expect the other to let them down or hurt them in some way. They get trapped in a rigid, monocular vision that makes the beloved seem like an opponent rather than a partner.[98]

After a bit of a time out, we got to the core of the problem—which had nothing to do with "brownies," or any of the other "subjects" of our disagreements, but rather with *how* we disagree and lose connection.

Something bigger is always going on: "Change starts with seeing the pattern, with focusing on the game rather than the ball."[99]

I said, "I'd love to feel like we are teammates, not opponents. Not at war."

He said he liked the team-not-war idea. And he had thought our failed "brownie" conversation was play, though I perceived it as war.

We agreed to remember that we're on the same team. We talked about needing to figure out how the other receives love. He reiterated that he loves me and, just as importantly, likes me.

I said I was so grateful that he daily tells me he loves me. That it means so much. "But honestly? I feel like you *don't* like me a lot of the time. I'm very glad to be wrong about that."

We hugged a good, long hug and ended the evening agreeing to be on the same team. And to name our team "Emmanuel"—God with us.

◆ ◆ ◆

we are so made that nothing contents us

—from "Hive" by Carolyn Forché[100]

While chatting with God (okay, complaining) about how slowly Jared and I are figuring things out, I sensed Him cosmically chuckling somewhere. Then, in the voice of Tevye from *Fiddler on the Roof,* He asked me, "What's your hurry, what's your worry?"

Humph.

But also: noted.

Mid-morning, I texted Jared a photo we'd taken of the two of us on Roxy Ann last spring. In the photo, the setting sun haloes us from behind. My caption: "Team Emmanuel."

His reply: "Definitely."

◆ ◆ ◆

On my walk, I realized: Jared is the only person who has ever straight-up thanked me for being myself.

Trip-prep for the coast. Cooler. Basket of snacks. Jared got off work early, so we were able to leave by 4:30—though it would have been even sooner if he'd found his shears. Apparently, he had a great big pair of broken shears he cuts his hair with. Apparently, he hasn't needed them since I moved in. And, apparently, they have gone missing.

I don't ever remember seeing them, though he described them in detail. I pointed out that there's a great pair of haircutting scissors in the bathroom drawer. After he continued opening cupboard doors and drawers for a while, he finally used the scissors to cut his hair.

I could feel the options arise in me: get miffed about him being miffed or…bless the trip. As we pulled out of the driveway, I chose to bless the trip.

We drove mostly in silence while Jared unwound from his work week. Long after dark, he was ready to talk. The topic of differences came up. How we're attracted to someone different from us so that we can grow.

We are beginning to learn that our differences "become the very force that serves to reveal, and then heal, whatever may have been in the way of…realizing unconditional love."[101]

◆ ◆ ◆

Our first morning at the inn, we poked through the bag of "continental breakfast" delivered to our door, which contained more sanitized plastic packaging than food. We sat at the little table, watching dawn brighten the dark town, river, and sea.

Eventually, a single car drove down one of the deserted streets.

In his hilarious, fake country accent, Jared said, "Look honey, there's a car!"

I laughed.

Once it was full daylight, we walked to the beach and were greeted with high winds. In middle school, I had lived on the Oregon coast, and this was the windiest I ever remembered it. Rivers of sand ran toward us as we faced south. As we returned north, the wind pushed our backs. We could lean back fully into the force of it and still be pushed forward.

Back in town, the air was still but cold. We got coffee and cookies at the coffee house. The weather held enough that it was almost pleasant to sit outside and enjoy them. Almost. After, we went back to the hotel to warm up. We each read our own books for a bit. Then I shared a passage from *Love Worth Making,* about the phases couples go through—how disappointment is part of getting to real love. "Us love," I like to call it.

We talked about the phases Niesje mentioned: how we continually cycle from infatuation to learning to disappointment to decision…and back again.

Jared said he struggles with disappointment in himself. I said I struggle with being disappointed in others, in circumstances. Interesting difference.

We walked down into town again for lunch, passing a tavern. Jared pointed out their "To-Go Cocktails" sign. I said that's maybe the only benefit of Covid!

We splurged on a whole crab at Tony's Crab Shack. Which, at $31 and barely bigger than a fist—legs included, turned out to be an expensive appetizer. It was so cold out on the picnic table that the second the server brought us our meal, the melted butter started to solidify. I mused aloud that a hot toddy would keep my fingers from freezing.

Jared remembered, "Hey, the tavern offered to-go cocktails."

Brilliant.

I walked across the street. To order alcoholic beverages to-go, the mysterious mandates required you to also order food. The savvy staff had figured out a good fix: the dollar peanut butter sandwich. No jelly, just Wonder Bread and peanut butter. Which turned out to be a good lunch supplement for Jared.

The conversation about disappointment came up again, and we related it to wanting to succeed at challenges. Jared said that's why he didn't want to get married for so long. He knew it would be a challenge—but he also knew he hadn't been ready for it. Eventually, he was ready because the risk was worth the gain.

The day gentled along. Soon it was time to think about dinner. We picked up take-out from Billy Smoothboars and enjoyed it back at the hotel with a movie. I can't remember ever having this swath of unrushed, untasked time with my husband. What a gift.

◆ ◆ ◆

During our shared quiet after breakfast, I thought of "good & good knitting." While dating last spring, Jared and I had brought Thai take-out to a park, where we watched the sun set. In my spirit, I heard the sound of knitting needles and had the sense that God was knitting our hearts together. Right after The Jam Fiasco, the knitting metaphor came to me again. That time, I "heard" a different sound: the knitting needles were undoing bad stitches—undoing a wrong row to return to the right design.

When I told this to Jared, he said it was hard but good knitting.

This weekend? Good & good.

We checked out of the inn and drove to Face Rock, but the winds were still gale force. So we decided to find the Whiskey Run Trails Jared had mentioned just north of us—and just inland.

Though you could hear the not-so-distant roar of the ocean, the air in the forest was eerily still. Not a leaf or pine needle moved in this mossy, fern-fronded magic-land. We walked over five miles alternating between dark, fairy-tale forests and open, deforested hills with new monoculture trees.

After, we drove to nearby Charleston's High Tide Café for fish and chips, on Andy & Linda's recommendation. Lo and behold: a covered outdoor patio with space heaters. And the best clam chowder I've ever tasted. And beer-battered rock fish that was heaven with a dollop of tartar sauce and a sprinkle of malt vinegar.

Then the drive home along the muddy, flooded Coquille River. Noting the low road through high marshes, I recalled the floods of 1996. That winter, I'd traveled back to the coast from Montana to visit my friend Molly for the holidays.

Jared remembered those floods. He'd been at a family house on the river, which was usually fifty feet above water level. But that year, river water lapped at the doorstep.

"I was in high school," he added.

"I was in college." I smiled, "Sometimes I forget I'm the older woman."

He said, "I've always dated older women, except for my last girlfriend." He paused and laughed. "I'm so mature."

I laughed, too. Then I added: "Remember that businessman in Redding I told you about? The one I edited for? I used to meet him and his wife for lunch each week to go over book drafts. One day, they mentioned they were praying for my future husband. The man said, 'He's like a young bottle of wine that needs a few more years to mature into a fine vintage.'"

I neglected to mention that was the spring after Jared told me he wasn't ready to grow up yet, and he just wanted to be friends.

There we were. And here we are.

And then we were back home.

Before bed, Jared huffed and puffed that he couldn't find his ear drops—which have been in his nightstand since I moved in (when I asked if I could move the things that were in what would be my nightstand into his).

I suggested he look in his nightstand drawer. He opened it and found them.

I confess that it has been hard for me to live in this house. I try to respect Jared's space while also being brave enough to enter into it—to share it. And though he's never said it, it has likely been hard for him to make space for me here. We've each had to unlearn some old ways of being.

In moments of difficulty, I want to remember this, from the authors of *Crucial Conversations*:

> We're asking you to fight your natural tendency to respond in kind. We're asking you to undo years of practice, maybe even eons of genetic shaping that prod you to take flight or pick a fight (when under attack) and recode the stimulus, "Ah, that's a sign that the other person feels unsafe." And then what? Do something to make it safe.[102]

And this from Ephesians 4:32: "Be kind to one another, tenderhearted, forgiving one another, as God in Christ forgave you."

Kairos: Kind/ness

Nothing can make our life, or the lives of other people, more beautiful than perpetual kindness.

—Leo Tolstoy

First Grade was a nightmare for me. It was the early eighties, and our family had moved from Oregon to Montana. I was tall and shy, and the popular Mean-Girl clique at my new school decided to hate me. I was bullied before our culture talked about bullying.

It was my first experience with ongoing emotional pain. It was also my first experience with ongoing physical pain: I was growing so fast that I only fit in the same pair of shoes for a matter of months (I was on my way to be six-foot-three by high school). My feet ached, especially at night. I often cried myself to sleep over the pain in my feet and the pain in my heart.

My Mom tucked me into bed every night. And while I lamented the school girls' meanness, she massaged my feet and taught me how to forgive them.

Forgive? I wanted straight-up revenge!

With gentleness, Mom persisted. Did I want to be like them?

No! Of course not.

Then I needed to forgive them.

This back and forth went on for months.

By Christmas break, I was maybe willing to forgive, but then Mom dropped another bombshell. She suggested I *pray* for the girls. What the heck? The very tormentors who were the source of my pain? No way.

But Mom is persistent—and almost always right. Eventually, I gave in. As I started praying for those girls, something shifted in my heart.

Mom helped me wonder what they might have gone through, what pain had been inflicted on them that *they* had not forgiven and now inflicted on someone else. Did I want to become part of that same cycle or break it?

How I answered that question certainly saved my emotional life.

Despite trying, I was never able to reconcile with those classmates. But that's okay. Forgiveness can happen regardless of reconciliation. More important is forgiving—it's the action we can take for ourselves, the heart-work we can do even if the other person does not. And it's worth doing; if we don't forgive, we grow bitter—not just hurting ourselves but also inflicting that unforgiven pain on someone else.

My Dad taught me about forgiveness when I was young, too. In fact, he modeled it. As he worked through his own issues, he sometimes lost his temper. And though he never did or said anything remotely awful, he knew what was in his own heart. Often, after a mild outburst, Dad would seek me and my brother out and apologize. Many times, I would hear a knock on my door and Dad's voice asking to come in. When I invited him inside, he'd come sit at the edge of my bed, apologize, and ask me to forgive him.

Here was my big, tall father—first a policeman and then a pastor, a man with strength and authority—asking a little girl to forgive him. He humbled himself and gave me that immense power. And always, I would smile and hug him and forgive him. In that exchange of grace, all was restored. To this day, I have not a single resentment toward my father. We dealt with everything as it came, and no bitterness built up.

In her book, *Beautiful Battlefields,* Bo Stern writes:

> Bitterness turns us into a brute beast. We lose sensitivity to God's voice. We can't hear anything over the sound of our own pain, and we trample people who may be just as wounded. Like a water buffalo at a tea party, we become all brawn and no brain; all power and no poise. At best, bitterness is disruptive and ineffective; at worst, it's lonely and destructive.[103]

She then notes two remedies to bitterness: forgiveness and gratitude:

> Forgiveness fills the hole that bitterness leaves behind, and it helps you see yourself more clearly.... The quickest route from bitterness to beauty is through the door of thanksgiving.[104]

My Mom & Dad are forgiveness superheroes. They taught me forgiveness, which kept me from bitterness, and I give continual thanks for that.

In fact, I believe forgiveness is the superpower we all possess that would change the world if we chose to use it.

I realize that not everyone had my parents to teach them how to forgive. That was a priceless gift. Still, I am often baffled when people don't believe in the power of forgiveness. That's like not believing in gravity. A supernatural truth is as true as a natural one. More so.

And for spouses to love each other well, we must forgive not only each other but also those who hurt us in the past...or we will end up hurting the one we love in the present.

> Love, the highest kind of love that matters most, is not—cannot be—determined by what others do, or

don't do toward us.... If we wish to love our partner unconditionally, meaning no matter what they manifest toward us—even if it seems uncaring—we must never return unkindness with unkindness.[105]

Dear, broken world: when people hurt us, may we respond not in kind but in kindness.

Chronos: February

When we returned from Bandon last night, Jared showed me a video of a flash mob concert singing "Ode to Joy."

On our drive home, I had told him that *joy* was my word for the year. Now I have an anthem!

This morning, when he came in to hug me goodbye, he pulled back to look me in the eye and thanked me for all my cleaning and picking up—he paused to smile—even if he can't find anything. Then, more seriously, he said, "I'm sorry for getting angry when I can't find something."

He finished, "So thank you, and I'm sorry."

"I *so* appreciate you saying that." I held him close again, fully forgiving.

When he left, a grace and spaciousness expanded in me, as if a few of those emotional cinder blocks had been lifted off my chest, and my heart had more oxygen to work with.

The power of apology and forgiveness!

Another quote from *Why Won't You Apologize?* is appropriate here:

The healing power of a *good* apology is also immediately recognizable. When someone offers me a genuine apology, I feel relieved and soothed. Whatever anger and resentment I may still be harboring melts away.[106]

Wholehearted agreement.

◆◆◆

After writing this morning, I walked with Hayley in the woods above her house. She told me the best argument story I've heard in a while. On a recent walk in the trails, she had overheard a 4- and 5-year-old pair of siblings talking. The older child, a girl, was picking ferns to feed the fairies...to her younger brother's consternation. He kept telling her to *stop!* The mice needed to eat them. She kept picking. Finally, he said in anger, "I hope you're happy—you're going to kill all the mice!" She retorted, "I hope *you're* happy—you're going to kill all the fairies!

Classic relationship fortune telling and all-or-nothing thinking!

When I came home, I found a letter from New Zealand in the mailbox. Joella! Her last lines: "May this season of spring, which will be upon you soon, bring renewed life and joy to you and your husband."

Well, isn't that the perfect blessing?

◆◆◆

Before bed, I applied a lavender-heavy essential oil blend Bobbi had given me that is supposed to help you sleep well.

As he kissed me, Jared said: "This is a compliment, but you smell like you tripped on a stick and fell in a lavender bush."

I laughed, "Nice preface!"

Joy always,

Joy everywhere—
Let joy kill you!
Keep away from the little deaths.

—from "Joy" by Carl Sandburg[107]

◆◆◆

I applied a new gasket around the wood stove door. A sooty adventure. Interesting: Jared recently bought a new gasket for the neck of his kayak drysuit. And I just noticed I need a new gasket for my Bialetti stovetop coffee maker.

It feels like the week earlier this winter when all the vehicles needed servicing at the same time. This seems to be the Time of Gaskets.

◆◆◆

Tackled the last of the interior paint touch-ups today. Finished the banisters just in time to make chili and cornbread before Gene & Debbie arrived.

After dinner, we all sat in the living room, and Gene played several songs on his guitar. My favorite: "It Is Well With My Soul." He told us the author wrote it after losing four of his children in a shipwreck. To be able to find peace in such tragedy.... Now I know why those lyrics hold such power.

◆◆◆

I listened to relationship podcasts while cleaning the dreaded shed. Spiders. Damp. Mold. Yuck.

But good gleanings from several episodes: before saying or doing something, ask yourself: will this make our relationship better or worse? And ask your partner questions about themselves: zero pressure for them, and you'll learn about them—and learn to not take what they do personally.

Jared is one-third done with the pavers on the back deck of the new house. One hundred pounds each, those pavers. He is mighty, and I told him so.

◆◆◆

After Jared pulled into the driveway, I heard him talking to our neighbors over the fence. When he came inside, he said, "They guessed I fixed their mailbox. The granddaughter said I was the greatest. At least somebody thinks I am."

I couldn't tell if he was joking. I smiled, "Many people think you're great. Me included."

Over dinner, I opened the deck of couple's conversation cards I'd bought and shuffled them. The one I drew to ask him, I kid you not: "What's one time lately that I've made you feel great about yourself and how can I do that more often?"

He didn't say anything for a while.

I laughed, "Obviously, I need to up my game!"

Then he mentioned not needing gratitude. How he doesn't understand it. When he elaborated, I discovered he thought my gratitude was the only way I was trying to make him feel great.

Oh boy.

He looked at the card on the table. "That's a terrible game."

Say grace.

I smiled, "It's not really a game. Don't worry: we don't have to do the whole deck. Thanks for trying it."

[Jared would like to add that he would have hidden those cards if I'd kept pulling them out. I would like to add that I have not pulled them out since! In fact, I gave them away.]

He asked, "What about you?"

I said, "Hmm. The first thing that comes to mind is an evening a few weeks ago. It was the day I felt like I had a funeral for my old self—it had been a rough day, emotionally. You got off work in a good mood, enjoyed dinner. I sat there just trying to hold it together. After the meal, you gave me a hug and said how glad you were to come home to me. That meant so much."

After tonight's meal, I washed the dishes while Jared stretched in front of the fire. I thought of him lifting cinder blocks and brick all day long and how grateful I am to do the household things— and for our easy division of labor. Which is no small thing. Come to think of it, one of the few seamless parts of our marriage has been sifting out who would do what. In our case, it's a complementary extension of Mr. Outdoorsy and Mrs. Indoorsy: my husband is happiest working outside the home, and I'm happiest working inside it. Something easy—how about *that?*

While Jared stretched his hamstrings and I started scouring the cast iron skillet, we talked about the difference between simple and easy, especially in building the house. How simple isn't always easy.

He looked up and said, "I thought of something." I wasn't sure what he was referring to. Turns out, it was the conversation card. "I feel great when I come home and I feel loved by you." I was immediately flooded with *good* emotions, and I had to focus as I scraped gravy from the skillet.

He continued. He enjoys how I make it easy for him to see family and friends here at the house by planning and cooking dinners. He loves that. And how, if we weren't together, he'd have been alone during Covid, coming home to an empty house.

I finally just left the skillet in the sink and came to sit next to him and lean my head on his shoulder. By then, he was clipping his heel calluses onto the hearth. Ah, the juxtaposition of romance and practicalities.

What can I do to make him feel great? Seems to be the very things he said he didn't care about when we were first married: coming home, *being* at home, anything to do with home. Maybe that's why he didn't immediately recognize that a welcoming, loving home makes him feel great.

And feelings are essential: "The focus of your feelings becomes the reality of your world."[108]

May we both figure out more ways to make each other feel great.

◆ ◆ ◆

The soapstone for the new house's kitchen counters arrived! And tomorrow, the toilets get installed. This means we will likely be moved in by month's end after all.

I read an odd generalization somewhere: that husbands often like to unwind with their wives around—but they don't necessarily need to be interacting with them. That might not be true for every couple, but it seems to apply to us. In the evening, I stretch or read while Jared does his digital stuff. Then, when he sets his laptop aside, I offer to read aloud a story while he stretches. And our current book, *Harris and Me,* is hilarious.

Understanding builds. As we kissed goodnight, I said, "Our neighbor was right. You *are* the greatest."

◆ ◆ ◆

Oh, the book *How to Improve Your Marriage Without Talking About It.* I've been mulling over it all week. So much of it echoes the classic exhortation to change yourself. How love will begin to change your partner—not *you* trying to change them.

Which echoes a line from *Crucial Conversations:* "the best way to work on 'us' is to start with 'me.'"[109]

Which also echoes *Independent Enough:*

> We don't realize that true happiness in relationships and life ultimately starts and ends with *us* doing the hard work to develop those characteristics about ourselves so we can meet the challenges most relationships bring…no matter how someone else is acting.[110]

All of these books have started to form one, big cross-check for the heart-math of love.

This morning, before we got out of bed, Jared thanked me for a good week. Then he said, "I love you, Anna."

I replied, "I love you too—so much."

And then he added, "Thank you for crawling through life with me." He paused before adding: "I feel lucky."

I smiled. Love was doing its work in both of us.

◆ ◆ ◆

Valentine's Day. Jared kayaked with the guys for most of the day. I was glad he got away to play, but I kind of wished he'd wanted to play with me.

Over dinner, he said he'd thought about getting me wine, but he figured I knew what I liked and could get whatever I wanted. Then he thought about getting me flowers but for some reason thought I didn't care about them.

I said, "The new house is the best Valentine's gift I could ask for."

We sat on the loveseat in front of the fire. At one point, I matched my breathing to his and noticed how much faster his is. How he's constantly wired for action. So I silently blessed him with rest.

◆ ◆ ◆

This morning, I called to see if it was an open burn day…and it was! I optimistically brought out a book to read, but a full day of burning required my full attention. Thankfully, I remembered a long stick of pitch wood Jared had found on one of our camping excursions. I crammed it down into the barrel as deep as I could, and it stayed lit when damp things refused to catch.

It was so gratifying to watch yard debris and moldy cardboard go up in smoke. It was also gratifying to wash ash from my hair after.

Jared and I shared a dinner of seafood chowder and cornbread and ended up in the living room, as usual. I stretched while he did some digital stuff, and then I read *Harris and Me* until bedtime.

After I closed the book, he lingered a while on the couch. Turns out: he was deciding what furniture to keep and what to sell. We agree on keeping the coffee table and the round oak table upstairs…but the agreements end there. I'd like to keep his antique tufted leather chairs—my favorite of the things he owns—but he said they're uncomfortable and kept telling me I shouldn't like them and *he* didn't want to keep them.

I started to get angry; here I was, trying to find elements of his décor that I *did* like (without emphasizing all the things I did *not*), and here he was trying to talk me out of liking them.

I remembered that I can only change myself. Time to practice holding my ground in equanimity. Since my husband likes logic, I stopped trying to convince him of the antique chairs' beauty. Instead, voice level, I said, "Well, they're more comfortable than the hard metal chairs at the kitchen island you like to sit at."

No reply. For once, I was fine with that.

◆ ◆ ◆

Paying attention to anger:

> Anger is something we feel. It exists for a reason and always deserves our respect and attention…. We all have a right to everything we feel, and certainly anger is no exception. There are questions about anger, however, that may be helpful to ask ourselves: What am I really angry about? What is the problem? And whose problem is it?... When I'm angry, how can I clearly communicate my position without becoming defensive or attacking?[111]

Let's just say I have so many answers to those questions!

Meanwhile, I'll be grateful for this: both Jared and I love the antique wooden steering wheel on the mantle. When my parents last came for lunch, Dad had guessed it was from a Model T Ford. He was right: Jared's great-grandfather's. A wonderful heirloom.

At least we both fully agree to keep *that*.

◆ ◆ ◆

The root of the word *emotion* is basically motion: "to move." A Captain Obvious etymology if there ever was one, but I had never thought of it before. Turns out, the original purpose of emotion was to trigger us to action. If we encounter a rattlesnake, the emotion of fear will move us out of its way. But when we don't use our emotions to move forward—physically *and* mentally—they can mire us in a bog of overthinking.

Marriage is helping me learn to move through my emotions, that's for sure.

And here's a not-so-obvious bit: "The fact is that *emotions are logical*."[112] I like that. And I like this:

> The most important part of your emotions is not how they make you feel but what they get you to do.[113]

So, to take charge of my emotional well-being today, I focused on good things, gave thanks for them, and prayed.

And yet...massive date night communication fail, *again*.

◆◆◆

Pouring rain outside and in my heart. I'll say it: cloudy with a chance of meatballs. Because that's what I made for dinner tonight.

This morning, Jared texted that if I needed anything at the store, he could pick it up. I didn't reply right away. I was still stewing over the harshness that had arisen in last night's conversation.

I had just read about relationship repair attempts: instead of saying "sorry," a person might offer to help with something or propose doing something together.

> Even the most entrenched non-apologizer may have a nonverbal way to try to defuse tension, reconnect after a fight, or show you through behavior that he or she is sorry and wants to make amends. Aim to make your default position one of generosity of spirit.[114]

I try!

My compassion rose as another downpour started this afternoon, and I knew Jared was out working in it. I finally texted that I didn't need anything, but I'd have coffee hot for him if he let me know when he was on his way home. He replied:

> I would love that.
> Home about 5:15.
> Thank you.

Definitely a repair attempt. Usually, his message would only be the middle line.

When he arrived, we kissed hello and hugged. When we pulled apart, I said, "I love you."

He said, "I love you, too. And I'm sorry. I don't know what for…"

I hugged him again. He added, "You don't need to tell me. There's probably a list."

There is. A long one. But I forgave it all.

> Dear Forgiveness, I saved a plate for you.
> Quit milling around the
> yard and come inside.
>
> —from "Litany in Which Certain Things Are Crossed Out" by Richard Siken[115]

◆◆◆

My studio! I'll have studio in the new house. On the house plans, it had been just an empty room with a utilitarian sink. But I cashed in one of my investments—a static one—so that I could have all the cabinets and standing desk installed before we move in. An even better investment.

It will be the first dedicated studio I've ever had.

◆◆◆

Spontaneous Sunday brunch with Jared's Dad and Linda at Gold Miner Restaurant.

Then home for a nap. A mellow day of rest. As I made an early dinner of nachos, Jared said from the couch, "It's like Bandon."

It is. This is the only other fully chill day of rest we've had since we've been married—no packing/unpacking from camping, no work on either house. Just blissful rest.

◆◆◆

Late afternoon, I met Jared and our builder, Ross, at the new house to decide where we wanted light dimmers. Jared was a bit in post-work-intensity mode after being at the grout pump all day, though I could tell he was trying to be kind. I made a comment not related to the task at hand, and he said with a smile, "Focus." But not long after, he told a story that took several minutes.

As we wound up, I noticed a small chunk of grout near his eye. I pointed it out from across the corner of the kitchen island—very intentionally *not* wiping it away, having been chastised for doing that once before.

He licked his thumb and held it out toward me, "Like Great Aunt Gertrude saying, 'You've got something in your eye.'"

I leaned back, kept my smile on and said, "I did *not* do that."

Ross quickly took his leave.

I drove home. Jared stayed to finish a few things.

Say grace.

I give thanks that the house is almost finished.

I give thanks that we are learning to communicate.

I give thanks that I can choose to be curious—not furious—about...everything!

Not long after I returned to the old house and started warming the dinner I'd prepped, Jared called. Said how great it was to see my joy for the new house. And...that he was sorry for being short. He's still working on the work-to-home transition.

I thanked him for saying so, accepted the apology, and added "I forgive you, like always. And I'm grateful you always forgive me.

Also, you're already much better about coming home than when we first got married!"

My heart was light when the call ended. Both for his heartfelt apology and for the fact that I had kept myself from a negative thought spiral and (mostly) had not taken anything personally.

It has taken us almost eight months!

◆ ◆ ◆

We move tomorrow.

For the final Friday night at this address, we ate steak and watched a save-the-world movie. Afterward, we sat in the darkness and Jared thanked me for all my help since we've been married—from cooking to shopping to bill pay—how it's given him time to help more with the family business.

A lovely thing to hear on our last night in this house.

Every exit...an entrance someplace else.

—Tom Stoppard

◆ ◆ ◆

Moving day chaos.

Thank you to family and flat-bed trucks! The weather held—and all the main furniture is in. Mom helped me line shelves and drawers. Dad had tweaked his back, but he still helped load his truck, sweet guy.

Alex and Andy and Abe (all "A" names, I just noticed), helped Jared schlep large things, including "He-Man-ing" the round oak table up onto the back deck and into the wide-enough double doors of my studio.

Alex mentioned how challenging it is to build a house. Andy

added that a high percentage of couples who build together end up divorcing. I received both of these comments as male compliments for making it through the stress!

Rachael brought bread and wine—her homemade sourdough and Kerrygold butter. She helped unpack kitchen things while Abe and Natalie unwrapped the barstools and named the robot vacuum Marlo.

Jared fetched chicken strips from Lil' Pantry to augment the bread. And then we all had a food coma and called it a day.

As everyone headed home, Jared returned to the old house and loaded up all his kayaks and bikes. My first glimpse of him driving up to the new house was with five kayaks and five bikes in his truck bed. Appropriate.

He had texted me on his way, "Almost home."

Home. *Our* home.

For dinner, we went to the Mexican restaurant across the river, Taqueria La Guacamaya. (Thankfully, indoor dining is now allowed again...for the moment.) Since it was my first time there, I ordered tortilla soup: my litmus test for Mexican fare. It was the best I've ever had.

Back home to build the first fire in the wood stove and watch the flames dance.

And then to bed, not knowing we'd sleep beneath the full Snow Moon, so bright you could read by its light through our curtainless windows, though we were too tired to touch a book.

◆ ◆ ◆

House firsts:

First love in full-moon, morning light.

First coffee.

First sunrise watched together, squished side by side in the big leather arm chair by the window.

First kiss at the front door, beneath the mistletoe Jared hung above it.

That afternoon, Sarah & Christer brought capital-C Champagne and corn chowder. We toasted the house on the front patio.

First Champagne toast in the pre-spring sunshine.

And later, first bath: the water orange from the well's high iron content.

So much beautiful new.

> May it be a house of courage,
> Where healing and growth are loved,
> Where dignity and forgiveness prevail
>
> —from "For a New Home" by John O'Donohue[116]

Kairos: The Gasket of Grace

I would like to suggest that gaskets are romantic.

I don't think I really knew what a gasket was until we had three needing to be replaced. First to go was Jared's kayak drysuit neck gasket (which I *really* didn't know about). Second was our wood stove door gasket (which I learned how to change). And third was my little stovetop coffee maker gasket (which melts if I accidentally leave the contraption on the burner too long).

Once things happen in threes, I start to pay special attention. And I research meaning. Turns out, the official definition of a gasket is a seal that fills the space between two or more mating surfaces.

Well, if that isn't a relationship metaphor!

A favorite of the way-too-many marriage books I've read is *The Zimzum of Love*. It explores *zimzum*—the dynamic energy field between two partners in marriage: the space between.[117] I tend to mention it like a broken record because I'm continually fascinated by the space between two people.

And basically, *zimzum* is like a gasket.

The best part of the gasket definition? It allows for less-than-perfect mating surfaces between two, irregular parts. Which could be said of the space between two, irregular people.

"So," I asked myself, "What is the gasket of marriage?"

First, remember that my husband and I are *very* different. We are learning to laugh about this.

He's Mr. Spontaneity. On a Friday after a long work week, he can grab a jar of peanut butter and head out camping on a whim. I am Mrs. Planner. If we are going camping, I like to A) know about it at least a day in advance and B) pack a cooler brimming with pesto, sliced aged cheddar, pre-chopped onions soaking in olive oil for morning scrambled eggs, driving snacks of sea-salt dark chocolate, a good bottle of wine, etc. etc.

He's Mr. DIY. Whether changing the car oil, installing a new dishwasher, or cutting his hair, he's a do-it-yourself kinda guy. I'm Mrs. Outsource-My-Weaknesses. I like to take the car in for its checkup to my trusty mechanic, hire a handyman to install anything that comes with a lengthy instruction manual and connects to electricity or water, and when I did briefly cut my own hair for a season, it just confirmed that I should leave some things to the professionals.

He's Mr. Down-to-Earth and says it like it is. I'm Mrs. Pie-in-the-Sky and tend to quote literature aloud. When we watched *Starsky & Hutch* one night, I recognized the start of a favorite Shakespeare line, quoted by Snoop Dogg, "To err is human…" and I spoke in time with the rest of it: "…to forgive, divine." At dinner parties now, my husband likes to say I quote Snoop Dogg, at which point, I start distinguishing between primary and secondary sources.

Whether expressed by a bard from the seventeenth century or the twenty-first, forgiveness is something my husband and I both agree on. It's the gasket of grace. Especially in marriage. And especially when two different people approach life in different ways—which is bound to lead to misunderstandings.

Maybe we don't need a lot of grace to love someone who's a lot like ourselves. That's pretty easy. Learning to love difference is a gift in that it *does* require a lot of grace. Maybe the more difference between two people, the more grace we can have—if we also choose to give it.

So whether I lean toward my poetic-academic love of Big Words and call it *zimzum*, or whether I lean toward the practical gasket, I know that whatever seals the space between us will be made of grace.

Chronos: March

I couldn't go back to sleep after Jared's 4:15 alarm, and so I began an all-over-the-place day in the new house: unpacking, getting overwhelmed, loading up and clearing the old house, back to the new house to let Mom in—she continues to line drawers and shelves for me, grand woman. And Dad brought lunch. Grand man.

Tired.

Coffee.

Back to the old place again after Jared got off work to help him take down the garage shop contents.

So glad I spent a month cleaning out the old garage.

And so glad to walk through our new doors.

> The soul's door
> swings open
> on its hinges.
>
> —from "The Beginning" by Mona Van Duyn[118]

◆ ◆ ◆

More house firsts:

First package in the mailbox: Saint Patrick's décor for the housewarming party (shamrock stickers).

First dance (solo) to Noah and the Whale's "5 Years Time" while prepping…

…first-date-night dinner in our new kitchen.

Today was also the Day of Waiting. I had to be home all morning to wait for Spectrum to install the Wi-Fi and all afternoon to wait for Home Depot to deliver the washer and dryer. It was a bright, blue-sky day, and I was overjoyed to not have to drive to the old house but to be able to unpack everything that had been hauled over to the new.

After installations and deliveries were finally done, I made time to enjoy a long bath with a glass of sparkly Accolade from the Applegate—the only kind of accolade I fancy these days. While soaking, I prayed for our date night and realized it was the eve of our eight-month anniversary.

I looked up the spiritual meaning of the number eight: new beginnings, new creation. And so, our first date night in the new house is the threshold of a new beginning.

◆ ◆ ◆

First dinner guests in the new house: Mike & Bobbi. I made Chicken Marbella. They brought all the rest: bacon green beans, salad, potatoes, blueberry crisp. So sweet of them.

During conversation, the subject of newness came up. I shared what I'd learned about the spiritual significance of the number eight and new things.

But Jared's comments about all the newness did not sound, um, positive.

I bit my tongue. Because newness had been hard for me too; the day I woke up married in his old place, I had a new town, new house, new *name.*[*] Now I have the chance to give grace as he works through newness.

And to *say* grace.

I give thanks for my husband's honesty.

I give thanks for misunderstandings that open us up to deeper understanding.

I give thanks for all the new we get to share—and that it will be good.

◆ ◆

While we were stretching this evening on the floor, I said how I loved that the robot vacuum, Marlo, can fit under the kitchen range and clean.

Jared said, "No one cares about that."

I said, "I do. Interior places are important to me."

I admit: I let his comment offend me.

(Future Me chooses to see the humor: another example of Mr. Outdoorsy and Mrs. Indoorsy. I am reminded of the song "5 Years Time" I danced to in front of that kitchen range, and I have a hunch that Future-Future Me will start to see the hilarity *as* things happens—or at least continue to drop her offenses!)

◆ ◆ ◆

Chris brought over the blue pine dining room table I'd

---

[*] After we married, I took Jared's last name and changed Elkins into my middle name—and now use that as my pen name.

commissioned from him. It was made from a few of the plank benches he and Shannon had set up at their wedding. The table was beautiful, though different from my original idea of two pieces of live-edge wood with a single seam down the middle—a play on "two become one." This was made of six, thinner pieces of irregular lengths, giving a snaggle-toothed edging to the ends. Jared liked them that way, and I'm trying to. Once again: surrender expectations.

Later, Jared and I ran a batch of errands together in his truck. We first swung by Pennington Farms for coffee and treats. Almost exactly a year ago, we'd stopped by the farm on the way to camp along the Upper Applegate River, and Gracie had taken a photo of us raising our Pennington coffee mugs together in front of the bakery. Cathy had framed the photo and given it to us after Jared proposed the following week.

On the hard days, I try to picture us that way: mid-toast, full of hope.

◆◆◆

Communion this evening was filled with lots of pauses as Jared prayed. Many thoughtful thanks and a dawning of the "okay-ness" of the new house—the "new" in general.

It was our first full communion *in* the house—with the last of the Pendleton Midnight from my parents and a RITZ cracker.

◆◆◆

Rejoice, again, my tired doleful soul.
Rejoice, yet, even while tonight grows cold.

—from "Against Acedia" by David K. Wheeler[119]

First family dinner in the new digs: Taco Tuesday. I didn't even set the table—mostly because the raw pine is so lovely, it looks best naked. But also because I felt worn out. Not just from the move but also from a malingering sense of disconnection between Jared and me during everything that led up to it.

I made taco meat and slow-cooked black beans and set out tortillas and cheese and chips.

Alex & Rachael brought margaritas and salsa. Mom & Dad brought ice cream and apple pie. Andy & Linda brought deviled eggs and wine. I am no longer a menu purist. In fact, I embrace the uncurated art of uncontrolled dinner assemblage.

Jared and I sat side by side at the most snaggle-toothed edge of the table, with the wood piece that juts out the furthest. I decided it makes for convenient extra surface area when two chairs are placed at that end.

During dinner, it came up that I'd first met Jared's brother and his wife and their kids at the Laughing Clam in Grants Pass ten years ago. They were eating dinner there as Rachael sang. Tonight, Rachael said I'd set the standard for Jared's girlfriends, and none of the others after me had met it.

I smiled. Bless you, my sister-in-law.

◆◆◆

Natalie's 16th birthday party at Alex & Rachael's. A beautiful day— just warm enough to eat burgers outside on their patio. Mom & Dad came. Andy & Linda brought a Plaisance Tempranillo, and Andy read the poetry label I'd written for it. But he started by reading the surgeon general's warning in a poetic voice first— clever.

After dinner, we all stood around the glowing fire pit as the sun sank—so lovely to share that warmth.

Family.

◆◆◆

Over Sunday breakfast, I asked what Jared's plans for the day were. He said he wanted to work on some things and then disappeared into the garage.

When he reappeared mid-morning, there was a contradiction I'll call "pie." It actually *did* have to do with pie. I won't bore any of us with the details, but at one point, I threw up my hands and said, "I can't keep track anymore."

I decided to go on a walk to slough off my rising anger before it grew.

I returned in relative peace, planning to make a second coffee and go soak in the tub. Jared was in the kitchen and warmly said, "I'm going to make some coffee to go with pie. Would you like some?"

This seemed to be a repair attempt.

I accepted it. We sat and drank our coffees and went on with our separate days.

◆ ◆ ◆

Have I mentioned we're throwing a housewarming party on Saint Patrick's Day? Two-and-a-half weeks after moving in?

It's actually 3 a.m. on the day of the party. I need to sleep, but I can't. Too many thoughts. Like about connection. I didn't need it from any human before marriage—I had it with God. Fully, beautifully. But marriage changed something—in a good way that I believe reflects divine union, though I haven't figured out why I often feel more disconnected than connected. Maybe still more False Selves to drop?

I wish I'd known this science from the book *Attached:*

> Getting attached means that our brain becomes wired to seek the support of our partner by ensuring the partner's psychological and physical proximity. If our partner fails

208

to reassure us, we are programed to continue our attempts to achieve closeness until the partner does.[120]

The authors go on to talk about the "dependency paradox": "The more effectively dependent people are on one another, the more independent and daring they become."[121]

That information would have helped me know I was not needy in my seeking to connect. That need is neural:

> Numerous studies show that once we become attached to someone, the two of us form one psychological unit. Our partner regulates our blood pressure, our heart rate, our breathing, and the levels of hormones in our blood.[122]

I love it when science confirms my hunches!

When Jared left for work this morning, he asked if I was okay. I said I didn't know, but I thanked him for asking.

I finished the ten-thousand-item-long checklist of Saint Patrick's Day party prep: get green helium balloons and tie them to the fence entrance since our new address doesn't reliably appear in navigation apps yet, stake solar lights by the adjacent field for overflow parking, start the cabbage and corned beef, open and shape the decorative green tissue thingies, slice the carrots, lay out the bottles of Guinness in buckets—ice! Get ice!—find a Celtic-folksy Pandora station. Get dressed!

Grace. Say grace.

For our first big gathering in the new house.

For the spring-splendid weather: low 60s and blue-skied.

For fifty friends and family under our roof.

Love.

Jared lit a bonfire at dusk. The local fire department came to say it was too big, just as our nephew Abe was heaving a massive log onto the fire.

Laughter.

Christina gave me a gorgeous gift: my poetry book, *Hope of Stones,* with sticky notes throughout, detailing her favorite parts, along with a letter. So sincerely thoughtful.

Being known.

◆ ◆ ◆

Note to future self: have date night the night *before* a big event, not the night after.

> If I have to heal myself completely every time before I
> start
>
> —from "Don't Let Me Be Wistful" by Dana Ward[123]

◆ ◆ ◆

I finally sat down and read the sticky notes Christina had placed throughout *Hope of Stones* and her accompanying letter. I was reminded of my love of spirit, of words, of connections.

Within two hours of reading her notes, I received an email that my book was a finalist for the Oregon Book Award's Stafford/Hall Award for Poetry. I felt the familiar, zingy feeling that surges through me when my art finds a home or blesses someone—a milder version of what I felt decades ago when I opened my mailbox to find the Fulbright Fellowship acceptance letter.

Now in mid-life, I try to avoid the highs and lows. But I'm all about gratitude, so I channeled the zing into thanks. And then, I hauled the last of the moving trash to the dumpster. There's a juxtaposition: poetry & trash. Life is probably about finding the poetry *in* the trash.

That evening, Jared and I watched *The Princess Bride,* one of the DVDs I'd found when unpacking. When Westley tells Buttercup, "As you wish,"[124] Jared scoffed; he couldn't believe any guy would ever say that.

I said, "I've never met a man who did. And I never expected to hear it from one."

Only later did I realize the first part of what I said was true, but the second was not. I hadn't consciously lied, but deep down, an old False-Self part of me *did* want my partner to just say, "As you wish." Which my True Self *doesn't* really want. Because getting our own way doesn't help us grow. And boy, is marriage a great way to grow!

How 'bout that.

◆◆◆

One act of thanksgiving, when things go wrong with us, is worth a thousand thanks when things are agreeable to our inclinations.
—Saint John of the Cross

Saturday morning. When I asked Jared what his day looked like, it was full of his own things.

After breakfast, we had a discussion about an automotive contradiction I'll call "cake." It was far more significant than last weekend's "pie." This was something we had discussed last summer that impacted me often, though Jared didn't remember it.

To his credit, he listened when I explained the "cake" contradiction and did not defend himself.

To my credit, I didn't defend myself, either. And I tried to stay respectful and contain my anger, though it was probably seeping through my pores—more for the accumulation of contradictions than this one specifically. I reminded myself that almost all sarcasm and criticism had ceased. Gratitude! Maybe the contradictions would, too. Regardless, I only get to control my own actions and reactions.

And though I've learned to give thanks for the good things, I am still learning to do so when things aren't *feeling* very good.

I have not mastered this. I often get mired in all the "feels"—which is partly how I finally recognized my Enneagram type of the feeler-Four. I am slowly seeing that I can be a conduit for feelings instead of a container.

Recently, I heard this helpful simile: feelings are like trains. You can be a passenger on the feeling-train and ride it to the end of the line, or you can be like the train station and let a feeling pass through you. I spent a lot of time on trains when living in Germany, where most through-trains stop at a station for exactly two minutes. So I decided to give myself permission to hold any heavy feelings for two minutes and then practice sending them on their way. I had no idea that was even an option! It's an unfamiliar freedom.

I'm also learning to remember that feelings aren't facts—even though they can *feel* that way.

> When the alarm goes off in the morning, we get up, even when we don't feel like getting up. Because we do what we don't feel like doing, does that make us hypocrites? No, it is a sign we are responsible people. Showing respectful behavior when we don't "feel respectful" is evidence of maturity, not hypocrisy.[125]

It feels easier to rise with the alarm than to maintain respect in some cases. But transcending feelings....

Say grace.

I give thanks for this first day of spring.

I give thanks for the madrone and oak trees on our land.

I even give thanks for that pesky "cake."

Jared left to go to the shop. Just before I headed out to deal with the "cake," he called and said if I had any issues with it on the way there to call him. He added, "I love you."

Behind his words, I also heard, "I care about you." Which felt good. And I let *that* feeling stick around as long as it wanted.

◆◆◆

Sunday. After making breakfast, I asked what Jared's day looked like. Again: his own things. And again, he disappeared into the garage.

That afternoon, he emerged and asked me to shuttle him to the end of Gold Ray Estates so he could kayak back to Gold Hill, where he would leave his truck. He put in where we'd stood last January near the eve of my trip to Mexico. That had also been a Sunday— one in which he'd made time to walk with me.

Back home, I readied the back slope to sow fescue seed. While raking and thinking of how little time we'd spent together this weekend or last, I moped, mulled (forgetting the two-minute maximum), and finally decided I need to say something. *Feel, Think, Do!*

But first, gratitude when I'm not feeling like it: I give thanks for the spring rains. For the seeds I get to plant. For how faithful and hardworking my husband is. For this rake. For these arms that can use it.

And thank you, Ann Voskamp:

> While I might not always feel joy, God asks me to give thanks in all things, because he knows that the *feeling* of joy begins in the *action* of thanksgiving…. The place where all the joy comes from is far deeper than that of feelings; joy comes from the place of the very presence of God. Joy is God and God is joy and joy doesn't negate all other emotions—joy *transcends* all other emotions.[126]

When Jared returned from kayaking, we shared dinner. He mentioned wanting to invite friends for dinner in the next week or two. I suggested an upcoming Thursday. Jared said maybe I'd missed it, but he was going to take future Tuesday and Thursday evenings with the guys.

This was news to me. I'd only heard that he'd be kayaking on Tuesdays. I clarified, "So you plan to be with the guys Tuesdays and Thursdays, leaving just Mondays for dinners with friends, and just Wednesday date night for us to connect—because you plan to be away every weekend until June."

"Until July."

"And so that leaves only Mondays to have friends over for dinner?"

"Or Fridays." He got up and started to rinse his dishes.

That was the last straw. "But that's the weekend. And you've asked me to not make weekend plans during the spring and summer so you can be gone, which includes Fridays." I took a deep breath. "So, I need to say something."

He sat back down.

I was all over the place, but I went for it. "All winter while you were working hard on this house, I worked hard on the old one. I tried to show my support. I cut back on time with friends…"

"I didn't ask you to do that."

"I know, but I was trying to be as much of a partner as I could, and since you couldn't get out with friends as much, I starting inviting only your friends over for dinner so you'd have a chance to connect with them…"

"Like I said, I didn't ask you to do that!"

"That was a way I was trying to love you. But you obviously didn't receive it as love, right?"

"No."

"That's my point. We have a disconnect in how we give and receive each other's love—and in how we make time for each other."

I remembered reading that "love thrives in the messy richness of *me, you,* and *us.*"[127]

The *me* part got a bit teachy: "It's not so much a 'me' or 'you' problem as an 'us' problem. And a big 'us' problem is still figuring out how to live together.

"Remember how we came up with Team Emmanuel? Most days, I don't feel like we're on the same team. Instead, I often feel like you consider me your opponent—that I'm in the way of your goals, and I'm getting kicked in the head with a soccer ball instead of running beside you.

"We need to figure out how to 'play' together, not against each other. This weekend, I tried to connect multiple times. I know you need your space—I do, too—but other than sharing a meal or two, you spent both days doing all the things you wanted—as if I were just a roommate you crossed paths with. I felt hurt just now when you announced your future schedule without checking in with me."

I concluded, "I feel hurt and diminished."

We were both quiet a while, trying to figure out who the heck this other person was and why they thought the way they did.

> The trick to achieving the kind of connection you want is to develop the advanced relationship skill of *binocular vision,* the artful ability to see your partner's perspective as well as your own.[128]

We had a ways to go before we started to see from the other's perspective. But what did happen right away: after this weekend, Jared started to check in with me when planning things…and even started to ask what I'd like to do.

And he just took Tuesday evenings with the guys, leaving Thursdays flexible.

How about that.

◆ ◆ ◆

Oh, the relinquishing of circumstantial happiness.

> There is a spiritual satisfaction that comes even in the midst of our trials. It is a demeanor that may not be as showy as gleeful happiness, but it is much less subject to moods and makes for much more permanent a disposition.[129]

Oh, to embrace joy.

I kept myself busy today in the back field. A perfect day for garden work: overcast with a light, misting rain at the end of seeding.

When Jared came home, I greeted him warmly. No matter my emotional maelstroms, I always great him warmly—both because connections help keep the maelstroms at bay in the first place, and I want our home to be a place he loves to enter.

I showed him the outside work I'd done, and he was grateful. Said he could bring in a truck of topsoil if I wanted, though he sounded tired even thinking of it. I assured him I can just move dirt around for now—plenty has been displaced since the build and needs smoothing anyway.

I made stir-fry for dinner. Though tired, he was kind and open.

I offered to read from *A Wind in the Door*. When I curled up on the couch, he came up to me, gently held the back of my head, and kissed me. He thanked me for dinner.

Smiling, I said, "I am happy to cook for you. And I'm happy to be kissed by you."

He added that he planned to talk to Alex about getting the van: "That might have been part of the confusion about schedules yesterday. I want to camp together on weekends—when you want."

I smiled. "I would love that. And when you want to do your hike-in kayak trips with the guys, also great. Other than that, I love spending time with you."

"I love spending time with you, too."

We were learning not just how to honor each other's time but how to create a new time zone of "us." Eventually, we decided that since I had the weekday work hours to fill as I wished (writer's bliss!), Jared had the weekends to fill as he wished (which he often shared with me). And we hit a decent weeknight rhythm. It took a while, but eventually, it all panned out.

◆ ◆ ◆

Joy is the simplest form of gratitude.

—Karl Barth

New development: I have no desire for accolades. I am trying to get excited about the Zoom reading for the Oregon Book Award finalists. If not for Covid, finalists would have been invited to Portland to attend an award ceremony at a lovely venue—one I walked by years ago, wanting so badly for an earlier book to win. And now...it's not that I don't want to win, but it just doesn't seem important.

I'm hoping that's a sign I'm letting more of my pride die off, another False Self. Speaking of letting go: I could let my CV end at The Year of Quarantine, never add to it again, and I'd be fine. Covid was a complete life reset. Incredible: this time last year, Jared and I weren't even engaged. In less than a year, we got engaged, got married, and built a house. And all during a global pandemic. No wonder we've had some rough patches.

Midway through the day, I texted Jared: "Thank you for your kindness and connection last night. I felt immensely loved by you."

I made meatloaf, mashed potatoes, and salad for dinner. Jared said he wanted to ask about the weekend (to ask!). He had mentioned Judd going to Mount Hood to kayak the Little White. And how he wanted to go and Mikey had offered to drive, and....

I interrupted, "That sounds great! I've been hoping you'd get a weekend to play." I added, "And I look forward to spring camping trips together once it's our turn with the van."

We finished *A Wind in the Door*. My spirit recognized so many parts from first reading it in the sixth grade, but this time I saw a depth I couldn't comprehend back then. Like the poetic litany toward the end as the protagonists try to save the mitochondria, the world. And the emphasis on "Be!"—which author Madeleine L'Engle left as a stand-alone word on its own line, multiple times.

Just this morning, on a phone call with Cindy, Psalm 46:10 came up: "Be still, and know that I am God." Before we can even be still, we must *be*.

◆◆◆

So much gardening and yard work I want to do. I don't miss my walks this season because I love amending this little acreage of earth. Smoothing the truck ruts and construction gouges. Letting the soil return to softness.

After working on the land all day, I took a bath and put on a little velvet dress in honor of date night. Jared came home in kindness. He showered and donned his nice pants, his Sperry shoes, and his gold wedding ring (he usually wears a silicon one for work).

We walked downtown to the River Station: our first date night walking into our new town. Live music. A lemon drop taste test between Yazi ginger and Thai basil. I mentioned our Team Emmanuel and asked if he had an idea for a mascot. He thought a moment and said: "A turtle. Like the tortoise and the hare. Slow but steady wins the race."

Perfect. And intriguing, coming from a man who likes to do things fast. Maybe emotional tortoise-ing?

We've had two offers on the old house. I told Jared that I trusted his financial decisions—and I am happy to participate any way he wants: to offer gut hunches, to bounce ideas off of, or to leave him free to make a final decision.

And then, handsome in his black suspenders, he said, "There's something I wanted to talk about."

He wants to give away a huge sum from the sale of the house.

I kissed him. Said he was the most generous person I knew.

It had been ages since the space between us had felt so open and connected. I tried to memorize the feeling at a cellular level.

Thai Basil won the lemon-drop taste test, and the Team Emmanuel Turtle won the evening.

Back at home, I looked up the spiritual significance of the turtle. It represents patience and wisdom, discernment and strength, and the expression of feelings. And it travels in both water and earth, remaining grounded in troubled times.

Yes to all.

> But just when the worst bears down
> you find a pretty bubble in your soup at noon,
> and outside at work a bird says "Hi!"
> Slowly the sun creeps along the floor;
> it is coming your way. It touches your shoe.
>
> —from "It's All Right" by William Stafford[130]

◆ ◆ ◆

Tonight, we took communion with a pepper cracker and the Redbreast whiskey our neighbors Dan & Dana had given us. We blessed our marriage, our new community, and the people we love.

Afterward, Jared got up to check his phone—it had chirped during communion. He came back to the couch and leaned over to kiss me, saying, "We just sold the old house."

So glad that chapter is over.

◆ ◆ ◆

I made molasses cookies to send off with the guys on their drive up to kayak the Little White this weekend. They all arrived right when Jared came home from work, and it was a whirlwind of loading and commotion. I wished them well. I am glad my hard-working husband can go play. And I am glad that I get the evening to sip wine on the stationary recumbent bike while watching a documentary—*my* kind of play!

◆ ◆ ◆

A gorgeous spring day. Woke to a text Jared had sent the night before: they'd arrived safely to Washington and he loved me. Yay to both.

And now for a weekend of yard work....

♦♦♦

Sunday night. Jared returned this evening. Over dinner, he mentioned that one of the older guys had told one of the younger, engaged guys to go off and travel before getting married. Jared had said nothing, but to me he mentioned—not for the first time— how he couldn't have imagined marrying so young. He had wanted to explore.

I'm glad we *both* got to explore.

I thought of the minuscule farae from *A Wind in the Door*: the tiny, personified parts of the mitochondria. How little Sporos kept resisting his destiny of Deepening. How he felt he would limit himself by taking root when he could move all over as he was— not realizing that by Deepening, he would be able to move farther, in ways beyond the physical. In fact, if the farae don't Deepen, their "universe" will die.

May my husband and I both Deepen.

♦♦♦

A poem and five errands before 10:30 this morning. Then four hours of wheelbarrowing—which is not conducive to blisters healing. Then making meatballs and spaghetti.

Sarah & Byron came for dinner. We gave them a tour of the house. While Jared was showing Byron another room, Sarah and I stood together at the patio, and I pointed out the view, apologizing that it was a bit marred by five, tarp-covered blobs of everything from the burn pile to the raft. I laughed and said I was trying to figure out how to live with the tarps.

Sarah shared valuable marriage counsel: she often prays that she either can care less about something or that God can take care of it—and *He* can take it up with her husband. Wisdom.

Over the meal, Byron asked how it had been, building the house.

I shared my father-in-law's comment about the stress a house-build can put on marriage—how divorce rates often increase during the process. Jared added that maybe some of those couples were younger. He didn't say we were wiser, but I like the implication.

He continued: being older had benefits and drawbacks. We knew ourselves—maybe too well. And we were used to being single and making all of our own decisions.

I added that we continually discover the Third Thing; we each start with our own ideas, but we figure out a new thing together, the Third Thing.

While giving our guests the tour earlier, we had all stopped to admire the back view of oak and madrone forests. All of a sudden, a silver fox jumped onto the log at the bottom of the field. We watched the fox stand *en pointe* in profile before he swooped and beat two hawks to a dead squirrel. He leapt away, dinner in his mouth.

I wonder about the spiritual significance of a gray fox?

◆ ◆ ◆

A gray fox is the only of its species that can climb trees. It reminds us that we need deep roots to climb to great heights. It helps navigate gray areas in our lives.

And it reminds me of a pair of Mary Oliver poems, published about two decades apart.

From my college-era copy of her book, *White Pine,* lines from "I

Found a Dead Fox" in the speaker's voice when she finds it:

> its posture—
> of looking,
> to the last possible moment,
>
> back into the world—
> made me want
> to sing something
> joyous and tender[131]

And from her later collection, *A Thousand Mornings,* lines from "Good-Bye Fox," in the fox's voice:

> You fuss over life with your clever
> words, mulling and chewing on its meaning, while
> we just live it.
>
> Oh![132]

Oh, indeed.

Oh, to live without fuss. But, oh, the marvelous mulling! And here I mull....

Oliver's two poems, with all those years between them, helped me answer a question that a couple of readers asked me about this book early in the editing: what would I think of a difficult scene in five years, ten years?

Like the younger Oliver, I have read so much into things. Like the older, wiser Oliver, I hope I will continue to expand my understanding of myself and my husband. Even just two-plus years married, I can look back at our first months of matrimony with so much more grace than I had at the time. If some of those difficulties happened in our tenth year, we would react differently, if at all. But they happened in year one. My original impressions of those things will always remain as I've written them here, but my interpretation of those things will change over time.

In the beginning, Jared and I were just learning each other's triggers and had no clue how to de-escalate tensions between us. I left a lot of my over-analytical process in these pages—and my questioning of Jared's process. That's all part of the raw relationship compost. I don't want to do the literary equivalent of spraying fake-floral air freshener over that compost. By sharing some of the muck (and what I first thought about it), I've hoped to show how we cultivated it into something far less stenchy. And eventually, into fragrant flowers—flaws 'n' all. Not Photoshopped. Not filtered.

Jared and I trust each other far more now than we did as newlyweds. We look forward to continually growing that trust together in all soils, all seasons.

◆◆◆

I worked all day on the land, amending literal soil. It was a breathtaking, 75-degree spring day.

A package came in the mail for us. The Penningtons had sent a sweet Easter gift: sprinkle cookies, an embosser with our new address, and a roll of gold seal stickers.

Jared and I ordered take-out dinner from La Guacamaya. His: two fish tacos with pico de gallo. Hers: the *hurache* with nopales. We brought our food to the Gold Hill river spot downstream from the bridge.

Jared asked how my writing was going, and I said I'd just written about having mistyped myself on the Enneagram for years (no wonder I hadn't explored it more). I was grateful for how marriage has opened a new understanding of myself and how I relate to others.

I am starting to see that "Marriage is the perfect opportunity to improve yourself. No other single setting in life can form more character."[133]

Kairos: The Personality of Process

Blobs, spots, specks, smudges, cracks, defects, mistakes, accidents, exceptions, and irregularities are the windows to other worlds.
—Bob Miller

One: In Which I Vent About the Enneagram (Though I Love It, Too)

If you know a bit about the Enneagram, you know that you are one of nine types—and that each type has specific fears and desires and motivations. Learning about this framework helps us understand ourselves and others.

However...I've also learned that you can come into this world as one number but can learn to adapt into another number that appears to serve you or others better. And then you can be very confused.

There are various schools of the Enneagram, and the number-types have different names according to which school you study. I believe I came into this world a Four—the Romantic or Individualist. But the world rewarded my ability to be a One: the Perfectionist or Reformer. I joke that I'm either a Perfecting Romantic or Romanic Perfectionist.*

---

* For fellow Enneagram geeks: in health, Fours access the good qualities of Ones. My problem was that I ignored the deep heart-needs of the Four and stayed top-heavy in the perfecting nature of a One.

From my school years through the first months of my marriage, I lived pretty well as a Perfectionist-Reformer. Even my creativity was highly structured; I'd embark on a series of 100 portraits, 30 days of painting-poems, et cetera, et-orderly-cetera.

It didn't help that most organized religion and education love measurable achievements. In grade school, I memorized whole chapters of Corinthians for the church version of the Girl Scouts, the Missionettes, earning badges to pin on my turquoise polyester sash. I worked to become high-school valedictorian. Then I worked even harder to become undergraduate *summa cum laude*. By grad school, I let myself breathe and settled for *magna cum laude*. And that was probably because, while I shaped my poetry thesis, I rediscovered a wild creativity longing to play free— uncaged by a rigid grid of quantification.

And then, decades later, I got married. Strange thing about marriage: your True Self emerges in a way it never did before. True union eventually squeezes out anything false. When two become one, a lot of shit has got to go.

Suffice it to say, that whatever façade we've built basically gets shaken off, and whatever's underneath probably has some black mold and maybe a rat or two, despite however many years we think we've done our spirit renovation.

Funny: I once published an essay on dating, drawing parallels between self-improvement and home-improvement. At the end of it, I naively concluded I had done my work and was "turnkey." Ha.

Also funny: I married an Eight, the Challenger. Challengers can call your bluff pretty darn well. Ha, ha, ha.

Two: In Which I Vent About Building a House (Though I Love It, Too)

This all leads me, most indirectly, to the process of building a house—before my husband and I had been married a year.

But before I get to that, I should also mention that it took me until my forties to see an obvious life pattern. During my college years, I worked as a housecleaner—for residential and commercial buildings. And then I worked as an editor in some capacity for longer than most starting editors have been alive. Cleaning and editing.

Basically, I trained myself to see the mess and the misspelled and to perfect them *all*. But such tasks, though they felt good when done, didn't feel good in the process; they felt exhausting and never-ending. I wouldn't so much celebrate as check off the completion of each round of "perfecting," even as I braced myself for the next round of trash and typos. Versus celebrating the process—mud 'n' all.

And let's just say that pointing out all the dirt and dialogue flaws is not a beneficial marriage skill. But the long-entrenched Perfectionist-Reformer in me was so used to doing this, it was hard to stop. It took me a while to be grateful for the fact that my husband doesn't really care if things are eat-off-the-floor clean or if the contraction *you're* is spelled like the possessive adjective *your*. "But these are my strengths!" a part of me kept shouting.

Meanwhile, behind the scenes, the truer part of myself kept saying she loved going off on muddy river adventures and not needing to analyze the etymology of the kayak term "boof." (This less uptight self will just shrug when the inevitable errors make it through countless edits of this very book.)

At the top of my suggested reading list for the Enneagram is *The Road Back to You*.* The One-Me never understood that title and never cared to read it. The Four-Me read it, jumping up and down for childlike joy, saying, "Yes! I'm back!"

Marriage has invited me to return to my creative being: my *True* Self, the Self who loves paint splatters and rough-edged canvas and impromptu word play for pure fun. The Self who knows that *all* of life is poetry, not just words on a page—or a specific page

---

* See Resource 3 for the full list.

count. *That* Self has risen up alongside our house.

Yes, finally, I get to the house. It has become my central metaphor for building a more authentic Self and marriage.

Last summer, we stood on the foundations—surrounded by heaps of displaced earth. Where wild grass had once grown in beautiful abandon, the hillside looked like a jagged scar. But we wanted to build something, and so we had to dig beneath the pretty surface. We had to make a mess.

Now, a brick home stands on that site, finished, after months of trucks and lumber. But nothing is ever finished, is it? The wake of construction rubble and ruts surrounding the house reminds me how ongoing building really is.

I am still struggling to love the messy process. But now that I've been building a house with someone *and* building a marriage with someone, I am beginning to get it.

I am also beginning to embrace both the integrated Reformer and the core Romantic in myself—and I consciously choose those two labels for the One and the Four. The One's drive for excellence helped ground the Four's often formless creative sensitivities. Maybe I'll mix it up and call myself a Romantic Reformer—head in the clouds but feet on the ground. Imperfectly trying to bring heaven to earth.

The two types in me have finally become one.

Union starts in our very own hearts.

Three: In Which I Don't Vent About Marriage (But Instead Write a Poem About It)

> O this strange bliss—
> brimming with
> mess & misspellings
> mud & wonder—
> I embrace all

your stains & stars.

Two become
one house
uniting
divided hearts.

We build
a mystery.

Real love often occurs when the feeling of love is lacking, when we act lovingly despite the fact that we don't feel loving.

—M. Scott Peck
The Road Less Traveled

The many facets of marriage furnish us with the experience necessary to finish the job. This is the work of a lifetime, not an overnight endeavor. It usually takes more patience and faith than we realize to sustain the effort without giving up in frustration. When both partners are willing to share fully in this process, concern about time fades into the background, as we become entranced by the joy of the process.

—Linda & Charlie Bloom
101 Things I Wish I Knew When I Got Married

How do I give up resentment for gratitude, gnawing anger for spilling joy?... To fully live—to live full of grace and joy and all that is beauty eternal. It is possible, wildly.

—Ann Voskamp
One Thousand Gifts

Part IV: The Wound That Heals Us

If we don't transform our pain, we will most certainly transmit it.
—Richard Rohr

As the first year of our marriage wound down, I remembered Westley's line to Buttercup in *Princess Bride:* "Life is pain, Highness. Anyone who says differently is selling something."[134]

If I were Buttercup, I'd retort: "Life is pain with a *purpose:* to be transformed into joy." And to back myself up, I'd quote *The Road Less Traveled:* "Grow in any dimension, and pain as well as joy will be your reward. A full life will be full of pain."[135]

I've mentioned my temptation to remove more of the rough patches from this book—and that was after already leaving out plenty from my original journal entries. There is a tension between honoring the privacy of our marriage and being honest enough to admit how hard it was. Jared wisely advised that it's best not to sugarcoat the rough stuff. He's right.

By sharing our story, we can let future newlyweds know they're not alone, but we can't save them from mistakes or pain—in fact, those things help teach us that "The capacity to feel joy grows in proportion to the capacity to experience pain."[136]

When I read an early version of *The Long Game of Joy* to Jared, we were each better able to see our individual woundings. While

Jared's wounds" are his to share, I have delved into many of mine. There will be more to unearth, I know. "Joy and pain, they are but two arteries of the one heart that pumps through all those who don't numb themselves to really living.[137]

That un-numbed process is painful. I often want a lightning-bolt healing. And sometimes I get one. But often, healing miracles are progressive—even painful as they progress. Like months of chiropractic visits for a pesky shoulder injury. Or months of newlywed God-work for a dislocated sense of worth...or loneliness, inadequacy, lack, loss, being misunderstood, misunderstanding, feeling incomplete, trying to complete another, failure, unfulfilling success, nonsense, disappointment with self, disappointment with spouse, disappointment with God.

All the negative, painful prefixes: dis-, un-, mis-, non-.

All the aching wounds.

And yet....

What's tough can toughen us up.

What tenderizes can make us tender.

Tough & tender.

Both/and.

There's often a whole lotta daily *chronos* slog before the *kairos* breakthrough. But over time, an oozing wound morphs from tender flesh to tough scar. Over time, we learn that "the transforming power of suffering and of joy are equally indispensable."[138]

In marriage, part of our long game is to heal ourselves and support our spouse as they heal—moving together toward the joy. Jared and I have done so much of that since we became husband and wife. We had no idea! In hindsight, I'm amazed that we began to see the fruit of our work before our first anniversary.

And right around our second anniversary, I read the book *Us*. By that time, I was able to laugh when I read this:[*]

> Love is like a Roto-Rooter…it will bring up to the surface every unhealed wound and fissure that has lodged inside your body. Nothing stimulates hurt quite the way love does…. We all marry our unfinished business.[139]

Choosing joy isn't ignoring all that's hard; it's being brave enough to have eyes of faith when it's hard, when it hurts, when we don't want to face our unfinished business.

Oh, the gaze of faith.

Oh, the faith of joy.

---

[*] I also laughed when I read the author's acknowledgments, in which he thanked his wife for the decades-long opportunity to work on himself!

Chronos: April

Doug & Jureen brought Thai takeout for dinner, and we lit a bonfire afterward—so happy to burn that pile down!

We tried to convince them to join us on the upcoming lower Rogue rafting adventure. Doug told us that, on a past trip, he had brought little bottles of Fireball whiskey when Jureen got cold. Brilliant. I promised to line my travel vest with whiskey and hand warmers if she came.

As the bonfire flames died and the embers glowed, we all moved closer. Jared stood next to me and put his arm around me.

Gladness tonight.

> I am not afraid of love
> or its consequence of light.

—from "The Creation Story" by Joy Harjo[140]

◆◆◆

Easter. And the anniversary of Jared's proposal to me—here on the land, where our house stands now. We actually slept in…and lingered. Delight.

Due to continued Covidness, we decided to skip church. Which is strange to do, especially on Easter, and especially for a pastor's daughter. But thankfully, God is not stuck in any building.

I suggested a walk, and Jared said he had an idea. Something told me his idea was not going to be an Easter-dress kind of walk, but I did not expect it to be a steep, off-piste, abandoned dirt bike trail snagged with blackberry brambles.

Still, I tried to be fully present. Though Jared says he doesn't like to hike or walk (too slow for him, I guess), when we do, he often shares about his life. On this walk, he told me about riding these trails as a kid on a dirt bike with his Dad, whom he usually only saw on weekends after his parents divorced.

Lightbulb: as a kid, weekends away meant time exploring with his Dad. That is the source of his love of weekend adventures. And that was worth the blackberry scratches.

> Our knowledge of our lovers' history and needs allows us to understand their thoughts and motivations. Once we can understand this, we may disagree with our lovers, but we will rarely hate them.[141]

We arrived to Andy & Linda's for a beautiful evening of prime rib and family.

On Resurrection Sunday, I choose to leave dead things in the tomb and reach for new life.

And to remember that "The secret of change is to focus all your energy not on fighting the old, but on building the new."[142]

◆ ◆ ◆

Jared pulled up to the house just before dinner with the picnic tables I'd bought earlier, bless him. I asked if he wanted help unloading. He said he was going to shower.

Later, he asked if I needed any help with dinner—Ben & Rebecca were coming.

I said, "Only with the picnic tables."

Again, he did not reply.

When Ben & Rebecca arrived, I asked where they want to sit. They chose outdoors, and I said, "We have brand new picnic tables!"

Jared smiled, "I was waiting for Ben to help unload them."

My smile might have been more of a grimace, "You could have told me."

"Nah."

Sigh.

In that moment, I wish I'd known this:

> You'll learn to see that every person is "both/and," not "either/or." This can be profoundly challenging, especially when someone comes along and starts pushing your buttons. Those individuals offer incredible gifts, though. Whatever irritates you about them—their behavior, speech, beliefs, or anything else—is the very thing you can learn to identify and then embrace in yourself.[143]

Or, instead of embracing the irritants, I can release them—both in myself and in my husband!

◆ ◆ ◆

My long list of errands ended with fetching grapefruit juice at our local market. I'd found a recipe for palomas, and I texted Jared that I'd be making date-night cocktails.

I set up blankets and pillows beneath the two oaks in the lower field, sunlight dapply through the branches, wildflower buds just beginning to burst open.

But when Jared arrived and I gave him the usual "welcome home" kiss and hug, it was like hugging a coat of armor.

Before dinner, I asked one, time-sensitive question about a website for…let's call it "licorice" to make it remotely interesting. I had mistaken the web address of the "licorice," and my mistake was not well received.

What I wish a certain *someone* had known this week: "If your spouse considers what you say to be disrespectful, it is."[144]

Say grace.

This time, I called to mind a good memory: our wedding-day photo shoot. Our photographer, Danny, had asked us to tell each other what we loved about our soon-to-be-spouse while he clicked away with his camera. I told Jared I loved his kind heart.

I know it's in there, beneath any behavior or armor. So I give thanks for his kind heart.

Jared helped me bring dinner and drinks down to the blanket. He prayed a repair-attempt blessing, thanking the Lord for me, for all I do, and for teaching us how to love.

How 'bout that.

◆ ◆ ◆

This evening, I asked if Jared wanted me to read a story.

"Sure. Or we could watch a nature show."

"A show sounds good. Would you like to share a drink?"

He did. And as I went over to the bar and asked which Scotch he wanted, he came up behind me and held me. I turned into him and told him how much I loved it when he did that.

On the funky futon I set up in the little TV room, we watched an undersea episode of *Our Planet*. Miracles of coral and schools of anchovies. Of Everglade bottlenose dolphins spiraling mud onto the water's surface.

Jared turned to hold me and continued to hold me for the rest of the show. I want to start documenting our moments of connection with the zeal of a marine biologist sighting manta rays in the deep.

◆◆◆

This morning, Jared asked what my day looked like. We've come a long way in less than a month!

"I kept it open," I said. "I figured you might have some things you want to do, but maybe we could get a walk in?"

He mused, "I wonder where we can find flowers...."

We ended up hiking Lower Table Rock in a spring peak of wildflowers. We shared beautiful, easy, open conversation about love and marriage. And how differently we communicate. How I am learning to care less about things—and he is learning to care more. How we both get to grow.

Back at home, we snacked. Me with coffee and cookies, he with coffee and brownie, peanut butter and RITZ.

He praised the versatility of peanut butter. I agreed, adding: "I tried almond butter for a while, but it was missing something."

He licked his spoon. "Peanuts."

I laughed.

Later we took communion. For the bread, I thanked the Lord for joy—how it is our strength. Jared blessed the protesters who have been making a ruckus at the Growers' Market, and I remembered

Rachael mentioning them and her revelation: it's kindness that leads to repentance. Not abrasion. Not shaming. So for the blood, I thanked God for His deep and strong kindness.

♦♦♦

Chicken cacciatore for dinner with my parents. Jared said multiple times how much he liked it. Will repeat.

We talked with Mom & Dad about convergence years and afterglow. Jared is entering convergence—all of his skills are at their peak, but he is also preparing to pass them on, to raise others up. And then will come the post-retirement afterglow—which my parents are entering. When it's no longer about doing but *being*—resting in the fruit of doing.

♦♦♦

Do not

tell me you are innocent of hunger. Desire
is the flesh, the fruit you cry for every night.

—from "Sinner, don't you weep" by Camille T. Dungy[145]

I am in love with the *Sacred Marriage* book. It reminds me where the ultimate source of love is:

Instead of being turned away from our spouse when…disillusionment sets in, we can be turned toward God…. Marital dissatisfaction, on whatever level, is best met with the prayer, *That's why I need you, God.*[146]

Gravel delivered: ten yards of it heaped in a gray pyramid outside the garage. By noon today, I'd moved half of it. I think that schlepping gravel must have some spiritual-relationship parallel.

♦♦♦

The Oregon Book Award poetry finalist's reading is tonight, via Zoom. As ever, readings hang heavy in me all the days leading up to them, but especially the day *of*.

For some reason, I thought to call Rogue River Fire District at 6:30 this morning, and voilà: burn day! So I decimated the rest of the tarp-covered burn pile in the three hours I had before Rachael came to walk with me.

All but the pallets are ashes. Now I only see *three* blobs of tarp-covered stuff outside: the wood pile, the brick pile, and the raft.

I planted, watered, and moved rocks in readiness for the twelve yards of topsoil coming tomorrow (Jared ordered some after all, and I told him I'd be happy to do the shoveling). Most all of me hurts a bit. But I also relish the physicality of the labor. In fact, while dreading the poetry reading, I wished to simply dig more. I remembered Seamus Heaney's poem, "Digging." The poet wrote of his father digging earth with a shovel and how he, the son, dug words with a pen. I wondered if I might write the reversal, back to shovel from pen. Or better: just do both and stop seeing life as either/or! Here's to the both/and.

I can love writing *and* not love giving readings in this season.

I can work the earth *and* the words.

I can be sad *and* joyful.

◆◆◆

I worked on the land from dawn to late afternoon. Almost decimated the gravel mountain. It was messy, heavy work. My poet-friend Renee calls this combo of yard work and gardening "yardening." I spent the day yardening.

When Jared came home, he said that *he* would have started with the soil instead of the gravel.

I replied, "Well, after shoveling gravel since 6:30 this morning, I was a bit tired by the time the soil was delivered."

Then later he said: "I thought you were going to drive the van up."

I took a deep breath. To install the van's camp bed, which he keeps down in the "cave," he had backed the van down through the deep construction ruts along the side of the house.

I exhaled. Granted, his statement about the van was not said in malice. But it was one of only two sentences he'd spoken to me since coming home—both of which felt like implied criticism—though some rational part of my brain knew they weren't.

I looked at him squarely and said, "You told me *not* to drive the van because of the ruts. Ruts I've been pick-axing and filling with gravel all day so the van won't get stuck. Which is also why I didn't get to the soil yet."

He said nothing—probably very smart of him—and went off to shower.

I walked down to the creek and tried to slough off my sadness. Dang it: I had taken things personally and forgotten my sense of humor. I remembered wise words:

> Truthfully, in over twenty-five years of counseling, I can't think of a client I've worked with whose communication style has not contributed to their problems, been part of their healing, or both.[147]

I'd love to get through the problems to the healing!

It was Thursday, our date night postponed because of my poetry reading last night. So we walked to The Millennial for dinner. I wasn't hungry, but I suggested Jared would like the pork lumpia. He did.

He was kind.

I tried not to be the melodramatic speaker of Lorca's poem:

> I want to cry my pain, and I tell you
> so you will love me and will cry for me
> in a dusk of nightingales
> with a dagger, with kisses and with you.

—from "The Poet Tells the Truth" by Federico García Lorca[148]

◆◆◆

Made it through my massive list—including prepping the van for its first camping use this season—and was giving the patio flowers a second watering when Jared came home.

After we climbed into the van, he reached for my hand, looked me in the eye and said, "Thank you." He paused before adding he was glad I could get away and rest after working so hard. I was touched. I was also surprised, which made me realize something: I've been outsourcing my moods. I know better, but I'd been confusing happiness—what happens, with joy—what's eternal.

I choose to choose joy, whatever happens.

We drove toward the Salmon River in Friday silence. Which was good. I needed to chat with God, who reminded me of this insight from Martin Buber:

> Marriage can never be renewed except by that which is always the source of all true marriage: that two humans beings reveal the You to one another.[149]

Ah, the reveal at the heart of revelation: the You invites us to *joy* in the divine. Joy turns verb.

Happiness is like cotton candy: it dissolves as soon as you taste it— a sugary treat that leaves a saccharine aftertaste on the tongue and spikes your blood sugar. But joy! Joy is like bittersweet chocolate that lingers on the taste buds and enriches your body with antioxidants.

Joy is the longing for God *and* the grace to survive the seasons when we can't feel Him—though He's always with us.

Emmanuel, God-With-Us.

Our constant.

Our only guarantee.

After Jared turned off the freeway and headed into forested highways, he started praying aloud out of the blue—a first. He thanked God for the weekend. For healing our spirits and minds. For what He is doing in us individually, in our relationship, in our friends.

Happiness.

And undergirding it: joy.

> Your joy is your sorrow unmasked
> …
>
> The deeper that sorrow carves into your being, the more joy you can contain.
> Is not the cup that holds your wine the very cup that was burned in the potter's oven?
>
> —from *The Prophet* by Kahlil Gibran[150]

◆ ◆ ◆

I enjoyed a day with complete spaciousness—I didn't even have to drive shuttle. Lingering morning. Coffee around the fire. Ben's sourdough waffles on the cast-iron griddle. Karen describing the process of making clarified butter and Mikey walking past, deadpanning: "Thanks for clarifying." Watching the guys don their kayak gear on the pebbled river bank and then putting in. Helping Brittany untangle little Ida's fishing line on the rocky shore. Ida bringing us small stones to admire—a glory of grays and whites and corals.

Then I went on a short walk and discovered a tiny private beach where I stayed alone for hours, dozing in the shade, dunking into the frigid water, and letting my hair dry in the sun.

I flipped back through the pocket-sized Moleskin notebook I take camping. Just before we married last year, Jared said he was grateful for our differences—and for how much we would get to learn from each other. How right he was!

After he returned from kayaking that evening, the two of us strolled down to the river, me with a tin cup of rosé, he with a beer. It was nearing sunset—or at least, the sun was nearing the mountain ridge, and we had the pebble beach to ourselves.

We watched the sparrows skim the water's surface as the sun sank. I held the moment close, knowing the joy beneath it, even after we walked back toward camp and Jared mentioned how little he wants of something I want so much of.

> You will not believe me when I tell you it's the wanting
> that you'll miss the most, once your lap is full of
> > everything
> you thought you'd go without.
>
> —from "Midlife Valentine" by Jen Stewart Fueston[151]

◆◆◆

Musing on wounds…

In his book, *The Wounded Healer,* Henri Nouwen writes:

> We live in a society in which loneliness has become one of the most painful human wounds.… The awareness of

loneliness might be a gift we must protect and guard, because our loneliness reveals to us an inner emptiness that can be destructive when misunderstood, but filled with promise for him who can tolerate its sweet pain. When we are impatient, when we want to give up our loneliness and try to overcome the separation and incompleteness we feel, too soon, we easily relate to our human world with devastating expectations.... Many marriages are ruined because neither partner was able to fulfill the often hidden hope that the other would take his or her loneliness away.[152]

I am finally learning to be grateful to my husband for *not* taking away my loneliness, which I have always had. That very loneliness, those "devastating expectations," feeling misunderstood—all of these draw me closer to God who is my joy. And when I draw closer to Him, I am able to see my husband through God's eyes. My husband does the same—drawing closer to God, seeing me through His eyes. Then, as we look at each other from heaven's perspective, we can start loving each other not just with our limited, expectation-laden love, but with God's pure stuff.

◆ ◆ ◆

Dinner at Dan & Janna's. We shared a balmy evening on their patio with chicken enchiladas and Symphonic Chronic beer.

Dan said he was lucky that Janna had a short-term memory—because he has to apologize and ask for forgiveness so often.

Neither Jared nor I are so lucky...I have a long-term memory, and he doesn't like to apologize!

I'm a fan of the apology:

To offer a serious apology, you need the inner strength to allow yourself to feel vulnerable. You need to be in touch with both your competence and your limitations. When you have fairly solid self-esteem you can admit to being in the wrong, without feeling like you're weakening the fabric of the self, or losing something to the other person.[153]

May I be a safe place for my husband to feel vulnerable.

◆ ◆ ◆

At lunch today, Dad asked, "Are you still happily married?"

"Most days," I said.

Well, some days.

Maybe not today.

Dear Reader: remember the difference between happiness and joy! And know that as painful as this scenario was, it was the turning point in our communication. I was about to learn this:

> God is love, but if we get it turned around, and make being loved into our god, we get lost in self. Death of self is always the pulse that keeps love alive…. The two become one to become stronger, to persevere and suffer and change and be sanctified and grow, rising to a new life together.[154]

I returned home from errands and saw that the new fire pit had arrived on the doorstep. Delight! It's smokeless and portable and contained, and I'd ordered it hoping it would arrive by today for date night. I wanted to surprise Jared with it as a (very) early anniversary gift—the better to get a head start on campfire season. I unpacked it and set it up, started the sweet potatoes baking, salted the ribeye steaks, and then went out foraging for wood on our land. We have so many fallen branches to clear, and they'll make ideal fuel for sitting around a fire with friends.

I didn't hear Jared pull up, and I had almost reached the new fire pit with a bucket of found wood when I looked up the hill and saw him open his truck door. I set down my bucket and went to greet him. He looked past me and said, "What the heck is that?"

I had reached him to give him a hug, but he strode past me to stand at the gift, saying "Don't tell me that's a fire pit!"

I froze. All sorts of thoughts flew through my head. I wondered if he thought it was an unnecessary expense, so I hastened to say, "It's a gift…." I didn't even get out that I had also gotten it for free because he started saying how much he hates fire pits.

And I froze again. What? Since when? I was so confused. "But it's the one I tried to get us last year for our road trip. It's portable. You can have a fire even when it's not fire season, on non-burn days. It's smokeless…"

He put his hand to his head in the shape of a gun and pulled an imaginary trigger.

It felt like lava and ice had filled my body simultaneously. I couldn't tell whether I was burning or freezing. I had about six seconds before the tears would gush, and I wanted so badly to communicate without crying. I started moving away, saying, "That was *not* the reaction I was going for." And I kept moving, down to the creek to try and figure out what on earth had just happened.

He doesn't like fire pits? We spend evenings around his brother's all the time. And around campfires. But that wasn't even the issue. I prayed for guidance (it might be more accurate to say I *begged* for it). God reminded me of this metaphor:

> Entranced as we are by the content of our struggles, we are blinded to what's going on in the big picture of our marriage, as if we are focusing on a single blue square in a mosaic, never stepping far back enough to know if we're looking at a picture of the sea, the sky, or the wing of a jay in flight.[155]

I was not going to get distracted by the single "square" of the fire pit. I wanted to address the bigger mosaic of our failed communication loop.

We are breaking that cycle tonight.

I rinsed my teary face in the creek water, belatedly wondering how clean it was, and walked back up to the house. I approached Jared in the kitchen as he was rummaging in a drawer.

With a smile, I said, "Hey, can we have a do-over?" I hugged him and said, "Welcome home. I got us a surprise as an early anniversary gift."

I paused and added, "And it really hurt when your response was to put an imaginary gun to your head and pull the trigger."

He said he didn't like fire pits.

We were *not* going to get stuck on the single squares. Back to the mosaic. I said, "I'm telling you, your response hurt."

He said some more about fire pits.

I wanted to run away, but I pressed in.

> Deal with difficult issues. Whenever you give in to another person to avoid a fight, you give away a little of your power. If you do this over time, you give away a lot of power and begin to resent the relationship. Avoiding conflict in the short run often has devastating long-term effects. In a firm but kind way, stick up for what you think is right. It will help keep the relationship balanced.[156]

I could no longer afford to stockpile resentment. I continued, "Whether it's a fire pit or a Guns 'n' Drugs sweatshirt, we're going to get and give a lot of things we don't want. It's not about those things. It's how we respond to them. And I'm telling you: your response to my gift hurt. I'm trying to let you know in the moment so these hurts don't build, but often, when I do, you ignore or reject my hurt."

This makes it feel unsafe for me to say what hurts—and so I try to let it go. But if I never mention anything, I won't grow in strength—and my husband won't grow in tenderness, so I'm not loving either of us well by saying nothing.

When dinner was ready, we sat out on the patio watching the sky and the birds, mostly silent.

At bedtime, Jared crawled under the sheets first and lay on his back, staring at the ceiling. I crawled in next to him.

"Hey," I said.

"Hey," he said. After a beat, he added, "I still don't like that glorified trash can, but I love you."

I moved toward him. "I love you too." I paused, deciding to finally say it: "Though, honestly, I don't always feel your love. Sometimes, I feel unseen." I paused, admitting the full truth, "Most of the time, actually."

A few seconds later he said, "That's not good. I'm sorry about that."

As soon as I heard that apology, a deep, heaving cry came out of me—the one from the Alvord. The cry of relief at being seen for who I was and what I felt—without having my feelings contradicted or denied.

After I was done, and while he still held me tightly, he said quietly, "Thank you for marrying me."

Remembering what I'd told Dad at lunch, I said "I'm glad I did." It was true. Anguish and all.

He added, "I don't know if you've noticed, but I'm not perfect."

I laughed, "Ditto."

Not long later, he said, "Thank you for loving me."

As before, I echoed his gratitude and kissed him. Later, before sleep, he added, "And thank you for your forgiveness."

"You are welcome. And same."

Bemusedly, he said, "Marriage is really weird."

I smiled. "It is. But it's the best—hardest-best—thing I've done. Thank you for sharing the adventure."

He said, "It's the best thing of my life. And I've certainly done dumber and harder things."

As I drifted to sleep, I thought of our night in the Alvord. How I'd set that little strand of lights by the van so that we'd have a point of reference to return to. In dark times, marriage is not so much about moving toward each other but about moving toward the Light—toward God. Especially when we can't see where the other person is. Because when we return to the Light, we will find each other.

◆ ◆ ◆

This morning as Jared hugged me goodbye, instead of saying the usual, "I love you," he looked at me a long while with love, letting me know I was seen.

> The world, a double blossom, opens:
> sadness of having come,
> joy of being here.
>
> —from "Concert in the Garden" by Octavio Paz[157]

◆◆◆

We didn't get on the road to camp until six. Once Jared was ready to talk, I told him about his Aunt Sue's visit that afternoon. My favorite line of hers: "Humor: don't leave home without it."

And I couldn't help but add, "She didn't like your last girlfriend." I reached over and squeezed his arm with a smile and a wink. "She's very glad you married me."

In all seriousness, Jared said, "I'm glad I married you, too."

A few beats later he added, "The one good thing about being with my last girlfriend was figuring out that I *did* want to be married. To grow and learn with someone. Because she didn't want that."

We talked about what we were learning with God. He mentioned that, even in the midst of his busiest season, God was teaching him how to rest.

I smiled, "Sounds like God: He seems to like a good paradox!"

Then he asked how my writing was going.

"Good," I said. "I'm thinking about a different way to organize the book. While shoveling soil today, I remembered an Instagram post I'd written last year. On a whim, I ended it with 'the long game of joy,' and a writer friend suggested that was the title of my next book. At the time, I stored it away for a future project. But now I think it's *this* book."

◆◆◆

Woke to overcast skies, thankful to be camping in the van and thankful it wasn't raining during breakfast. Someone had a fire going. The guys coordinated their shuttles.

This was not a balmy swimming weekend. But I did get in a walk between rain showers. Without a wheelbarrow full of gravel or soil, I felt bouncy-light.

When the rain started back up, I returned to camp and curled up in the van, finishing *Sacred Marriage* and starting *Hold Me Tight.* It was heaven to have nothing to do but read.

◆ ◆ ◆

On the drive home, I wanted so-o-o-o much talk about marriage. I often feel stuck, and I'd love to figure things out together. But I know that I like to talk about relationships more than my husband, so I restrained myself and only shared one favorite quote from *Sacred Marriage* about differences:

> Too often...when a mismatched couple gets together, they start judging each other instead of learning from each other. They in essence ask, "Why can't you be more like me?" instead of asking, "How can I become more like Christ?"[158]

The continual heart-shift from judgment to wonder.

◆ ◆ ◆

My hands felt like oven mits from moving the last of the gravel yesterday. Giving my arms a rest, I decided to work on less intense household things. I also decided to tweak an old motto: Expect the best, *respond with the positive.*

◆ ◆ ◆

Midday, I texted Jared: "I love you, and you're my so-much-more-than-coffee hero." (I call him my "coffee hero" when we camp and he makes me coffee first thing.)

For dinner, we ate elk burgers on the bench the Penningtons had given us. As the sun began to set, Jared suggested we walk down to the creek. We brought the last of the palomas with us. He showed interest in the paths I'd created and what I'd planted.

We walked across the creek and up into the huge field above it, wondering what that land might become someday.

Back home, I asked him to tell me about more of his photos. I'd pulled out a box of them—I plan to make a photo collage, blending photos from our lives. We sat, side by side, looking at images of him as a toddler and on soccer teams. I said how much I enjoyed getting to hear about his childhood.

He reached for me, resting his hand on my leg. On the stereo, Tom Petty's voice began to fill the room with "Learning to Fly."

Jared began to speak, "Well, I'll start and see where it ends…" And for a second, I thought he was referring to the song lyrics.

But then he began a lovely litany of gratitude that lasted for several songs:

Thank you for being a helper.

Thank you for keeping the house tidy and always beautiful.

Thank you for paying the bills.

Thank you for doing the grocery shopping and cooking—I know you like cooking, but I'm sure it's a lot of work.

Thank you for spending time with my friends—who I hope have become your friends.

Thank you for driving time—how we can talk or be silent together.

Thank you for your prayers. I love praying with you, but also seeing what you pray for. It's fun watching your prayers come true.

[By now, my tears were splashing on his shoulder.]

Thank you for not planning everything, even though you love to plan. For being game to go camping last minute.

Thank you for reading to me in the evenings—which I hope you enjoy, too!

Thank you for not letting me get away with stuff. For helping me grow.

Thank you for giving me my freedom.

Thank you for supporting the things I love even if you don't understand them.

Thank you for respecting me.

Thank you for being yourself.

Thank you for being content—not the bad kind, but the good kind. I don't know much about your work, but I'm glad you do it and that it brings you joy.

I can't remember how it ended. In fact, I'm not even sure he reached the end. There were swaths of silence between some elements of his list, and I didn't want to interrupt.

When the silence felt final, I whispered, "That was so beautiful. I feel loved. I feel seen. I feel cherished." And then, trying not to drip snot all over him, I added, "and I need to get a tissue before I kiss you." Which I did.

As the song says, we're starting out on dirty (and gravelly) roads, but we're learning to fly.

◆◆◆

To understand is to stand under the sky
of your own desires.

—from "Sky Inside" by Molly Peacock[159]

I woke glowing from the gratitude list last night. It stayed with me all day.

In one of his powerful sermons, Bill Johnson said: "Thankfulness helps to create hope. And hope is the joyful anticipation of good."

I am discovering that Jared spends time thinking of what to thank me for—his gratitude is worth far more than an average, casual "thank you." And it's one of the ways he flips his usual mode of *Do, Think, Feel.* Just as I have been learning to flip my mode of *Feel, Think, Do*—especially when *Do* is saying something in the moment.

Chris & Shannon came for dinner, and we celebrated the purchase of their first house together with wild salmon, salad, and jalapeño-cheddar bread.

We talked about how God is in everything with us—from birth to sex. He isn't afraid of those messy actions. In fact, He created them.

We mused on God's designs for marriage.

Jared said that, as a single guy, he hadn't really understood the Church teachings on marriage as a representation of union with God. But now he is beginning to.

I remembered my last trip to Switzerland a couple of springs ago, days after Jared reconnected with me. I had traveled to Aarau to teach a poetry workshop for an arts-and-faith conference. At the end of the event, I took a train to Lausanne and then on to Aigle, soaking up the familiar views along Lake Geneva. And then the bus—ascending the mountains on roads so curvy and narrow, I'd always marveled how that big vehicle could take the turns. And finally to a tiny village inhabited by more milk cows than humans, where dear friends let me stay in their chalet while they were out of the country. It was just a few chalets down the mountain from l'Abri, where I'd spent many seasons studying and working over the years. It is a fairy-tale nook of the world, that mountainside, with its geranium-filled window-boxes, alpenglow sunsets, and cows wearing bells on steep pastures.

I had the chalet to myself. I had pre-sold subscriptions to what I called "The Word-Painting Project." I would create a painting-poem of encouragement every day, make postcards of them when I returned home, and mail them to subscribers over the summer. It was most all of my dreams come true. I was doing what I loved all the day long: waking with God and coffee, writing all morning, hiking and painting all afternoon, and watching the sun set with wine. Bliss.

One evening, sipping chilled Chasselas on the balcony, my feet up on the decorative balustrade with its traditional floral cut outs, I acknowledged the perfection of the moment—all the things I like the way I like them.

And in that moment of recognition, I saw that seeming "perfection" for what it was: a beautiful illusion. On paper, this self-made, solo retreat was idyllic. But in spirit, it was way too much in my control. I wasn't experiencing perfection but rather the false peace that comes when you disconnect from anything unpeaceful.

And also: my biggest dream was still missing. Marriage.

Long prior to that trip, I had not only accepted being single, I had also chosen to devote my desire for romance into loving God. But there, in that high-elevation light, I saw that staying single wasn't how I'd best grow in love for Him. I saw that my dream had not "expired" after all.

Somehow, the moment I acknowledged the limits of that orderly time of solitude, I knew I was finally ready for the messier, shared reality of loving a partner—and in doing so, loving God in a new, more expansive way.

It's relatively easy to have a mountaintop experience of the divine when you're alone on a literal mountain. In fact, this was the same mountain where I'd once discovered C. S. Lewis's thoughts on joy.[160]

I had certainly learned wonderful things in my solo retreats over the years and in my time alone with God. But....

As Gary Thomas writes in *Sacred Marriage:*

> There has been an undeniable prejudice that to become *truly* holy, to earnestly pursue sanctity, one must embrace the single life.[161]

A few pages later, he counters that prejudice:

> Being so close to someone—which marriage necessitates—may be the greatest spiritual challenge in the world.[162]

I should share the subtitle of his book: *What if God Designed Marriage to Make Us Holy More than to Make Us Happy?* What if, as Thomas suggests, marriage is actually one, big sanctification process?

Elizabeth Gilbert speculates a similar thing in her book, *Committed:*

> With all respect to the Buddha and to the early Christian celibates, I sometimes wonder if all this teaching about nonattachment and the spiritual importance of monastic solitude might be denying us something quite vital. Maybe all that renunciation of intimacy denies us the opportunity to ever experience that very earthbound, domesticated, dirt-under-fingernails gift of difficult, long-term, daily forgiveness.... Maybe creating a big enough space within your consciousness to hold and accept someone's contradictions—someone's idiocies, even—is a kind of divine act. Perhaps transcendence can be found not only on solitary mountaintops or in

monastic settings, but also at your own kitchen table, in the daily acceptance of your partner's most tiresome, irritating faults.[163]

What if, indeed?

Kairos: All of the Above

On one of the rare weekends we weren't camping this season, Jared and I attended an outdoor service at church. We sat beneath an umbrella on a gorgeous morning, the blue sky broad above us.

Our friend, Niesje was leading worship. Before beginning a song about bringing heaven to earth, she reminded the congregation that, with God, anything can happen.

God often speaks to me in wordplay (I like to call Him the Wordsmith). As Niesje spoke, I heard in my heart the phrase "all of the above." Such words and phrases arrive with layers of meaning that take me a moment to unfurl.

One layer to "all of the above" was heaven, as in: all of what is higher, all of what is possible. At that moment, beneath the expansive sky, I was reminded of the vastness of possibility.

But "all of the above" also referred to that pesky option on multiple-choice tests.

I was never a natural test-taker. I could study in school, and I did—hard. But because I didn't have the knack of knowing what test makers wanted, I spent far too much time trying to memorize things instead of learning their context.

When required to answer essay questions, I could "show" my

work and explain nuances, which helped. But for multiple choice tests, there is just one right answer. Pretty black and white. Unless there is the shades-of-gray option D: "all of the above."

In school, I loved and hated "all of the above." It meant there was more than one correct answer (which I secretly believed about most everything). But it also meant I'd have to know the subject well enough to know whether A, B, and C were all correct, too.

That Sunday beneath the heavens, I saw how easy it is to slip back into old patterns of limited, either/or thinking—of believing there's just one right answer.

> Either/or thinking is a red flag, an indication that our thoughts and feelings are under the control of fear and not Love.[164]

I was reminded that God—Love—is big enough to be both/and—even big enough to offer an alphabet-length set of options and for *all* of them to be possible! Love is big enough to offer all of the above.

I was recently reading about dialectics, which is basically a fancy way to say both/and thinking. It's the paradox of seemingly contradictory things being true at once, like feeling sad *and* hopeful at the same time. In other words, there is usually more than one "correct" answer—or at least more than one way to arrive at it.

Life will throw tests at us—both essay *and* multiple choice. But it helps to remember that God offers more answers than any test key. It also helps to remember that He is not sitting around in heaven with a big red pen, waiting to tally our mistakes and write a low score across our lives. In fact, I have a feeling God isn't into tests the way humans are. For some reason, we seem to like them. So here's a test on subject matter I'm trying not to memorize but to embody:

A. God is not a test-maker waiting to fail us
B. God is Love, and Love is BIG: bigger than our

closed either/or thinking *and* bigger than our most open and noble imaginings

C. He invites us to dream with Him and heaven— to get to know Him well *and* to embrace the mystery of what we do not know

D. All of the above

Chronos: May

Jared and I went to the Growers' Market together for the first time since last summer. He knows so many people in Grants Pass that we barely moved six feet in 40 minutes. Such communal goodness.

And happy bounty: asparagus, pear cider, Manny's wooden spoons, Pennington jam.

◆◆◆

Today I'm flying low and I'm
not saying a word.
I'm letting all the voodoos of ambition sleep.

—from "Today" by Mary Oliver[165]

A lingering Sunday morning. Breakfast of bacon and eggs. After eating, Jared said, "I'm going to…or…what do you think if I get in a bike ride this morning and then we walk this afternoon?

Nicely done.

I smiled big. "That sounds great."

Our walk turned out to be up Aunt Sue's "roads." She and Uncle Tom live at the base of a mountain near us. Old, steep forest roads rise behind their house. But poison oak grew everywhere. When we returned, I put our clothes in the washer and prayed we wouldn't wake the next day with blistery skin (thankfully, we didn't).

Jared and I shared a quiet evening. I wrote while he started reading my book, *Hope of Stones*. I hadn't mentioned that the OPB announcement of the Oregon Book Awards was tonight, and I would find out whether my collection won. For some reason, I didn't want to listen to it live.

When Jared paused reading, I asked if there was anything he wanted prayer for this week. His response was the usual: his work crew. He then asked me, and I said I'd like prayer for my hands. They still don't work well after all that wheelbarrowing and pickaxing. He came over and sat with me and simply prayed aloud. It was lovely. Better than listening to an announcement. Which I did check before bed to find...that my book had won.

I told him, and he said, "Hey, I was reading your book while they announced it!"

He hugged me and asked how the award made me feel.

I said, "Good, I guess. I don't know."

Strangely, I didn't know. An award like that is an honor in the literary world. Winning it did make me happy—but it didn't really alter my joy. Maybe I really *have* let go of ambitions—the accolades the world tells us we should want.

And maybe I really have returned to my True Self; since I was a little girl, I've wanted to write and paint and love—not in that order and not for praise or pay.

In bed, curled into our goodnight spoon, Jared said—in his fake country accent, "I haven't read many poetry books, but yours is a darn good one."

I laughed and said, "That's my favorite review."

I try to decipher the meaning of hope rising up again
making music in me

—from "The Long Approach" by Maxine Kumin[166]

Dear Niesje came for lunch. I told her of my rediscovery of Enneagram Four-ness. How it made so much more sense in my life—and in my marriage.

She laughed, "I knew you were a Four!" She is, too.

She mentioned something she'd recently learned about the Enneagram. Without going off into geeky goodness, let's just say I was inspired and reminded that our growth is one, big, beautiful cycle. (And may I say again: I really wish I'd done a deeper study of the Enneagram long before marriage.)

Niesje also shared a realization that the depth of a Four can be a gift to others. Instead of expecting people to want to go to the same depths as she does, she can share her depths with them—even as they share their gifts with her.

People don't have to have the same core-deep experience of the world as Fours to truly connect with us? Revelation!

I had all this in my mind when Jared returned from kayaking—my heart full of the odd possibility that I could embrace my need to don emotional scuba gear and go to oceanic depths about…well, most everything but without demanding that he join me. I was relieved—and he probably would be, too.

As I washed the dinner dishes, Jared came up behind me and put his hands on my hips and his chin on my shoulder. I took that as a divine confirmation.

◆◆◆

Cinco de Mayo: date night and…the day the sale of the old house closed!

For a celebratory dinner, I mixed palomas and we called in a take-out order to Taqueria La Guacamaya. Even though the governor closed the state back down, the restaurant was able to set up tents in the parking lot and serve a boisterous holiday crowd. We were glad to see the restaurant doing well.

We brought our food to the Gold Hill river spot and sat in the spring-hot sun.

I asked how Jared's burrito was. He nodded at it in supreme appreciation. Then he acknowledged the harsh way he used to tell me when he didn't like certain foods. I said he was far better about that—and I hope I am far better about not taking it personally. I am happy to hear what he does and doesn't like, as long as it is said with kindness.

We talked about how loving others as we want to be loved doesn't always work. Especially with those closest to us, we need to learn to love them the way *they* need to be loved.

And we can check in with Holy Spirit moment-by-moment, conversation-by-conversation, for the best way to speak to people.

We listened to the river as late-day light poured across the water, everything molten gold. I kept thinking about communication, remembering how Jared has helped me grow in strength, and I have helped him grow in tenderness. My past tenderness often got mired in self-absorbed sensitivity; he helped me climb out of that. In fact, had I married someone with my same tendencies to over-feel and overthink, we'd have likely mired each other in an emotional bog. I'm glad to be in the flowing river of growth instead.

◆ ◆ ◆

I tried to start packing for the annual, multi-day rafting trip. But it's hard to imagine a non-summer water adventure. I'm excited…but also don't want to have freezing toes for days.

◆◆◆

Jared came home and was kind, even though it sounded like he'd had a terrible day—which made his kindness even more powerful. He shared a bit about the situation while he tried to eat his meatloaf, but eventually he set down his fork and said, "I'm too mad about work to eat."

I'm so glad we'll get out on the river this weekend.

◆◆◆

The weather was ideal for spring rafting. Blue skies. A few puffy white clouds. I had lined my travel vest with Fireball whiskey and Little Hotties Hand Warmers. Didn't need the hand warmers.

There were twenty people and nine boats—two of which were kayaks. Jared likes to kayak for this annual spring trip when the river is high, so I was a passenger in my father-in-law's boat. I called him Captain Andy—appropriate, since he had served as a Coastie in the Coast Guard.

The day's run was a lovely mix of quiet and conversation. Of still and rushing waters. Of turtles sunning on rocks. Of geese and goslings. And always ahead of us: the ever-V of sky made by shore-side mountains angling down into the river.

Andy and I talked about the importance of having guy- and girlfriends in marriage and not expecting a spouse to be everything to us. I remembered Esther Perel's oft-quoted wisdom: "Today we turn to one person to provide what an entire village once did: a sense of grounding, meaning, and continuity."[167] I am glad that both Jared and I have strong and healthy friendships.

We arrived to Black Bar Lodge. At water level, all you could see was a cove of rocks—the lodge was hidden further up the mountain. We "parked" (I kept using car terms) in a steep nook and clambered up the bank.

Happy hour on the lawn: Dark 'n' Stormies and "serious appetizers" and talk.

Exhausted by 8 p.m.

And I think cabin C's "queen" bed is really just a full.

♦ ♦ ♦

After a cozy morning in bed, I took my coffee and walked around the grounds, passing a mass of flowers that looked as if their petals had been painted with a watercolor brush. Spring finery.

We were all back on the water after breakfast. I enjoyed listening to Andy's Coast Guard stories and how he took Alex and Jared on their first river trips when they each turned five.

We stopped for lunch some-rocky-where near a creek. Beth & Jason and a few other folks hiked up to a waterfall. I overheard Jared talking to Larry about rethinking risk—physical, adventurous risk—now that he's married. Hmmm.

Late afternoon stop at writer Zane Gray's historic cabin, where Jared picked me sprigs of rosemary and mint and wild iris.

It was a bit cloudier today—grateful for the tarp to cover my "waterproof" pants.

When we arrived to Marial Lodge, a group of us walked up to Inspiration Point to see the double waterfalls Jared had once run in his kayak.

More wild irises. Happy hour on the deck. Andy's good wine came out.

Someone asked how Jared and I met. I looked at my husband and smiled. "I'd like to hear *you* tell the story."

When he got to the part where he walked away a decade ago, he said he'd known he had a good thing, but he wasn't ready for it. He finished by saying that, a few years ago, he realized he *did* want to get married.

Interesting: before Jared returned to my life, I had finally let go of my desire for marriage. I had grown entranced by mystics and the contemplative life, and I had prepared myself for union with God without union with man. And before I returned to Jared's life, he had finally let go of his desire for bachelorhood and embraced the idea of marriage.

How about that?

Then Anne asked us what surprised us most about marriage.

I had asked my friend, Kadance, that very same question before I married. I quoted her answer now: "I thought I had it all together!" Laughter. I added that I'd known marriage echoed union with God, but I hadn't realized union started with being undivided in myself—with letting go of the divisive False Selves that get in the way of wholehearted oneness.

Jared said what surprised him was how differently we made decisions but how we came up with the Third Thing—something better than what we'd each thought of separately.

Luke asked for an example. The patios on our new house. At first, I had wanted wood decks, but Jared didn't want any external wood he'd have to refinish someday, so he voted for composite, which I didn't like the look of. We ended up with exposed concrete: durable ("bomb proof," to quote Jared) and somehow beautiful.

In *Heart of Love,* I'd read about the *vesica pisces:* the shared space made by two, slightly overlapping circles, like that of a Venn

Diagram. The author illustrates healthy relationships using this shape. He calls it:

> Unity Within Duality: The two spheres remain separate but connected. (The *vesica pisces* is the third shape created by the joining of the two.)[168]

I recognized that shape as the Third Thing. And I also recognized it from my studies of medieval art, when I had learned the name of that shape as *mandorla*—from the Italian word for *almond*. Medieval artists often painted Christ inside the almond-shaped mandorla, which represented a kind of vehicle that moved between heaven and earth.

The *vesica pisces*. The mandorla. Whatever name it goes by, the shape represents union. This is why Jared and I are often delighted when we come up with the Third Thing. The idea we create together is always better than what either of us could create on our own, and it's made possible in the shared space between us.

◆◆◆

Twin beds are not conducive to snuggling, but I got into Jared's anyway this morning. At one point, he raised up his head, looked me in the eyes, and said, "I love you so much."

Ditto, my dear.

Breakfast was served on two-tiered turntables stacked with fresh blueberry muffins, homemade blackberry jam, egg casserole, bacon, honeydew, and melon.

Then early on the water for the long last day. Which turned out to be so warm, that when we stopped for lunch at Tate Creek Falls, I dunked in the creek pool at the base of the waterfall *and* in the river after, happily abandoning my "waterproof" pants for bare legs the rest of the blue-sky day.

And then, after a bit more river, we came to the take-out, and the trip ended. After the goodbyes, we emerged at Gold Beach and drove to Brookings for an early dinner at Zola's before the long drive home along the Smith River.

When Jared and I pulled onto our road, I said, "Home!"

And he added, "Sweet home."

> This is the country we return to when
> For a moment we forget ourselves,
> When we watch the sleeping kitten quiver
> After long play, or rain comes down warm.
>
> —from "Humility" by Fred Chappell[169]

◆ ◆ ◆

This evening, Jared suggested communion. Happily. I brought out a RITZ and the last of the Clonakilty Ben & Rebecca had given us. Jared thanked God for hope: hope that I would grow more in love with God and hope that he would grow more in love with God. He closed by asking that God's goodness in our lives and marriage draw people to Him. That he didn't even know what that looked like, but he was excited to find out.

◆ ◆ ◆

For date-night dinner, we called in a take-out order to The Millennial, walked down to pick it up, and then continued on to find the confluence of Evans Creek and the Rogue. It was a bit of scramble, involving underpasses and train tracks, but when we found it, we had a pebble beach all to ourselves. We dunked in.

Strange: in the confluence, the water at our feet was warm, but up at our thighs, it was cold. Also strange: the mysterious confluence that is marriage.

◆ ◆ ◆

I met Christina at Cathedral Hills to walk this morning. She asked me how marriage was going. I said I hadn't experienced the legendary "honeymoon stage." It had been hard from the start, but it's so much better now.

She suggested it's better to get hard stuff out of the way and then enjoy the good later.

Wise perspective.

◆ ◆ ◆

Departure day for my husband, who is heading off to Idaho in a van with a group of nine guys and their smelly kayak gear. I am so glad to be staying home.

I cooked Jared bacon and eggs before he left at six. He had stuffed his drybags full of kayak gear and enough jerky, salami, and sausage that—he surmised—he won't poop all week.

Boyz.

After he left, I started tackling the tarped woodpile. By midday, I had stacked all the wood on narrow pallets along the wall of the patio. Six pallets long.

Then I was finally able to get to the ruts beneath the former woodpile and start leveling those. That evening, Jared sent a photo of kayaks with the text: "Made it. Love you."

Have fun, my love.

◆ ◆ ◆

After days and days of work, I finished the side yard! And now there is only one tarp-covered blob out there.

Jared called to say they had just finished their three-day run down the South Fork Salmon: 66 river miles—28 of them today. They were getting beer and burgers and then driving up to camp before running the Lochsa.

He mentioned how good it was to get away, "From work, not from you," he was quick to add. I told him I was so glad he could be away, too. It sounded like he'd had time to catch up with himself.

He said, "I miss you."

I said the same—and that it was a new kind of missing. Different from when he'd been working out of town in Chiloquin or Coquille last fall. "Maybe it's because we're closer now, but it's a bittersweet missing. Since there's no distance in the spirit, maybe it's knowing that you're close even when you're far away. If that makes any sense."

I'm pretty sure Enneagram-Four-Me often sounds confusing. Before we hung up, I thanked him for trying to figure me out. Since I can barely figure myself out, that's a daunting task. But, as I like to remind him, I married a man who likes a challenge!

As I often do, I thought of union with God. I love how Brother Lawrence describes it:

> This union is not a mere fleeting emotion…. It is, instead, a state of soul—if I can but find words—that is deeply spiritual and yet very simple, which fills us with a joy that is undisturbed, and with a love that is very humble and very reverent.[170]

Life goal: undisturbed joy.

That evening, I watched the clouds move above the trees, giddy in love with God, speaking aloud my gratitude to Him. Reasserting that He is and always will be my first love and the one who knows the deepest corners of my heart. That my husband and I can love each other even if we never fully know each other. And that our huge differences will continue to teach us each to love even better.

I laughed aloud in joy. I'm pretty sure God was laughing, too.

> And when I hear you laugh I know again
> you are the letters of every word I use, you
> the source and form of every poem.

—from "A Little Book of Hours" by John F. Deane[171]

◆◆◆

When Jared arrived home, I think we both felt a teensy bit shy of each other. Nine days apart—the longest span since being married.

I had just made tea and cookies, so we enjoyed those while he told me about the trip. The great water. The guy-dynamics. The pouring rain and the sunshine.

He asked what I'd planned to do this afternoon. I said, "Make cookies and organize my studio. Cookies are done, and my studio can wait. I'm happy to do whatever you like."

He suggested a walk, so we ended up walking seven miles of the local bike trail that follows the river. We had a good conversation, and I was especially pleased to hear these two parts:

While talking with a friend who had just gone through a divorce, Jared had mentioned he was learning that even when your partner says something completely different from what you think, you can trust they are saying it from a place of love. His friend said it would have been nice to know that.

Jared also said this river trip was easier than our fall road trip, but he hadn't grown as much with just the guys. He marveled at the different ways men and women think. Beautifully, his marveling was filled with respect.

◆◆◆

Late Sunday afternoon, we decided to swing by the river and then see if anywhere in downtown Grants Pass was open for dinner. Except for The Haul, it was like a ghost town.

So The Haul it was. I took a deep breath, remembering The Jam Fiasco there in January (and, in fact, had just transcribed my handwritten journal notes from that evening). Thankfully, the glitchy QR code system was no longer in place; we could order inside.

Jared didn't have a mask with him, so he got us an outdoor table, and I was in charge of the orders. When I entered the restaurant, I felt a hint of panic as I waited in the long line; I could feel Jared's order disappearing from my brain.

"Stop it," I told myself. And I listened. I remembered that The Jam Fiasco had been forgiven and finished. And I remembered Jared's fried chicken sandwich and beer choice.

And all was well.

◆◆◆

This evening, Jared asked if we could talk about the brick patio design. Nice timing. For three months since moving in, I've not brought up any landscaping desires I couldn't do alone. I wanted him to have time to recoup from the grueling season of working on the house in addition to his regular work.

We mostly agreed on the brick patio planters, and we did a good job of listening to each other. When I misunderstood his desire for ground cover, he sighed, "It's been a while since we worked on the house. I forgot how hard it is to make decisions together." But he softened his statement with a half-smile.

I came up to him, hugged him, looked him in the eyes, and said with a smile of my own, "Hey, we make great decisions together." I squeezed him.

He laughed.

◆ ◆ ◆

Today, without saying why, I *will* say I am trying really hard to learn this from *Loving Bravely:*

> What's most essential when it comes to healthy intimate communication is not some fancy set of skills. *It's relational self-awareness*—the ability and willingness to look honestly at what tends to set you off in your intimate relationship and how you handle yourself when you feel upset.[172]

◆ ◆ ◆

Celebrating the brothers' birthdays tonight. Though Alex is a few years older than Jared, they were born within a week of each other. Tradition is dinner at River's Edge with Andy & Linda. I donned my back-up wedding dress: a simple, silky wrap dress. Though it's only tea-party formal, it's a bit overkill. Still, there haven't been many occasions to wear it in the Time of Covid.

After Jared showered and dressed, he came up to me in the kitchen and reached for me. We kissed and I said, "You look very handsome." He hugged me and said in his fake country accent, "You look so pretty. And you smell like a woman."

I laughed and thanked him. I have avoided wearing fragrances because Jared once complained about perfume. But tonight, I'd applied the scent Linda had given me for my birthday. After yesterday, I felt a childish urge to do something I loved that he didn't. I was almost annoyed that he *liked* the scent—because he'd once said he didn't like *any*. But I sent the annoyance away.

He held me a few beats longer than usual, and when he pulled back, he looked me in the eyes and said, "I love you."

And, though I am the first to admit I can read non-existent subtext into anything, I sensed that this "I love you" also meant he was trying to figure out how I needed to be loved.

We're learning how to play the long game together.

> There is good news in the slight male advantage in focusing on facts relatively free of emotion, coupled with the slight female advantage in processing facts in the deeper emotional context: We make a good team.[173]

River's Edge was packed. Linda had reserved seats out on the deck, and the river glistened beside us in early evening sunlight.

The topic of weekends away came up. Jared said he'd had all of April and May to play on the weekends. With a smile, I added that he'd had all of March, too.

Alex asked what *I* got in the deal.

I furrowed my brow and laughed, "I'm not sure…"

He smiled, "You can keep renegotiating the contract."

Smart man. I'm going to quote him later.

Then gifts came up. Rachael told the story of the necklace Alex had given her. Jared said, "At least it's not a hoodie!" and he reached for my hand as we laughed. Rachael said she sensed a story. Jared explained he'd gotten me a hoodie for my birthday from our local pharmacy.

I added the definitive detail: "It said 'Guns 'n' Drugs' on it. But I liked the lip balm he got with it!"

◆◆◆

Friday afternoons = departure prep for camping. It was almost five when Jared got home, and let's just say this homecoming was massively disconnected.

I could feel the hurt rising up in me. But the second my inner dialogue began its familiar grievance—arguing that there's always time for quick kindness—I caught myself and stopped. Jared probably had something to finish before we departed.

So I did the opposite of what I felt after that "greeting." I kissed him, said "Welcome home," and left him to whatever he was evidently focused on. The authors of *How to Improve Your Marriage Without Talking About It* noted that men live on the brink of shame and women on the brink of fear. This has all sorts of ramifications for the communication loops we find ourselves in, and their solution resonated with my ever-hope of focusing on the positive. This is a long quote, but it's gold:

> When a surge of emotion *feels* like it's hijacking your body and making you react in a nonloving, noncompassionate way, it may feel good to discharge the emotion and react in the moment, even though the lasting effects can be devastating to your relationship and even harmful to your health. To help in this seemingly daunting but highly rewarding task, we offer the skill of *emotion transformation....* When your partner is on the precipice of fear or shame but coming off as angry, critical, irritable, or resentful, practicing emotional transformation will prevent you from falling into the fear-shame trap. That's when the fear in one of you stimulates shame in the other and vice versa.... When you feel like giving up, you can transform that troublesome emotion by making a *small* improvement; when you feel like casting blame, redirect to some form of appreciation; when you feel like withdrawing, redirect toward connecting; or when you feel like attacking, redirect to protection.[174]

And it worked. When we finally got on the road, Jared was delighted to be done with the last of his admin, and he blessed the trip warmly. I was able to let go of my fear that he doesn't want to connect. And I avoided saying—even thinking!—something that my husband would interpret as shaming for his terse homecoming.

After we passed through Scott Valley, the Josh Garrels song, "Morning Light" came on the stereo. I had never heard it, and it immediately caught my heart. So many good songs have the lyrical equivalent of "Everything's going to be all right."

It is.

Especially because I'm starting to see the innocence behind my husband's words and actions—as in: they are not intended to wound or hurt. They usually have nothing to do with me. That, and we each hold the immense power of forgiveness and can use it at will.

◆◆◆

My husband turns forty today. Welcome to my decade!

We drove to Greys Falls and hiked down to a rocky shore of the Trinity, where Jared sunned himself on a boulder and I alternated stretching with dunking in the rock pool.

Then we drove up to Cedar Flat so he could kayak back to Greys Falls. After he launched, I enjoyed a perfect swimming spot—a calm eddy so wide I could swim large ovals for laps. When done, I hiked back up to the van, dripping wet, and drove with the windows rolled down and the music cranked up, and "Morning Light" came back on again. It was an exhilaration of music, sunlight, and river water in my hair.

I returned to the place we'd chosen to camp, making everything as celebratory as I could by setting the picnic table with a little tablecloth, coffee, and the birthday cake the Penningtons had sent Jared (pink—with sprinkles!).

I hung the hammock and read until Jared's projected return time of 5 p.m. Right on time, he emerged through the trees with his bright red kayak.

As he took off his drysuit, he wondered aloud if we should drive to the Salmon tonight to meet up with the crew there.

I said, "Whatever the birthday boy wants."

But thankfully, he wanted to enjoy his cake and coffee and decided to stay.

He was in the mood to talk. And I was happy to listen. He told me a lovely thing: "You let me be myself, and as I better myself, I learn to love you better." I'd never thought of that.

We discussed the difference between "kind" and "nice." How kindness has love and strength behind it, but niceness is often a Band-Aid way to avoid doing the hard thing.

He lit a fire in the pit, burning not just the foraged wood I'd brought from our land but also fallen branches from the campsite outskirts.

He mentioned reconsidering his love of high-risk activities and that he wants to be responsible. But he loves how exhilarating those things were.

I suggested things might shift as we age. That exhilaration could expand from physical to include mental and spiritual.

Before bed, he peed on the fire and said, "A great way to end my birthday."

Boyz.

◆ ◆ ◆

This warm morning, we enjoyed the scenic drive along the Trinity and Klamath to the Salmon. Once there, we spotted Eric's pop-up van at a large group camp site a ways above the river. Some of the crew had gone on an early bike ride; Eric and Gabe were heading down to the river with the others.

So many people, I couldn't keep track of who went with whom. Dogs. Kids. Cornhole on the riverbank stones. Dozing in the shade. Beer cooling in the river. Bluest skies as the sun shifted to shade the entire bank.

We all stayed down by the water until evening, it was still so hot up above.

When Jared and I walked back up to the campsite to make dinner with the boisterous group, Jared said he was glad we got to have last night alone together.

I was glad too—and glad *he* was.

This has been a good and mellow month.

[Jared would like to add that this month was mellow because he got to kayak a lot!]

Kairos: Peace Like That

We are all one question, and the answer seems to be love—a connection between things.

—Mary Rueffle

I'm a metaphorical girl—I see connections everywhere. This year, I learned the word *apophenia:* the tendency to look for connections among unrelated things. I'm pretty sure I have a not-so-mild case of it, as evidenced by my last book: a cross-century conversation in poems among a Spanish nun, a French Architect, and an American poet.

Whether through simile or metaphor, I am constantly comparing unlike things to better understand abstractions. In fact, here's a metaphor: our marriage *is* apophenia!

Which brings me to rivers. I spend a *lot* of time on rivers since I married a man who loves them. And this spring, I've wondered about that metaphorical comparison of "peace like a river" in Scripture.[175] Spend time on even a single river, and you realize that rivers are varied: one section might be placid as a pond. The next might be a whitewater "boulder garden" your husband inexplicably wishes to kayak through.

Peace like *which part* of the river?

Like *all* of it. Peace in *all* the river sections, from frog water to Class-V rapids.

And peace in the snags—the fallen trees and root masses that accumulate along a shore. They can impede progress. But they can also create little eddies of stillness out of the fast current and give you a place to pause before you continue your journey.

I kid you not, I had that snag realization by a river one morning, and that same afternoon, Jared and I got into a massive snag-fight. We got caught on the jagged edges of stuff we'd let accumulate along our shore, but once we pressed through, we found a pool of peace. Someday, we may even remember that there can be peace *in* the snags, too.

I have an old hymn stuck on repeat in my heart: "When Peace, Like a River." That song has always held power for me. It was originally titled "It Is Well With My Soul" for its famous refrain. But I didn't learn why it was so powerful until this winter, when a friend came for dinner and played us the song on his guitar, telling the back story.

Horatio Spafford wrote the hymn in the nineteenth century. He was a prosperous businessman in Chicago. He and his wife had a son and four daughters. Things were going well—until they weren't. They lost their son to scarlet fever. Then, the Great Chicago Fire destroyed all of Horatio's real estate, wiping out his life savings. He decided to take his family to England to start over. Right before he planned to leave, a business deal arose that could help his family, so he sent his wife ahead of him with their four daughters.

The boat carrying his family shipwrecked. His wife survived, but *all* of their daughters died.

As soon as he received the news, Horatio took the next ship to be with his wife. At one point on the voyage, the captain told him they had reached the spot where his children had drowned. And there—in the place of his deep loss and sorrow—he wrote a hymn of peace. Here are the first lines:

> When peace like a river attendeth my way,
> When sorrows like sea billows roll;

Whatever my lot, Thou hast taught me to know
It is well, it is well, with my soul.

That man's faith takes my breath away. It makes me game to learn
the currents of peace like a river.

From placids to rapids, I'm all in.

Chronos: June…and Then Some

Before we left for Jared's birthday weekend, I had given him a watercolor painting of our communion elements—whiskey & RITZ—and a family-sized bag of Sour Patch Kids.

Eating the candy tonight, he told me, "Sour Patch gummies are a better way to end dinner than a salad."

I laughed, "There are even green ones—you could say you're eating the rainbow!"

◆◆◆

Hidden Valley High School Class of 2021 graduation.

Since we were family of the valedictorian—our bright niece, Noel—we had honorary seating down on the black track tarmac…in triple-digit, record-breaking heat.

I melted. From the heat but also from all of the young hope through-lining the student speeches. And though I'm not a fan of crowds, it was actually a treat to be outside with hundreds of people after all the Covid-banned gatherings.

After the ceremony, while waiting for the family to take their photos, Jared and I ran into a volleyball friend of his from their own high-school days. She introduced us to her husband, and

Jared introduced his new wife.

Before they left, I heard her say to Jared that he was a little slow.

After they walked away, I asked "Slow at what?"

"Getting married."

I laughed, remembering his resistance to marriage years ago. Since I spent my life wanting to get married and he only recently wanted to, it will likely take a while for his old resistance to wear down and for all of my old expectations to wear down. We're leveling the playing field. And turtle-slow but steady, we're learning that "We live and move and have our being in a unified field of love."[176]

◆ ◆ ◆

We've been married eleven months.

Morning revelation: I'm the rhythm section, and Jared's the riffs. Rhythm & Riffs.

Suzanne Stabile writes: "Don't we all want the one or two infallible rules for how to love and be loved? But love is improvisation."[177] Despite my being less naturally inclined to improvisation, I think my husband and I are both getting better at it.

I've lost track of how many metaphors I've used for marriage so far—from rivers to games to house-building. I willfully mix them all into a batch of understanding.

◆ ◆ ◆

Whatever is singing
is found, awaiting the return
of whatever is lost.

—from "The Law That Marries All Things" by Wendell Berry[178]

On the way to camp on the Illinois River, we stopped by the Growers' Market. It was the last time we would "meet" at the Pennington Farm stand. They have been a cornerstone of the local markets for thirty years, but they are finally going to close that chapter and focus on their farm and bakery. It was as if they were graduating, and—in some odd way—as if Jared and I were, too.

After we made our rounds, we ended up at El Charro Viejo's stand where Jared loves the burritos. He recognized his friend Antonio, who used to work at Rogue Roasters. I remembered meeting him at the old G Street locale a decade ago with Jared, on our way to the coast.

Antonio is now a filmmaker working in Brazil. His friend Max was sitting with him, and their two sets of kids were running around, happy and wild. Jared introduced me as his wife, and everyone said their congratulations. Max said he'd just read a newspaper article about a woman who had traveled the world and recently married and was writing every day during the first year of her marriage because it is the greatest adventure....

I realized he was quoting from the interview answers I'd given to the *Grants Pass Daily Courier* after *Hope of Stones* won the Oregon Book Award. Rachael had texted me Kelsey's photo of the article that came out yesterday. I hadn't picked up a copy yet. I started to say that might be me when Max said, "Wait, is that you?"

They had run a huge photo of me instead of the book cover. I took my sunglasses off, "A small world! I haven't even read the finished piece!"

We sat down with the two men and talked while their kids zoomed about in a frenzy of friendship, asking for bites of burritos and for dollars to buy honey sticks. It was a sunny, summer morning, and it felt like pre-Covid life.

After a while, we said our goodbyes and drove toward the river. I told Jared that Max had picked up on what I'd learned from travel writer Tim Cahill about arriving to a new country for the first time: take contemporaneous notes because you'll never have those first impressions again. That advice had been part of my inspiration to write every single day for our first year of marriage.

Jared nodded. He said, "It's like kayaking. You can never ride the river blind twice."

Turns out, that's why you don't always scout new rivers—so you can experience them wholly new. A chance you only get once.

I thought of the marriage parallels. It's probably good you can't scout marriage, either. It's also one of the benefits to making a commitment without knowing what you're getting into. When you enter a shoreless gorge, you stay the course even when you smash up against rocks. Thankfully, there are plenty of tranquil riverbanks downstream, too.

As we had last year, we stopped at Six Mile so Jared could kayak to a gravel bar downriver where I'd meet him with the van. I walked down to the water with him to dunk in. After he climbed into his boat, he glided up to me, and we kissed.

Later, while driving high above the river on the one-lane road, I spotted him down through the trees, far below on the water. In a rare moment, he looked up and saw me, and we waved to each other, both of us going in the same direction but on our own routes.

I arrived to the take-out and got the van stuck on a stone. Which wasn't hard to do—the entire river bar was made of stones. I managed to move the melon-sized one I'd caught on and then get the van in place. It's always a relief to park and know I don't have to drive in wild places again for the day.

This stretch of river has wide swaths I love to swim in, but soon the wind picked up, and the water looked like it was flowing upstream. Swimming became clavicle-slapping chore. I clambered out and pumped up the stand-up paddleboard to use as a landlocked floaty-bed. I enjoyed the soft sun and solitude until Jared arrived.

Later that afternoon, I would get quietly mad about a petty thing that arose between us. But I tried not to dwell on it and instead to dwell on all the good parts of the day.

> What brings love to our relationship and sows the seeds for forgiveness is simple: appreciating absolutely everything we can about the person we are with each and every day. There is nothing simpler to do, and no more powerful gift you can offer to your partner....We make an agreement with ourselves to look at our partners through the eyes of love. The eyes of love reveal our partners to be wounded individuals who make mistakes, not terrible people trying to do harm. [179]

And so, I kept my ire to myself. I figured it was mostly mine, anyway. I tried to look at my husband with the eyes of love and to appreciate his knowledge of rivers and his love of camping.

I reminded myself that joy is a practice. It's also one of the fruits of the Spirit:

> In life, we often want to partake of the good fruit without putting in any of the labor.... But life is much more like a garden than a grocery store. Our marriages require us to engage in the work before we ever see good fruit.... I can't just grab the fruits I want like I would in the produce department. This fruit is not a product to consume; it's evidence. It's the proof that the Holy Spirit is already at work in our lives. It doesn't simply appear. [180]

Later that summer, I would finish the photo collage of Jared and me from our childhoods through to our marriage. I spangled the snapshots across a cluster of hexagonal cork boards, making a honeycomb of history. I wanted to find the parallels in our lives. Each photo of Jared is hung next to a similar photo of me. A few of the pairings:

Husband as a toddler showing the camera his hands and face covered in frosting	*Wife as a toddler at the kitchen sink, showing the camera her hands covered in soap suds*
Husband as a teenager standing beneath a massive palm tree leaf in Costa Rica	*Wife as a teenager standing beneath a massive palm tree leaf in Jamaica*
Husband as a twenty-something with dreadlocks when he lived in Australia	*Wife as a twenty-something with a Halloween beehive when she lived in North Carolina*

Husband and wife standing together at their wedding

It took me far longer than I care to admit to create this collage. But I knew that doing so was about more than covering a blank wall— it was about seeing patterns and connections across time. Looking for the good, celebrating it. Seeing what Jared and I had made of our lives separately and knowing that we could make something of our lives together. There was even a photo of toddler-Jared waving at the camera. It was as if he was waving across time—like today-Jared waving at me from the river below on our different but parallel routes.

Joy is a life-long game.

◆ ◆ ◆

In the morning, the gravel bar filled up with a zoo of a group launching their inflatable kayaks. A blur of boats and coolers and conversations. In a brief lull, Jared, who was finishing *Hope of Stones,* asked me what one of my lines meant. It was from one of the last poems and reads: "plot a heart of possibility."[181]

I said it had to do with planner-me learning to relinquish my idea of how things should be. Of realizing the limitations of my imagination and learning to partner with heaven for things I don't even know to dream of.

Jared nodded. He reiterated that he wasn't a planner, but that he could see this idea applying to how he thought of the future.

By midday, we finally had the beach to ourselves. While I read, Jared lay back on the sand. I thought he was dozing, but after a while he said he was pulling my line of poetry throughout his life: starting with us, then friends, work, and the future.

How lovely.

We had one last swim before driving back up the hills away from the river and into the heat. My skin still cool from the water, I referenced a conversation we'd had earlier about what people get addicted to. I wondered if I was addicted to sadness—to melancholy. Though I hoped that some of the fruit of it is my writing and art.

Jared was quiet for several winding stretches of road. Eventually, he spoke. He said he didn't perceive me as sad but that I'd worked through my melancholy to find joy. That I had a *chosen* joy—one I'd fought for. One that's contagious and rooted in years of growth and gratitude. A joy that others gravitate toward. He had always thought overly-happy-acting people were actually miserable—they hadn't fought through their sadness, were just masking it.

It was such a considered and deep reply. I was reminded that my husband can dive into the depths, too.

C. S. Lewis was right: "Joy is the serious business of heaven."[182]

Back home, between taking communion on the patio and reading from *Black Beauty*, I told Jared, "I want to thank you again for all your hard work." I hugged him and said what a delight it was to be able to write without having to edit everyone else's writing. How very grateful I was. He held me tightly far longer than usual. When he finally released me, he looked me in the eye and said, "I love you."

I had expressed this specific gratitude before, but I think he heard it in a new way tonight. This time, between the lines of his "I love you," I heard "thank you."

Saying grace together.

In *Atlas of the Heart,* Brené Brown writes:

> We need happy moments and happiness in our lives; however, I'm growing more convinced that the pursuit of happiness may get in the way of deeper, more meaningful experiences like joy and gratitude.... In our research we found that everyone who showed a deep capacity for joy had one thing in common: They practiced gratitude.[183]

◆◆◆

Doug & Jureen came for dinner. Over chicken cacciatore, we talked about men's love languages often being quality time and recreational companionship. (With a nod to *The Five Love Languages* and *His Needs, Her Needs,* respectively.)

The couple had just celebrated their 33rd anniversary, so I asked them to tell us something they had learned about marriage. Jureen was quick to answer: "That your partner loves you—and even when it doesn't feel like it, they are responding to you from a heart of love. That you can trust that."

Jared agreed, acknowledging that he maybe doesn't always come across as loving even though he loves me. It felt like he especially wanted me to hear that, to have faith in him.

> Did I not say
> the night we fell into the same dream
> that the earth
> on which we walk in confidence
> will heave beneath our feet,
> jar us from the dream
> and bring to birth
> all we could never have imagined?

Did I not say
I love you?

—from "After Reading the Love Poems of Dov Ben-
Zamir" by Alim Maghrebi Habibi[184]

◆◆◆

I drove to the Applegate to see Christina. We sat on her porch,
framed by a riot of fragrant wild roses I'd once painted in
watercolor. So strange to drive forty-five minutes to see her when
I used to drive just a few. All those years of dinners beneath her
oak tree, of hatching writing projects.

We marveled that we "got away with" Deep Travel Workshops
without any major catastrophes. And though I'm immensely glad
for those travel-writing years, I'm immensely glad now to nest.

◆◆◆

What I am happy I figured out the first week of marriage,
confirmed in *The Proper Care and Feeding of Husbands:*

> The truth is that wives generally overwhelm their
> husbands with communication. Much of what motivates
> that communication might be better dealt with through
> personal circumspection, triaged for significance,
> selected for true communication (connecting) value,
> whittled down to its essence, timed better, and expressed
> more appropriately.[185]

I do plenty of whittling generally, but in the hour after Jared gets
home from work, I quickly learned to whittle down even the vital
queries, too. When I first moved in with him after our wedding, I
had a backlog of questions about practical things, like which
payment method to use for utilities and what days of the week
worked for entertaining and which brand of milk did he like? I
actually wrote down a list of questions and spaced them out over
weeks, prioritizing for immediacy and maxing a couple of
questions per evening, after he'd had time to decompress.

Now, I sometimes mix it up, using this suggestion from *Soul Mates:* "A general principal in soul-work is to bring the endless fertility of imagination to whatever is under consideration."[186]

Today when Jared walked in the door, I kissed him hello and broke my norm, asking two questions right away—but fun ones: "What time would you like dinner, and when would you like your drink?"

Answers: "5:30 and now."

Sometimes the soul-work is easy!

◆ ◆ ◆

> Desire is a tricky thing, the boiling of the body's wants,
>   more praise, more hands holding the knives
> away.

—from "Notes on the Below" by Ada Limón[187]

Jared came home and went right back out for a bike ride. How to fulfill his love language of quality time and his need for recreational companionship when I don't like to speed down mountains or rapids? And when he says he dislikes my favorite activities: walking and swimming? To his credit, he'll walk with me now and then. And to my credit, I drive shuttle for him now and then.

I'm a solitude-loving introvert. I don't need heaps of time with my husband, but I do need some. Romantic me, the only person I want to get my romance with is him. Every other interpersonal need, I try to spread equally among my "village" of friends and family, being there for them, too. I'm very careful not to expect Jared to be my everything, and I'm glad he doesn't expect that of me, either. Still….

We're reading *Peter Pan.* And oh, Mrs. Darling's hidden kiss that Mr. Darling missed!

What I wish I'd known then was my own epiphany later that year: my need for romance is just as strong as my husband's need for adventure. And it was important that I finally articulate that need, giving it the same significance as Jared's oft-articulated need for adventure. That was a light-bulb moment for both of us, helping me to honor his desire to career off of things and helping him to honor my desire for candles and bossa nova music.

Another thing I didn't yet know: on a future weekend getaway, *Jared* would light the candle I brought. All things are possible!

And I am continuing to remember (oh, how we forget) that as long as I stay connected to God, I have everlasting romance.

Bernard of Clairvaux, in his book on Song of Songs, explains Solomon's mysterious line about kissing with the kiss of his mouth: "it is the uniting of God with man."[188] *Aha.* Once again: the reminder that God is my first love, my true union. When I remember and live from that knowing, I can love my husband well.

And Mrs. Darling's kiss can become visible.

◆◆◆

When the wind blows, you put up your sail, and when it doesn't, you row.

—Saint Teresa of Ávila

Rainy day. After a morning of writing and indoor-choring, I read all of *Independent Enough* on the stationary bike. Oh my. So much insight. Turns out, we choose a partner who needs the same amount of closeness/distance we do—even though one often looks like the pursuer. The one who withdraws keeps that same space between us. If the pursuer backs away, the previous withdrawer now pursues.[189]

I knew a bit about this in dating, but I didn't know the

"measurement" of the distance stayed relatively constant throughout a relationship—or that we choose someone who needs the same amount of space between us.

♦ ♦ ♦

It's been hard to transcribe my handwritten journals from our difficult days. But: I can know if I have truly forgiven by how my heart feels as I reread past angst. Often, I have more forgiving to do. If any ire rises, I choose to be grateful for the sight and insight.

(Future Me, inserting herself here in late revisions, can now smile when rereading the rough stuff—and can see just how far we've come. Example: after our first year of marriage, my husband got far better about homecomings, and I got far better about not taking it personally when he wasn't.)

This evening we drove to Noel's graduation party and stayed for three hours.

I mostly talked with the married ladies, trying to glean wisdom. Janna, Rachael, and Carmella had all married so early in life. They're all younger than I and have been married an average of twenty years. *Twenty.* They grew up with their husbands.

Jared and I...we did *not* grow up with each other. In one way, that's good: we figured ourselves out, we know who we are, we lived full lives. But we also had to unlearn some things...and learn how to be united.

I shared the Teflon-Velcro metaphor I'd read about. How our brain is designed to be Velcro for the bad (to remember and prevent future danger) but Teflon for the good (no need to use energy to save good info). How I'd love to reverse that.

Thank goodness for neuroplasticity.

♦ ♦ ♦

Healing is a new ill…

—from "Perfect Harmony" by Ibn ʿArabî[190]

I am slowly getting to know various views from our new house. Through the rain this morning, I noticed a mountain ridgeline of trees I'd never seen. It took clouds resting on it to became visible. I am delighted for the rain in this dry year, but I'm not always delighted for emotional storm fronts or circumstantial ones. And yet, they always reveal some new view in my soul and spirit—like that ridgeline.

This wasn't an emotionally "rainy" day, but I had a feeling this observation would come in handy.

Early afternoon, I decided to walk the Skycrest Trail, which I hadn't been to since we'd lived in Grants Pass. I could almost feel the hurt I'd tried to shed there. Just up from the trailhead, I noticed a post: "Healing in Progress" with a notice to please stay on the trails. Then, farther up, I found a bell hanging from a tree with a note thanking a liver doner who saved the life of a young girl. Healing is in the air today. By the time I left the trail, those old hurts had finally left, too.

The neuroscientist Dr. Caroline Leaf posts Instagram memes I love. Like this one: "It's not your responsibility to heal others, but it is your responsibility to heal the parts of you that resonate with their brokenness."[191] And this: "Hard truth: often healing requires you taking responsibility for the role you played in your own suffering."[192] Truth and truth.

Back home, I hung corner shelves in the master bedroom—to hold books on marriage and things of spirit. My goal is that everything in our room be about and for the two of us.

For dinner, Jared and I met the young engaged couple Barrett & Clara at The Haul. A perfect summer evening of soft sun.

Barrett said people were surprised when he introduced them to his fiancé. Jared said people were surprised when he introduced them to his wife.

I added, "They often get googly-eyed and take a step back—the bachelor finally married!"

Jared mused that a bonus to marrying young was probably being able to share experiences and memories as you grew up together. He said he'd made memories with friends and random people at home and while traveling. But many of those people aren't in his life anymore. Barrett & Clara would be able to share all those growing years.

I think that was the first time he talked about his bachelorhood without idealizing it. The playing field *is* leveling.

◆ ◆ ◆

Over dinner, I bemoaned our second lost date night this month (graduations, birthdays) and said I was glad that we could get away together for our anniversary weekend.

Jared asked how I wanted to celebrate. I had figured we'd be camping somewhere until I discovered, just this week, that he would have three days off, not just the regular two. I said it would be fun to camp a couple of nights and then stay somewhere nice...but hotels would be booked this close to the holiday weekend.

I didn't add that, had I known *earlier* he had a three-day weekend, I could have made reservations somewhere. No matter. I've learned that good things can come to both those who plan for them *and* to those who don't.

I've also learned that though I'm the planner, I can get fixed on what's happened. And though Jared doesn't like to plan, he can be fixed on what's next. We're learning to connect in the moment.

◆ ◆ ◆

On my Woodlands walk, I had a revelation about risk-taking. It's a river metaphor, of course. Physically, I avoid rapids and love to swim in the calm frog water while Jared loves to kayak down Class-V waterfalls and is bored in the smooth sections. But emotionally, I head for the rapids, and he's often fine with the frog water. This helps me understand our differences a bit more. And I see how we're learning to meet in the middle riffles.

Today, I swam in emotional rapids. I had no idea how my own Monday observation about cloudy emotional states would apply to myself!

I didn't know I would have the chance to accept the invitation to begin with forgiveness:

> Forgiveness is a skill, a way of preserving clarity, sanity and generosity in an individual life, a beautiful question and a way of shaping the mind to a future we want for ourselves…we might as well begin forgiving right at the beginning of any drama rather than put ourselves through the full cycle of festering, incapacitation, reluctant healing and eventual blessing.[193]

For date-night dinner, I'd marinated lamb steaks, asparagus, and garlic scapes. Made cucumber raita and set out a bowl of grapes. Laid blankets and pillows beneath the lower oaks.

But…during the meal, I tried not to flinch every time Jared said, "I don't care."

I asked if he would like "avocados." Silence.

Trying to keep kindness in my voice, I said, "You know it really helps me when you answer my questions."

Nothing.

I looked at him. "Your silence is hard."

"I just don't care."

I said, now with an edge to my voice, "And that's even harder." I took a deep breath. "Not tonight, it's getting late, but soon we need to talk about the bigger issue of 'toast'—and also about the 'avocados' and other 'toppings.' Because I can't handle the silence anymore."

I was angry. But beneath anger is almost always pain, a wound. I would not let this wound fester.

> You could define faith a hundred different ways. I like to think of it as a kind of inner coherence that allows you to keep your balance in a relationship. That doesn't mean you'll be happy all the time. It just means that when you're miserable, you'll still be able to stand your ground—and to trust that the eventual outcome will be okay.[194]

In the middle of my misery, I was surprised to find myself wondering if there were marriage angels. If so, I think they might be some of the strongest guardians of all.

◆ ◆ ◆

> their grief and pain
> made accurate by their joy.

—from "The Cruel Plumage" by Wendell Berry[195]

I felt lighter when I woke this morning. Nothing changed, circumstantially, but I brought up the circumstance—I didn't keep it inside and ruminate. I've been mad at Jared for his silences, yet in my own way, I've sometimes been silent, too—I've been afraid that when I share what I feel, I'll be argued out of it. And that's been my error: not speaking my heart. Circumstances may never change, but if both of us can feel brave and safe to share what we feel about them, something tells me it is more likely they *will* change.

Jared kissed me twice before departing for work.

As I tried to fall back asleep before my alarm went off, I thought again of healing:

> A good relationship is not one in which the raw parts of ourselves are avoided. A good relationship is one in which they are handled. And a *great relationship* is one in which they are *healed*.[196]

When faint dawn light started to suffuse the bedroom, I blinked. I had hung two of my own paintings of angels on the wall—each one a gestural watercolor in cerulean blue. I created them a few years ago for an annual art show, titling them, vaguely, "The Naming of Angels." I hadn't realized they were waiting to reveal their identity: "The Marriage Angels."

By the time my alarm rang, I was smiling. I had remembered the through-line of joy.

There would be no talking about "toast" tonight because we had dinner guests, Chris & Shannon. Which turned out to be a godsend. Over salmon and gnocchi, we all ended up talking about marriage. About it being hard. Chris & Shannon said they've talked to long-married couples who check in with a therapist at least every couple of years.

I nodded, "That's wise. It's like a chiropractic adjustment—keeps you aligned."

If union with God is our greatest goal, and marriage is a mirror of that union, we probably need to be vigilant about connection and communication to keep *both* unions aligned.

◆◆◆

Jared and I drove to the upper Applegate River, hoping for the boondock camp site we'd scouted last summer, but it was taken. He decided to continue further up the forest road and found an even better spot with an immaculate fire pit, a stack of firewood, and access down to our own private waterfall and series of pools. Well done.

We had swapped the van back to Alex and family for their summer travels and were now in tent season. But tonight was clear and mosquito-free—no tent needed.

Since we'd brought the work truck, Jared suggested sleeping in the truck bed. Despite having to sweep out chunks of cement, it was a good idea; amid the tall pines spread a circle of night sky, and we'd be able to look up at a swath of stars.

We filled the air mattress and made up the bed. Then Jared built a campfire, and I set out dinner. We lingered a long while, with silence and fire beneath the half moon. Silence from me: trying to keep from saying anything about "toast" until the morning. Silence from him...because he was asleep in his chair.

Say grace.

I give thanks for my husband's hard work, his faithfulness.

I give thanks that he also makes time to play and rest.

I even give thanks for the different ways we each approach work and rest.

I didn't sleep well that night. The air mattress hadn't filled enough, and the truck bed was hard beneath it. I was also cumulatively sad—sadness that had gathered during our whole year of marriage about the "toast."

At one point in the night, I let out a silent, wide-mouth scream. I'm not sure who or what I was "screaming" at, but doing it made me feel better enough to sleep. The gift in staying awake late: I saw the thick slather of stars.

And I swallow stars. I eat stars.

I breathe stars. I survive on stars.
They sound precisely, humming in my nose,
in my throat, on my tongue. *Stars, stars.*

—from "Place and Proximity" by Pattiann Rogers[197]

◆◆◆

For me, today was one of the most pivotal days of our marriage. It was certainly the hardest conversation I hadn't wanted to have.

Our Team Emmanuel mascot is telling: the creature's hard, protective armor covers a soft, vulnerable core. To move forward, it has to emerge from its shell—its shield. Otherwise, it just stays stuck in the same place. Nothing like marriage to prod us forward! I just have to remind myself of how far we've come, even when our speed feels tortoise-paced.

Slow but steady….

> Courage is a big part of faith. It takes courage to have
> faith, and faith in turn rewards you with courage. It's like
> a muscle. The more you use it, the stronger it gets.[198]

We lit a morning fire. Alongside the firewood, a previous camper had stacked huge sugar-pine cones. I was enamored of the way they burned—the orange glow from their core backlighting petal-like scales as they turned to ash. Fire flowers.

After we finished breakfast I said, "So I've been thinking about Wednesday night and how we need to talk about 'toast.'"

When I got to the part about it being hard for me to hear his silence and his not caring, he was…silent.

I waited.

Eventually he said he hadn't understood why I was mad the other night.

I took a deep breath. "Please try to understand: I asked if you wanted 'avocados,' and you said nothing. And when you finally answered, you said you don't care. Can you try to imagine how that might feel to me—the silence, the not caring? I want to connect. I want to know your heart. I know there are wonderful things in there. And I know you can be a good communicator. You often say things that sound like poetry."

"Maybe when I know what I'm talking about."

"Not just then—and not just about things. Of spirit, of wonder. You've spoken lines I later wrote down because they were so profound. But most times, I feel like there's a shield up, and you keep me at arm's length."

He said, "I feel like you want us to be this tight little unit," and he held up his hands, cupped to make a little ball which he orbited around in front of himself, "and go everywhere and do everything together all the time."

I made a face, "That sounds awful! I don't want that, and I don't think you do."

"No, I don't!"

"That means we're not aware of each other's wants or needs. Which is why we've got to figure them out. So that we can love each other well."

And so we talked about them.

> It is important to argue well about our differences. Not arguing or arguing poorly can actually be worse than a good disagreement. In a healthy couple, each forgives the other for being different and even for being themselves. To do this we need to communicate well and on a regular and ongoing basis.[199]

It was probably the best discussion of difference we've had, even

303

though we both threw in a few "you" statements and got a bit defensive. Whatever. We also both stayed engaged and present as the whole year's differences over "toast" and its "toppings" went into the refining fire, each piece slowly catching like the pinecone scales.

We sat there until we had both spoken and listened to all we could.

After, we stood and hugged. I thanked him for listening to me. He said he was sorry he had hurt me. I said the same. He said I hadn't hurt him—he was just trying to understand.

I'm so glad the shield was down. He pulled back from the hug just far enough to look me in the eyes and said, "I love you."

I smiled. "I'm learning that."

And this time, in his "I love you," I also heard that he's willing to keep loving me—even when he doesn't understand me and I completely exasperate him.

My reply of "I love you" echoed all that subtext.

We ended up spending a gentle morning down on the river rocks, in just the right amount of sun and shade. We read. We stretched. An easy peace. Butterflies flew all around, alighting on each of us multiple times. One came to land on Jared's foot as he lay on a boulder, and it stayed there for a full minute, opening and closing its wings in a kind of wild anointing.

Our marriage wings are starting to take shape. There's a reason I hung a butterfly in the master bedroom: to remind us of continual transformation. And there's a reason I've dogeared Rita Dove's poem, "Geometry." The last lines of it:

> the windows have hinged into butterflies,
> sunlight glinting where they've intersected.
> They are going to some point true and unproven.[200]

After a picnic lunch, we took a last dip in the river and drove home with the windows down and our hair drying in hot wind.

Back at the house, while we cleaned camp stuff and prepped to have my family over for dinner, Jared came up to me in the kitchen and held me.

I thanked him for listening to me.

He released me and looked me in the eyes. He apologized for not engaging with the topic of "toast." He hadn't realized how important it was to me.

I leaned into him again. I added it's kind of amazing how different we are. But how good that can be.

> Another reality…is the virtual certainty that your lover will not love you exactly the way you want to be loved…. Let go, love as best you can, and join your lover in creating your future.[201]

My parents and visiting aunt and uncle were coming for an early dinner at our place. I hadn't seen Aunt Carol and Uncle Dwain for years, and it was a delight to catch up and introduce them to my husband and tell them to pass on my love to my cousin Heather when they next saw her.

As I was giving a tour of the house, Uncle Dwain pulled me aside and said, "I like the look in Jared's eye. You've got a good one."

Yes I do.

◆◆◆

In high-school art class, I was informally voted the most likely to marry a cardigan-wearing history professor. But I chose an alternate life.

Life really is a choose-your-own-adventure book, a genre I hated in middle school: turn the wrong page, and you're dead. Yet had I chosen the professorial life, I would have been dead in a different way: safe in predictability but dead to adventure. Not to say academia isn't a place of growth, it just wouldn't have been for me, obsessed as I was with plans and calendars and *chronos*.

Instead, I chose a wilder life with room for loads of *kairos* interventions. And I chose a man who doesn't own a cardigan!

> What you can plan
> is too small
> for you to live.
>
> —from "What to Remember When Waking" by David Whyte[202]

◆ ◆ ◆

Big family dinner: DIY Greek salads and grilled chicken. Before the meal, everyone gathered in the kitchen, and we all began organically to stop talking and form a circle. It was fun to watch.

Jared and I had our arms around each other, and he said a lovely, simple grace, full of gratitude for God's love—which we need.

◆ ◆ ◆

On Tuesdays, when Jared kayaks with his friends, I hang out with mine. This week, I invited Kadance over for champagne. I shared how Jared and I had come up with Team Emmanuel and the turtle mascot for our marriage. Slow but steady.

She added that she sees an image of God with His hands on both of our backs, pushing us gently forward into our marriage. That it might feel turtle-paced right now, but there will be a season of acceleration, too.

I mentioned once keeping a gratitude journal, and Kadance said she keeps a joy journal: a record of three things each day that bring her joy. Ah, the link between gratitude and joy.

◆ ◆ ◆

Revelation watching the sunrise: women can let men into them physically. Men can let women into them emotionally.

◆ ◆ ◆

Ridiculous forecast for this June weekend: 113 degrees?

Dinner at Dan & Janna's. I threw my swimsuit in my purse, remembering their pool and guessing we'd eat outside. So hot.

Jared didn't even bother to put on his T-shirt—just his swim trunks. When we arrived, Dan came out in just his swim trunks, too. They chest-bumped hellos and ran immediately to cannonball into the pool with Ender and Jude. Boyz.

Janna wisely suggested waiting until the more volatile splashing had receded and the big boyz were in their floaties, at which point, she and Evie and I joined them, bringing out beverages.

We ate in our swimsuits on the patio. Bountiful surf-n-turf dinner of sausage, salmon, steak, and shrimp.

The kids mentioned a TV show they like and asked if Jared and I had seen it. We told them we don't have cable TV. Neither of us watch much, just movies now and then. Ender asked why.

I said, "Well, for me...I once watched too much TV, so I decided to give it up for a year. And after that, I've never really wanted it. For a stretch in my twenties, if I felt I was too dependent on something, I'd give it up for a year." I paused and laughed, "But after doing that with coffee, I loved it even more!"

Ender asked, with sincerity, "Are you going to give up Jared?"

I smiled at the thoughtful question, "Nope, I'm keeping him."

◆◆◆

We'll be camping on the upper Rogue this weekend in record-breaking, triple-digit heat. The breath-catching cold of that river section will be welcome.

We arrived at dusk, and by then, even all the boondocking campsites were taken. But we found what looked like a dirt-bike trail, so I said I'd hop out and see if it went anywhere. If you were willing to brave tree limbs thwacking you in the face and tree sap coating your flip-flops, you could emerge to a clearing right on the river. Alas, you couldn't easily *get* to the water: it was a steep, grassy bank down into wood snags. Still. It was late, and this was it.

We pitched the tent, sipped Kentucky Mules, and read from *Peter Pan* while swatting at no-see-ums.

◆◆◆

Woke to a morning that promised to be hot. We walked the trail that links to Natural Bridge, and at a waterfall, we spotted a rainbow in the gorge mist. Jared leaned in to kiss me, and after, I kept my face pressed to his neck for a long while, enjoying the grace of the day.

After lunch, we drove up to Jared's put-in. He geared up to kayak. I waved and started walking to the bridge to watch him descend.

"Hold up," he said, with a smile. "A goodbye kiss." And, with his kayak over his shoulder, he stepped toward me—the first time he had reminded *me* of a goodbye kiss. The burden of firsts feels like it has lifted.

From the middle of the bridge, I watched him put in and descend a large succession of waterfalls. After he passed beneath me, I yelled down, "I love you," and he looked up and waved.

So many little, kind connections.

I drove to the take-out and walked up the trail again. It was hurt-hot by midday, and the little beach I remembered seeing that morning seemed far away.

Finally, I made it there—overheated and relieved. I'd brought a bottle of rosé to keep chilled in the water and a hammock to hang in the shade. I spent the afternoon alternately reading and dunking in the river until I heard Jared approach from the trail. He promptly jumped into the water, and threw some squishy river algae at me with a big grin.

I screeched and dodged it, laughing. "Boyz!"

◆◆◆

When we woke and embraced, just before the sun broke through the trees, Jared said, "I think this is my favorite part of camping— the morning light, and this." He squeezed me.

I squeezed him back, "Me too."

One of Jared's fellow masons, Randy, was getting married that morning at 11 a.m. We decamped early, stopping by the bridge for one last dip in the river. I hesitated before plunging into the frigid water, saying I was always glad I did, but that never made it easier.

From further upstream, Jared said, "It's like this year. It hasn't been easy, but it's been good," and then he slipped in to swim down the current toward me.

Well said.

On our drive home, a text popped up on Jared's phone. Dustin & Eva had an extra permit to raft the lower Rogue River next weekend—our one-year anniversary. Did we want to come?

Jared looked at me, eyebrow raised. As I'd answered a similar invitation the night of our wedding, I said, "Sure!"

We made it to Randy's outdoor wedding with time to spare. Jared's brother, Alex, officiated, and he did a beautiful job. He shared a list of "love is" bits, including:

Love is bringing home flowers on a Tuesday, just because.

Love is taking out the trash without being asked.

Love is gutting the fish you didn't catch.

Love is telling someone when they have spinach in their teeth. (I almost elbowed Jared: he won't tell me when I have something in my teeth!)

It had already been oppressively hot when the ceremony started, and the reception got hotter. I gravitated toward the barrels of ice holding a quickly dwindling number of sodas. I rubbed ice over my arms and neck while rotating in front of the water misters.

After the cake was cut, I told Jared I was about to melt. He was good and quick and we said our goodbyes.

Back home, he mused, "My Grandmother wanted me to get married. But she also said, 'Good luck!'" He echoed the dismissive way people say that when they don't really believe there is any luck to be had.

I said I didn't think it was luck. Marriage is a lot of work—but it works if the goal is moving closer to God together.

Some couples who've been married for decades skip the sanctification process; they live like roommates, unwilling to be vulnerable enough to let each other in, to do the deeper work. Versus the couples who have been married for decades and have spent that time pressing in to God and shedding the things that hold them back from fully knowing Him and each other. Jared and I know examples of both kinds of relationships.

We ended up having a good conversation about our differences with zero defenses and plenty of appreciation. Mr. Wild and Mrs. Refined, rubbing off on each other. We're on our way to being pretty well rounded someday.

Jared said that after we'd had dinner with Barrett & Clara, he'd marveled at the way he and I could be together with others—how our differences complement each other.

Complement: the perfect verb.

He suggested communion, and so: whiskey & RITZ, holiness & joy. For the bread, I gave thanks for the miracle that God is continually sanctifying us, especially in marriage. For the blood, I gave thanks for Christ's suffering, which He endured for the joy set before Him—also a miracle. And I admitted that I hadn't been focused on the joy as much as I want to be. I invited God to keep revealing His joy.

Ann Voskamp opens up a deeper understanding of communion, Eucharist:

> *Eucharisteo*, thanksgiving, envelopes the Greek word for grace, *charis*. But it also holds its derivative, the Greek word *chara*, meaning "joy." *Joy*. Ah…yes. I might be needing me some of that. That might be what the quest for more is all about—that which Augustine claimed, "Without exception…all try their hardest to reach the same goal, that is joy".... Deep *chara* joy is found only at the table of the *euCHARisteo*—the table of thanksgiving.... Is the height of my *chara* joy dependent on the depths of my eucharisto thanks?[203]

I believe so.

And I believe the Unified Field of marriage is a pretty good place to practice gratitude-grace.

and we rose up like wheat,

acre after acre of gold,
and we harvested,
we harvested.

—from "Us" by Anne Sexton[204]

◆◆◆

Sunrise revelation: the Enneagram Four's weakness is envy, and it took me a while to relate to that because I don't desire what others have. Which I learned isn't necessarily how Fours envy: they tend to envy the way others move through the world more easily (less intensely) than they do. But I never wanted to move through the world less intensely—I wanted to find others who also wanted to engage the crazy-but-maybe-possible task of bringing heaven to earth. Others who were not content with the way everything is and is done.

Just this minute, I see that my envy is for goodness and beauty, and when I don't think I have those, I get stuck on all that is bad and ugly. In essence: I'm envious of a perfect world, fully connected to God. I'm envious of heaven. Heaven envy.

Maybe envy shows us what is missing, what we seek. And the Four seeks equanimity—preferably in a good and beautiful setting! I envy that which brings equanimity.

And I can see that one of the ways I've tried to bring heaven to earth in my marriage is by being a bit "teachy." I could say my old teaching habits die hard—and are likely annoying! But I could also say I try to see my husband as God sees him—and to hold him to that higher standard. Sure, that will benefit me—as my growth will benefit Jared. But those benefits are a byproduct of the greater miracle of each of us growing into our True-Self identities.

Of course, even though I want heaven's best in our marriage, I'd be arrogant to think I always know what that is. I *do* know that it's not my business to do Jared's work for him or for him to do mine—though I've invited him to call forth my best self as well.

Sometimes we get it right, sometimes we get it wrong. As with all of it: slow but steady.

Which reminds me...I painted a watercolor tortoise for a redux anniversary gift: Team Emmanuel.

◆ ◆ ◆

What I want to be true for myself each day: I am filled with joy, receiving God's love, and loving my husband and others well.

During a midday attempt to snap out of a negativity spiral, I received a text from Jared suggesting some lovely evening activities.

And so, lines *not* from Neruda's single song of despair but from one of his twenty love poems:

> No one saw us this evening hand in hand
> while the blue night dropped on the world.[205]

◆ ◆ ◆

Maybe it was because of how peaceful my heart was this morning that the unpeaceful conversation this evening didn't bother me as much as it would have a year ago. Maybe I've learned something after all!

Let's call the conversation topic "rotten tomatoes" because who wants to eat those? Not me. I was proud of myself: I stayed curious and didn't get furious. I mostly didn't take things personally. I almost kept my sense of humor.

How about *that?*

> We automatically look for the one to blame, the person who "started it," but relationships don't work that way. Both observers are right and both are wrong. Relationships operate in a circular, not linear fashion, the

behavior of each person provoking and reinforcing the behavior of the other. The real question is not who started it, or who is to blame, but rather what each person can do to change his or her steps in the dance.[206]

Well, this person is changing her steps from insta-anger and insta-sadness to curiosity-in-love.

◆ ◆ ◆

discovering
again in one place

the history of my pain,
my ordeal, my grace,
unable to resist

seeing what is past

—from "What Love Intended" by Eavan Boland[207]

I woke still confused about how the "rotten tomatoes" conversation had happened—and a bit miffed that it happened just before our anniversary weekend.

But.

I don't want to stay stuck in Boland's lines of poetry, "unable to resist // seeing what is past." I choose to resist the past, to release the pain, and to keep my grace on. I choose to exchange confusion for peace.

I watered the six new sequoias—a process I dislike. It requires three trips of lugging heavy sets of water buckets across the driveway and down the gully through thistles and bristles. But I do it anyway—like so many worthwhile things that have nothing to do with circumstantial happiness.

As I heaved the last water bucket over the last tree, I tried to not mull over last night's conversation. I reminded myself: "When the past calls, let it go to voicemail. It has nothing new to say to you."[208]

And so, I chose joy-despite-circumstance.

Right then, Jared texted: "Just wanna say I love you."

I replied, "That means so very much at this exact moment. Thank you. I love you, too."

Dr. Emily Nagoski writes:

> I want to understand the brain mechanism underlying joy.... But the science can only lead us as far as to the edge of what is known. What I've learned...is that joy is what happens when you jump off the edge of what is known into the adventure of what is true.[209]

Ah, the adventure of what is true.

It took me all day to finish the watering, prep the food, and pack for the rafting trip. I was outside giving the seedlings a second watering when Jared pulled up. He came up to me, held me with intention, and a long time later pulled back to say, "I love you."

I could hear whole worlds in those three words. I hugged him again, returned the love, and said, "This is the best homecoming to date."

And we drove to the river.

As we traveled the familiar country roads, I saw that marriage has no arrival. We never pass a final exam or graduate into happily-ever-after. Some days, we'll link our "happily" to what happens. Other days, we'll remember transcending joy. And someday, we may even embody the Greek meaning of joy—the God-sourced "culmination of being."

Meanwhile, there will be good moments and bad ones—always. That's why we vowed to stay in the game, for better or for worse.

◆◆◆

We bitch about our difficulties along the rough surface of our path, we curse every sharp stone underneath, until at some point in our maturation, we finally look down to see they are diamonds.

—Frank Jude Boccio

Today is the last day of the first year of our marriage. For riverside breakfast, we eat peaches with yogurt and oats. My spork still has yogurt on it when Jared packs things up. He licks it and looks at me with a gleam in his eye, "Love licks your spork clean for you."

It does.

The group packs up and we all get back on the water. Jared is my raft captain, as he was on the weekend of our wedding; exactly one year later, this trip is a bit of déjà vu.

Late afternoon, we pass Zane Gray's cabin where we'd stopped this spring with the other rafting group. Hands on the oars, Jared nods to the cabin and asks if every writer needs a remote place like that to write.

I say, "It depends." I've written in solitude from the coast of Spain to the craggy Alps and written in community at residencies from California to Vermont. I figure it out as I speak: "For me, there are times it's helpful to have a long swath of silence to keep a project full in my mind, but I think the more realistic way of writing I've grown into is the daily kind—amid chores and errands, friends and family."

Maybe the idea that you have to retreat to write is similar to the illusion that to be one with God you should leave the world behind and live a monastic life. When really, it's in the daily interactions— pesky as some of them are—where the true growth and creativity are found. If relationships and love are the most important things in this life, then I want to be able to make my art amid them.

As we float along, Jared turns the raft backwards, something he's done for much of the flat water, the better to use his legs to help power the rowing. Facing upstream, I watch the water we've just floated down. All of a sudden, the leaves on the shore trees clarify, the water surface sharpens. In the heat of the day, I shiver with epiphany.

I'm not just looking back at the river, but at the whole year since our first journey down these waters together. How we have come not just river miles, but marriage miles. We've come through wild whitewater, where we had to watch for signs of invisible rocks beneath the surface. We've come through smooth waters, where we took breaks to rest and feast.

Maybe joy is keeping our eye on the moment, without reaching for the past or the future. It's knowing that we'll come down rough waters again, but we'll have learned more since the last run—learned better how to enter rapids, when to hold on tight, and when to lean back and relax.

Our first year has a few hours left in it. Jared and I don't yet know we'll see a bear meander past our camp tonight at dusk, our whole group watching in silent awe.

We don't yet know the glow of moon rocks rubbed together in the dark.

We don't yet know the specific Goodness & Mercy that wait for us tomorrow—and all the days of our marriage.

Yet we choose to keep choosing each other.

"Love is a decision."[210] That's the one thing my husband and I have known from the day of our wedding.

And each day since, we choose again to say, "I do."

Kairos: For the Joy

If love is an act of imagination, then intimacy is an act of fruition. It waits for the high to subside so it can patiently insert itself into the relationship. The seeds of intimacy are time and repetition. We choose each other again and again, and so create a community of two.... It's the act of choosing, the freedom involved in choosing, that keeps a relationship alive.

—Ester Perel
Mating in Captivity

On the morning of our one-year anniversary, somewhere on the Rogue River, I say of the last-minute rafting trip, "I'm glad this worked out."

Jared looks at me from beneath the brim of his straw cowboy hat and says, "I'm glad *we* work out—and that we work it out."

"See! You speak in perfect one-liners."

He grins.

After the river trip, we head to the ocean to spend the night at a hotel on the beach. (I found an available room after all!)

Our first year of marriage has been bookended with mirror adventures. We began with a reserved hotel followed by a last-minute rafting trip; we ended with a last-minute rafting trip followed by a reserved hotel. Mrs. Planner & Mr. Spontaneity.

I love going to the ocean. It is often a metaphor for forgiveness: it's vast and capable of holding more than we can imagine. Like God's love—so big, so timeless, that His brief *chronos* suffering while He walked this earth in human form was worth the *kairos* joy set before Him.

If someone chose to be crucified on a literal Cross to forgive me, I can choose to crucify my pride and False Selves—and to forgive. I can remember my wise Mom saying she now gets excited about the hard things because she knows she will learn some new aspect of God's heart as she presses toward Him.

Richard Rohr writes about the archetypal journey of heroes and heroines—which very much applies to husbands and wives:

> They are almost always wounded in some way and encounter a major dilemma, and the whole story largely pivots around the resolution of the trials that result. There is always a wounding. And the great epiphany is that the wound becomes the secret key, even sacred, a wound that changes them dramatically. Which, by the way, is the precise meaning of the wounds of Jesus.[211]

For my wedding bouquet last year, I foraged for greenery and yarrow in the Jacksonville Woodlands. Yarrow survives drought and heat and grows wild under beating sun. It shares the coupled meanings of healing and love. The two go together.

Marriage truly is a marvelous-hard healing process—if we forgive the wounds. Because it's the wound that heals us, and it's sorrow that teaches us to cultivate joy.

Our sorrows are worth the joy set before us.

The Catch

There is no perfect soul mate, no flawless lover. We are all stumbling around, treading on each other's toes as we are learning to love.
—Dr. Sue Johnson

We all want to find a partner who's a catch—the right one. But the catch is: we each *become* the right one.

During our first year as husband and wife, Jared often said that marriage is weird. He was more right than he knew. The Old English word *wyrd* is the root of our present-day *weird*. It originally meant "becoming." Which looks weird. Which looks like the first year of marriage—especially for two people who married later in life, who've each done their own "becoming" and who are now trying to become one.

And how do we become? We drop our False Selves. We invite our True Self to love others by forgiving their faults, and we thank others for revealing our own.

> The hardest spiritual work in the world is...to encounter another human being not as someone you can use, change, fix, help, save, enroll, convince or control, but simply as someone who can spring you from the prison of yourself, if you will allow it.... It may be the only real spiritual discipline there is.[212]

And it's a healing discipline. By the last round of editing this book, my once-festering wounds had healed into scar-stories.

In her poem, "For What Binds Us," Jane Hirshfield writes of proud flesh: the torn skin of horses that heals to be stronger than when "untested." The final stanza of that poem:

> And when two people have loved each other
> see how it is like a
> scar between their bodies,
> stronger, darker, and proud;
> how the black cord makes of them a single fabric
> that nothing can tear or mend.[213]

Our scars are evidence of all we have healed.

Not long after our first anniversary, I told Jared I was thinking of using the painting of our Team Emmanuel turtle as the book's cover image. I hesitated, "But it's a bit quirky and imperfect."

His wise reply: "Well, marriage is quirky and imperfect."

It is. Though something tells me we'll get better at it. Especially if we keep playing the long game of joy by choosing to grow together in grace, faith, and forgiveness. Bonus points if we go for Olympic forgiveness—to not just forgive but also bless.

And so, a marriage blessing to end:

> May Goodness & Mercy chase us down & lift us up.
> May we treat our troubles as Grace-Growers.
> May we give thanks for the good during the bad.
> May we see with the eyes of faith.
> May we release the false & choose the true.
> May we heal our wounds with the balm of forgiveness.
> May our sorrows teach us joy.
> May we love with Love.

The one who blesses others is abundantly blessed.
—Proverbs 11:25 (MSG)

Gratitude

To all those I quoted in these pages: for sharing your wisdom with the world.

To everyone I've ever asked about marriage: for sharing your heart.

To Lavinia: for spotting this book title in my own Instagram post!

To Tim: for the travel-writing advice—who knew it would apply to marriage?

To Bobbi: for encouraging me to look into the Enneagram and "introducing" me to Richard Rohr.

To Sarah & Byron: for being our marriage "godparents."

To my new family: Kayt; Andy & Linda; Alex & Rachael, Noel, Natalie and Abe.

To Niesje, Mindy, Amy, Doug, Alex, Sarah L., Cindy, Christina, and Mom & Dad: a beautiful mix of readers and counselors and editors who helped me write with honesty and honor.

And to my husband, Jared: who is becoming the man of my dreams, even as he helps me become the woman of his.

Marriage Resources

Note: I have no affiliation with any of the resources that follow, and the only thing I "get" from sharing them here is deep joy at imagining what it would be like if we all could understand ourselves and each other better.

Resource 1: Scriptures for Wisdom

Scriptures are from the ESV unless otherwise noted.

1 Chronicles 16:34 (MSG)
Give thanks to God—he is good and his love never quits.

Colossians 3:12-13 (TPT)
You are always and dearly loved by God! So robe yourself with virtues of God, since you have been divinely chosen to be holy. Be merciful as you endeavor to understand others, and be compassionate, showing kindness toward all. Be gentle and humble, unoffendable in your patience with others.

Tolerate the weaknesses of those in the family of faith, forgiving one another in the same way you have been graciously forgiven by Jesus Christ. If you find fault with someone, release this same gift of forgiveness to them.

Colossians 3:15
And let the peace of Christ rule in your hearts…. And be thankful.

1 Corinthians 13:4-8a
Love is patient and kind; love does not envy or boast; it is not arrogant or rude. It does not insist on its own way; it is not irritable or resentful; it does not rejoice at wrongdoing, but rejoices with the truth. Love bears all things, believes all things, hopes all things, endures all things. Love never ends.

1 Corinthians 16:14
Let all that you do be done in love.

2 Corinthians 9:8 (TPT)
Yes, God is more than ready to overwhelm you with every form of grace, so that you will have more than enough of everything—every moment and in every way. He will make you overflow with abundance in every good thing you do.

2 Corinthians 12:9
But he said to me, "My grace is sufficient for you, for my power is made perfect in weakness." Therefore I will boast all the more gladly of my weaknesses, so that the power of Christ may rest upon me.

Deuteronomy 31:8 (MSG)
"God is…right there with you. He won't let you down; he won't leave you. Don't be intimidated. Don't worry."

Ephesians 2:8
For by grace you have been saved through faith. And this is not your own doing; it is the gift of God.

Ephesians 4:1b-3
Walk in a manner worthy of the calling to which you have been called, with all humility and gentleness, with patience, bearing with one another in love, eager to maintain the unity of the Spirit in the bond of peace.

Ephesians 4:31-32
Let all bitterness and wrath and anger and clamor and slander be put away from you, along with all malice. Be kind to one another, tenderhearted, forgiving one another, as God in Christ forgave you.

Ephesians 5:2 (MSG)
Mostly what God does is love you. Keep company with him and learn a life of love. Observe how Christ loved us. His love was not

cautious but extravagant. He didn't love in order to get something from us but to give everything of himself to us. Love like that.

Galatians 5:22-23a
But the fruit of the Spirit is love, joy, peace, patience, kindness, goodness, faithfulness, gentleness, self-control.

Galatians 5:22-23a (TPT)
But the fruit produced by the Holy Spirit within you is divine love in all its varied expressions: joy that overflows, peace that subdues, patience that endures, kindness in action, a life full of virtue, faith that prevails, gentleness of heart, and strength of spirit.

Hebrews 11:1
Now faith is the assurance of things hoped for, the conviction of things not seen.

Hebrews 11:1 (TPT)
Now faith brings our hopes into reality and becomes the foundation needed to acquire the things we long for. It is all the evidence required to prove what is still unseen.

Isaiah 40:29-31
He gives power to the faint,
and to him who has no might he increases strength.
Even youths shall faint and be weary,
and young men shall fall exhausted;
but they who wait for the LORD shall renew their strength;
they shall mount up with wings like eagles;
they shall run and not be weary;
they shall walk and not faint.

James 4:6b
"God opposes the proud but gives grace to the humble."

James 5:16 (TPT)
Confess and acknowledge how you have offended one another

and then pray for one another to be instantly healed, for tremendous power is released through the passionate, heartfelt prayer of a godly believer!

1 John 4:16
So we have come to know and to believe the love that God has for us. God is love, and whoever abides in love abides in God, and God abides in him.

John 1:16 (TPT)
And from the overflow of his fullness we received grace heaped upon more grace!

John 13:34
A new commandment I give to you, that you love one another: just as I have loved you, you also are to love one another.

John 14:27 (TPT)
"I leave the gift of peace with you—my peace. Not the kind of fragile peace given by the world, but my perfect peace. Don't yield to fear or be troubled in your hearts—instead, be courageous!"

Luke 6:37
"Judge not, and you will not be judged; condemn not, and you will not be condemned; forgive, and you will be forgiven."

Luke 17:3 (TPT)
"If you see him going the wrong direction, cry out and correct him. If there is true repentance on his part, forgive him."

Matthew 5:7
"Blessed are the merciful, for they shall receive mercy."

I Peter 4:8
Above all, keep loving one another earnestly, since love covers a multitude of sins.

1 Peter 5:10

And after you have suffered a little while, the God of all grace, who has called you to his eternal glory in Christ, will himself restore, confirm, strengthen, and establish you.

Philippians 2:14
Do all things without grumbling or disputing.

Philippians 4:6-9 (MSG)
Don't fret or worry. Instead of worrying, pray. Let petitions and praises shape your worries into prayers, letting God know your concerns. Before you know it, a sense of God's wholeness, everything coming together for good, will come and settle you down. It's wonderful what happens when Christ displaces worry at the center of your life.

Summing it all up, friends, I'd say you'll do best by filling your minds and meditating on things true, noble, reputable, authentic, compelling, gracious—the best, not the worst; the beautiful, not the ugly; things to praise, not things to curse. Put into practice what you learned from me, what you heard and saw and realized. Do that, and God, who makes everything work together, will work you into his most excellent harmonies.

Philippians 4:6-9 (TPT)
Don't be pulled in different directions or worried about a thing. Be saturated in prayer throughout the day, offering your faith-filled requests before God with overflowing gratitude. Tell him every detail of your life, then God's wonderful peace that transcends human understanding will make the answers known to you though Jesus Christ.

Keep your thoughts continually fixed on all that is authentic and real, honorable and admirable, beautiful and respectful, pure and holy, merciful and kind. And fasten your thoughts on every glorious work of God, praising him always. Put into practice the example of all that you have heard from me or seen in my life and the God of peace will be with you in all things.

Proverbs 3:5-6
Trust in the LORD with all your heart,
and do not lean on your own understanding.
In all your ways acknowledge him,
and he will make straight your paths.

Proverbs 15:1-4 (MSG)
A gentle response defuses anger,
but a sharp tongue kindles a temper-fire.
Knowledge flows like spring water from the wise;
fools are leaky faucets, dripping nonsense.
God doesn't miss a thing—
he's alert to good and evil alike.
Kind words heal and help;
cutting words wound and maim.

Proverbs 17:9 (TPT)
Love overlooks the mistakes of others, but dwelling on the failures
of others devastates.

Proverbs 28:13 (TPT)
If you cover up your sin you'll never do well. But if you confess
your sins and forsake them, you will be kissed by mercy.

Psalm 16:7-11 (NIV)
I will praise the LORD, who counsels me;
even at night my heart instructs me.
I keep my eyes always on the LORD.
With him at my right hand, I will not be shaken.
Therefore my heart is glad and my tongue rejoices;
my body also will rest secure,
because you will not abandon me to the realm of the dead,
nor will you let your faithful one see decay.
You make known to me the path of life;
you will fill me with joy in your presence,
with eternal pleasures at your right hand.

Psalm 34:8 (NIV)

Taste and see that the LORD is good; blessed is the one who takes refuge in him.

Psalm 37:3-4
Trust in the LORD, and do good;
    dwell in the land and befriend faithfulness.
Delight yourself in the LORD,
    and he will give you the desires of your heart.

Psalm 91:1-2
He who dwells in the shelter of the Most High
    will abide in the shadow of the Almighty.
I will say to the LORD, "My refuge and my fortress,
    my God, in whom I trust."

Psalm 94:19 (TPT)
Whenever my busy thoughts were out of control, the soothing comfort of your presence calmed me down and overwhelmed me with delight.

Psalm 107:1
Oh give thanks to the LORD, for he is good, for his steadfast love endures forever!

Romans 8:28
And we know that for those who love God all things work together for good, for those who are called according to his purpose.

Romans 12:12
Rejoice in hope, be patient in tribulation, be constant in prayer.

Romans 12:17 (TPT)
Never hold a grudge or try to get even, but plan your life around the noblest way to benefit others.

1 Thessalonians 5:15-18
See that no one repays anyone evil for evil, but always seek to do good to one another and to everyone. Rejoice always, pray without

ceasing, give thanks in all circumstances; for this is the will of God in Christ Jesus for you.

Song of Songs 6:3a
I am my beloved's and my beloved is mine.

Resource 2: Help for Healing

Organizations

Emmaus Road Ministries: "Come home to your heart." *EmmausRoadMinistries.org*

International Forgiveness Institute: "Healing hearts, building peace." *InternationalForgiveness.com*

Heart Sync: "Healing through synchronizing broken and divided hearts." *HeartSyncMinistries.org*

SOZO: "Saved. Healed. Delivered." *BethelSozo.com*

Prayers

The following are my short & sweet adaptations of much, much longer prayers I've found over the years. Feel free to craft your own adaptations from these.

The Exchange Prayer:

When you start to behave or feel badly, ask God:

Am I believing a lie?

If you sense a yes, ask Him: What truth do you have for me in exchange?

And then wait for the positive opposite of that lie to land in your spirit.

Prayer for Breaking off Soul Ties:
(Specifically for a Former Relationship)

I thank _____ *(name of ex-partner)* for helping me to grow.

I release any remaining attachment between them and me. I give back to them any parts of their soul I took on—knowingly or unknowingly—during our relationship.

Pause: imagine sending back anything that is not yours to keep.

May the space I had taken up in them now be filled with holy peace.

I take back any parts of my soul I gave up—knowingly or unknowingly—during our relationship.

Pause: imagine taking back anything that is yours: innocence, faith, joy, hope, rest, courage, etc.

May the space they had taken up in me now be filled with holy peace.

May we both continue to grow on our separate paths.

*Also: get rid of anything your ex gave you.

Listening Prayer:

Quiet your thoughts, focus on God's presence, and imagine resting in the embrace of Love.

Thank you, God, for _____ *(any good thing in your life at present).*

I have a question about_____ *(whatever is on your heart).* I would love to hear your wisdom.

Be still. Listen. Wait.

Have a journal handy and write whatever comes: it may be an impression, an image, a word, a memory.

If you sense an answer but worry that you're making it up, "cross-check" it with God's character, with Scripture, with a trusted friend.

If He asks you to do something, do it.

If you don't hear anything right away, thank Him for the opportunity to spend time getting to know His heart.

Whatever you do or don't hear, release expectations of when and how He might answer your question. Remember to keep your focus not on the gift but on the Giver.

Resource 3: The Enneagram for Understanding

Books

A great Enneagram primer is *The Road Back to You: An Enneagram Journey to Self-Discovery*. The authors explain: "The true purpose of the Enneagram is to reveal to you your shadow side and offer spiritual counsel on how to open it to the transformative light of grace."[214]

The Path Between Us: An Enneagram Journey to Healthy Relationships shows how to navigate relationships: "The Enneagram doesn't just tell us who we are—it tells us who we can be." And it "helps us to identify our blind spots when it comes to dealing with our feelings and the feelings of others." [215]

The Journey Toward Wholeness: Enneagram Wisdom for Stress, Balance, and Transformation expands on the healing process. The author writes: "Years of studying the wisdom of the Enneagram have led me to an ever-deepening understanding of how we are broken and how we can be healed, often at exactly the same time. The Enneagram reveals who you are and who you can become. If you don't know yourself, how will you ever know who you are in relation to others and who you are in relation to God?"[216]

The Sacred Enneagram shares contemplative practices to help us return to our truest selves: "Often misunderstood as simply a personality tool to describe quirks and traits of people's individuality.... The contemporary Enneagram of Personality illustrates the nine ways we get lost, but also the nine ways we can come home to our True Self. Put another way, it exposes nine ways we lie to ourselves about who we think we are, nine ways we can come clean about those illusions, and nine ways we can find our way back to God."[217] (Author Christopher L. Heuertz also wrote an accompanying workbook.)

Elisabeth Bennett has written separate **devotionals for each of the nine Enneagram types**. (Pro tip: read the devotional not just for your own number but also for your partner's! Which I did for my husband's number Eight.) She writes: "Personality is a kind of shield we pick up, and hide behind. It is functional, even protective at times.... However, we cling to this personality like it's our key to survival, and nothing has proved us wrong so far. It's the only tool we've ever had, and the shield has scratches and dents to prove its worth.... The Enneagram talks about childhood wounds and how we pick up a particular shield as a reaction to those wounds."[218]

For a year-long, comprehensive devotional, dive into *Hearing God Speak: 52-Week Interactive Enneagram Devotional*. Authors Eve Annunciato and Jackie Brewster share weekly Scriptures and guidance for all nine numbers: "As you begin to hear God's message with new awareness, you will recognize cycles and triggers in your life that have kept you bound. This acknowledgement will help you find freedom, allowing you to embrace your uniqueness and others' differences."[219] (The authors also have a podcast, *Speaking of the Enneagram*.)

If you want to geek out and go really deep, you can learn about archetypes, types, and subtypes in Beatrice Chestnut's *The Complete Enneagram*. This resource "describes a vision and a method that advances the goal of greater self-awareness and clarifies the path to achieving it in a way that inspires you to move forward on your own journey of personal evolution."[220]

For a lovely, simplified, illustrated look at how the Enneagram helps us be more compassionate, check out **Kindness: A Guide for Humans Based on the Enneagram**. Author Frank De Luca writes: "I wrote this book…to encourage you to get to know the people in your life better. See life through their eyes, not yours."[221]

Websites

The Enneagram Institute: *EnneagramInstitute.com*

The Narrative Enneagram: *NarrativeEnneagram.org*

Sleeping At Last: songs for each number of the Enneagram (this is how I finally recognized my own type): *SleepingAtLast.com* or via online streaming platforms

And you can also find **Richard Rohr's** Enneagram teachings on YouTube

Resource 4: Questions to Ask Ourselves

What if I choose to become unoffendable?

What if I learn to let things go?

What if I not only learn to let things go but to not grab hold of them in the first place?

Will what I am about to say help or harm our relationship?

What if I am responsible not just for my own joy but for my own pain?

What if I looked at my marriage from heaven's perspective?

What if my spouse's motivations are innocent?

How can I love my spouse in the way they best receive love?

What am I building with my spouse that is eternal?

And write your own...

Resource 5: Books to Read

Of all the relationship books I referenced, these Sweet Sixteen are my favorites. Get them. Read them. Tell others about them. They will change your marriage.

1. *Attached: The New Science of Adult Attachment and How It Can Help You Find—and Keep—Love,* Amir Levine and Rachel S. F. Heller
2. *Crucial Conversations: Tools for Talking When Stakes Are High,* Patterson, Grenny, McMillan, and Switzler
3. *The Five Love Languages: The Secret to Love that Lasts,* Gary Chapman
4. *Forgive for Love: The Missing Ingredient for a Healthy and Lasting Relationship,* Dr. Fred Luskin
5. *Getting the Love You Want: A Guide for Couples,* Harville Hendrix and Helen LaKelly Hunt
6. *The Heart of Love: How to Go Beyond Fantasy to Find True Fulfillment,* John F. DeMartini
7. *His Needs, Her Needs: Building a Marriage That Lasts,* Willard F. Harley, Jr., PhD
8. *How to Improve Your Marriage Without Talking About It,* Patricia Love and Steven Stosny
9. *It Takes One to Tango: How I Rescued My Marriage with (Almost) No Help from My Spouse—and How You Can, Too,* Winifred M. Reilly
10. *The Labyrinth of Love: The Path to a Soulful Relationship,* Chelsea Wakefield, PhD

11. *Love Sense: The Revolutionary New Science of Romantic Relationships*, Dr. Sue Johnson
12. *Love Worth Making: How to Have Ridiculously Great Sex in a Long-Lasting Relationship*, Stephen Snyder
13. *Relationship Magic: Waking Up Together*, Guy Finley
14. *Sacred Marriage: What if God Designed Marriage to Make Us Holy More than to Make Us Happy?* Gary Thomas
15. *Why Won't You Apologize? Healing Big Betrayals and Everyday Hurts*, Harriet Lerner, PhD
16. *The Zimzum of Love: A New Way of Understanding Marriage*, Rob and Kristen Bell

Resource 6: Our Fifty-Year Letter

Before our wedding, my father asked us to write a letter to ourselves fifty years into marriage. This our prophecy and our promise.

Dear Us in fifty years:

We may not know exactly what to hope for in the next decades, but we do know we want to become better and better at receiving God's love and extending it toward each other and those around us.

We are excited to grow as we explore each other's different ways of being, of living, of hearing from God.

As Jared said before we got engaged, "We don't have to be on the same page as long as we're writing the same story."

Here's what we'd love to be true now and when we next read this:

We fill our story with the fruit of the spirit. Just as we anticipate planting a garden and trees on our new land, we anticipate cultivating love, joy, peace, patience, kindness, goodness, faithfulness, gentleness, and self-control in our marriage.

We love each other with God's love.

We keep God first, then each other, then family, then friends.

We try to see each other from the vantage of being seated with Christ—from heaven's best.

We communicate with kindness and grace.

When we mess up, we extend and receive mercy.

We seek wise counsel from Godly people when needed.

We build trust together.

We know that our marriage is about more than just the two of us, and we share our blessings with others—in physical and spiritual ways.

We continually move toward union with God and with each other.

And we hope we've shared plenty of laughter, adventure, and unexpected delights!

With & in love,

Anna & Jared

Notes

A note on these notes: I quote from many sources. I don't necessarily agree with everything in these sources, but truth can be found in many places. Even in imperfect books. Even in imperfect people. Thank goodness, right?

We Fought About *What?*

1   Winifred M. Reilly, *It Takes One to Tango: How I Rescued My Marriage with (Almost) No Help from My Spouse—and How You Can, Too* (Gallery Books, 2017), 236.

2   Adam Grant, *Think Again: The Power of Knowing What You Don't Know* (Penguin Audio, 2021), Audiobook.

Part I: Meet the Players

3   Rob Bell, *Everything is Spiritual* (Macmillan Audio, 2020), Audiobook.

Chronos: July

4   Susan Cain, *Bittersweet: How Sorrow and Longing Make Us Whole* (Crown, 2022), 243.

5   John O'Donohue, "For a New Beginning," *To Bless the Space Between Us: A Book of Blessings* (Doubleday, 2008), 14.

6   John F. DeMartini, *The Heart of Love: How to Go Beyond Fantasy to Find True Fulfillment* (Hay House, 2007), 21.

7   Alexandra H. Solomon, *Loving Bravely: 20 Lessons of Self-Discovery to Help You Get the Love You Want* (New Harbinger Publications, 2017), 211.

8   Dorianne Laux, "What We Carry," *What We Carry* (BOA Editions, 1994), 20.

9   Alain de Botton, @TheSchoolOfLife, "Why You Will Marry the Wrong Person," Video on *YouTube,* https://www.youtube.com/watch?v=-EvvPZFdjyk.

10 Chelsea Wakefield, PhD, *The Labyrinth of Love: The Path to a Soulful Relationship* (Chiron Publications, 2021), 197.

11 Dr. Kevin Leman, *Sheet Music: Uncovering the Secrets of Sexual Intimacy in Marriage* (Tyndale Momentum, 2008), 10.

12 Jalal ad-Din Muhammad Rumi, "Love Dogs," *The Essential Rumi* Translated by Coleman Barks and John Moyne (HarperOne, 1995), 155.

Kairos: The Corn Dog Compromise

13   Alexander Schmemann, *For the Life of the World* (St Vladimir's Seminary Press, 2018), 111.

Chronos: August

14   Robert Hass, "Time and Materials," *Time and Materials* (Ecco, 2007), 26.
15   Alexandra H. Solomon, *Loving Bravely: 20 Lessons of Self-Discovery to Help You Get the Love You Want* (New Harbinger Publications, 2017), 155.
16   Allison A. Armstrong. *The Amazing Development of Men* (PAX Programs, 2012), Audiobook.
17   Li-Young Lee, "Living with Her," *Behind My Eyes* (W. W. Norton & Co, 2008), 99.
18   Allison A. Armstrong, *The Queen's Code* (PAX Programs, 2012), 64.
19   Seamus Heaney, "St Kevin and the Blackbird," *Spirit Level* (The Noonday Press, 1996), 25.
20   Luci Shaw, "Writing the River," *Sea Glass: New & Selected Poems* (WordFarm, 2016), 129.
21   Marie Forleo, *Everything is Figureoutable* (Portfolio/Penguin, 2020), 179.
22   Pablo Neruda, "The Song of Despair," *Twenty Love Poems and a Song of Despair*, Translated by W.S. Merwin (Penguin Books, 2004), 89.

Kairos: My Hardest-Best Classroom

23   Terrence Real, *The New Rules of Marriage: What You Need to Know to Make Love Work* (Ballantine Books, 2008), 40.

Chronos: September

24   Rick Hanson, PhD, "Take in the Good," *The Practical Science of Lasting Happiness,* https://www.rickhanson.net/take-in-the-good/.
25   Elizabeth Libbey, "The Act of Letting Go," *Poetry Foundation,* https://www.poetryfoundation.org/poetrymagazine/browse?contentId=35445.
26   Alison A. Armstrong, *The Queen's Code* (PAX Programs, 2012), 44.
27   Jack Gilbert, "A Brief for the Defense," *The Poetry of Impermanence, Mindfulness, and Joy,* Edited by John Brehm (Wisdom Publications, 2017), 170-171.
28   Beatrice Chestnut, PhD, *The Complete Enneagram: 27 Paths to Greater Self-Knowledge* (She Writes Press, 2013), 299.
29   Ruth Stone, "The Wound," *What Loves Comes To: New & Selected*

Poems (Copper Canyon Press, 2008), 238.

30 Desmond Tutu, quoted by Evelyn Lau in "A look back at Desmond Tutu's greatest quotes, from kindness to forgiveness," *The National News*, December 26, 2021, https://www.thenationalnews.com/arts-culture/books/2021/12/26/a-look-back-at-desmond-tutus-greatest-quotes-from-kindness-to-forgiveness/.

31 Mac Barnett, *What is Love?* Illustrated by Carson Ellis (Chronicle Books, 2021), No page numbers in this illustrated book.

32 Guy Finley, *Relationship Magic: Waking Up Together* (Llewellyn Publications, 2018), 247.

Part II: Marriage as Metamorphosis

33 Richard Rohr, *Immortal Diamond: The Search for Our True Self* (Jossey-Bass, 2013). 211.

34 Richard Rohr, *Falling Upward: A Spirituality for the Two Halves of Life* (Dreamscape Media, 2011), Audiobook.

Chronos: October

35 Rainer Maria Rilke, "The Silence," *The Book of Images,* Translated by Edward Snow (North Pont Press, 1991), 27.

36 Stan Tatkin, *Your Brain on Love: The Neurobiology of Healthy Relationships* (Sounds True, 2013), Audiobook.

37 Wendell Berry, "Manifesto: The Mad Farmer Liberation Front," *A Country of Marriage* (Counterpoint, 2013), 15.

38 Terry Tempest Williams, *When Women Were Birds: Fifty-Four Variations on Voice* (Picador, 2012), 175.

39 Antoine Saint-Exupéry, *The Little Prince,* Translated by Katharine Woods (Harcourt Brace & Company, 1971), 87.

40 Rob and Kristen Bell, *The Zimzum of Love,* (HarperAudio, 2014), Audiobook.

41 Chelsea Wakefield, PhD, *The Labyrinth of Love: The Path to a Soulful Relationship* (Chiron Publications, 2021), 133-134.

42 Harville Hendrix and Helen LaKelly Hunt, *Getting the Love You Want: A Guide for Couples* (St. Martin's Griffin, 2019), 12-13.

43 Richard Rohr, *Immortal Diamond: The Search for Our True Self* (Jossey-Bass, 2013), 161-162.

44 Romeo Oriogun, "Flyway," *Poetry* (June 2022), 248.

45 Czeslaw Milosz, "Love," *New and Collected Poems 1931-2001* (Ecco, 2001), 50.

46 John Gottman, PhD and Nan Silver, *The Seven Principles for Making a Marriage Work,* (Tantor Audio, 2020), Audiobook.

47 Adedayo Agarau, "before the dark," *Poetry* (July/August 2022), 380.

48 Dr. Daniel G. Amen, *Change Your Brain Change Your Life: The Breakthrough Program for Conquering Anxiety, Depression, Obsessiveness, Lake of Focus, Anger, and Memory Problems* (Harmony, 2015), 313.

49 Dr. Kerry Howells, "Moving Past Resentment to Grateful Living," *Gratefulness.org,* https://gratefulness.org/grateful-living/grateful-living-through-moving-past-resentment/?mc_cid=d7c2b7e9fa&mc_eid=b497390611.

Chronos: November

50 Anne Waldman, "Light & Shadow," *Poetry Foundation,* https://www.poetryfoundation.org/poetrymagazine/browse?contentId=32677.

51 Patricia Love and Steven Stosny, *How to Improve Your Marriage Without Talking About It* (Harmony Books, 2007), 141.

52 Alison A. Armstrong, *The Queen's Code* (PAX Programs, 2012), 316.

53 Elamin Abdelmahmoud, *Son of Elsewhere: A Memoir in Pieces* (Random House Audio, 2022), Audiobook.

54 Anna Elkins, *Living Large on Little: How to See the Invitation in Limitation* (Wordbody, 2019), 18.

55 Brother David Steindl-Rast, *Gratefulness, the Heart of Prayer: An Approach to Life in Fullness* (Paulist Press, 1984), 204.

56 Elisabeth Bennett, *The Individualist: Growing as an Enneagram 4* (Whitaker House, 2020), 144.

57 Jo Piazza, *How to Be Married: What I Learned from Real Women on Five Continents About Surviving My First (Really Hard) Year of Marriage* (Harmony Books, 2017), 254.

58 Guy Finley, *Relationship Magic: Waking Up Together* (Llewellyn Publications, 2018), 63.

59 Chelsea Wakefield, PhD, *The Labyrinth of Love: The Path to a Soulful Relationship* (Chiron Publications, 2021), 158.

60 Lucia Perillo, "I could name some names," *The Poetry of Impermanence, Mindfulness, and Joy,* Edited by John Brehm. (Wisdom Publications, 2017), 61.

61 A. W. Tozer, *The Pursuit of God* (Aneko Press, 2016), Audiobook.

62 Harriet Lerner, PhD, *Why Won't You Apologize? Healing Big Betrayals and Everyday Hurts* (Gallery Books, 2017), 56.

63 Chelsea Wakefield, PhD, *The Labyrinth of Love: The Path to a Soulful Relationship* (Chiron Publications, 2021), 107.

64 Robert Farrar Capon, *The Supper of the Lamb: A Culinary Reflection* (The Modern Library, 2002), 86.

65 Emily Porter St. John, "Differentia," *Poetry Foundation,*

https://www.poetryfoundation.org/poetrymagazine/browse?content
Id=22933.

66 Guy Finley, *Relationship Magic: Waking Up Together* (Llewellyn
Publications, 2018), 139.

67 Rick Johnson, *Becoming Your Spouse's Better Half: Why Differences
Make a Marriage Great* (Revell, 2010), 11.

68 Ibid., 208.

69 Ephesians 3:20 TLB.

70 Linda and Charlie Bloom, *101 Things I Wish I Knew When I Got
Married: Simple Lessons to Make Love Last* (New World Library,
2004), xxvii.

71 A. W. Tozer, *The Pursuit of God* (Aneko Press, 2016), Audiobook.

Chronos: December

72 Parker Palmer, *Let Your Life Speak: Listening for the Voice of
Vocation* (John Wiley & Sons, 2000), 5.

73 Abdellatif Lâabi, "Just Love," *The World's Embrace: Selected Poems,*
Translated by Anne George, et al. (City Lights Books, 2003), 65.

74 Mary Oppen, *Meaning A Life: An Autobiography* (New Directions,
2020), 258.

Part III: Comm(union)

75 Matthew 26:26; Luke 22:19-20; I Corinthians 11:25.

76 Alexander Schmemann, *For the Life of the World* (St. Vladimir's
Seminary Press, 2018), 106.

77 Annie Dillard, *Teaching a Stone to Talk: Expeditions and Encounters*
(Harper Perennial, 2008), 19-20.

78 Richard Rohr, *Falling Upward: A Spirituality for the Two Halves of
Life* (Dreamscape Media, 2011), Audiobook.

Chronos: January

79 Zbigniew Herbert, "I Would Like to Describe," *Selected Poems:
Zbigniew Herbert,* Translated by Czeslaw Milosz and Peter Dale
Scott (The Ecco Press, 1967), 38.

80 Dr. Daniel G. Amen, *Change Your Brain Change Your Life: The
Breakthrough Program for Conquering Anxiety, Depression,
Obsessiveness, Lake of Focus, Anger, and Memory Problems*
(Harmony, 2015), 40.

81 David Schnarch, PhD, *Passionate Marriage: Keeping Love &
Intimacy Alive in Committed Relationships* (W. W. Norton & Co.,
2000), 324.

82 Heather Havrilesky, *Foreverland: On the Divine Tedium of Marriage* (HarperAudio, 2022), Audiobook.

83 Denise Levertov, "Dialogue," *Denise Levertov: Poems 1968-1972* (New Directions, 1971), 88.

84 Winifred M. Reilly, *It Takes One to Tango: How I Rescued My Marriage with (Almost) No Help from My Spouse—and How You Can, Too* (Gallery Books, 2017), 105.

85 Richard Rohr, *Immortal Diamond: The Search for Our True Self* (Jossey-Bass, 2013), 47-48.

86 Ibid., 64.

87 Suzanne Stabile, *The Journey Toward Wholeness: Enneagram Wisdom for Stress, Balance, and Transformation* (InterVarsity Press, 2021), 231.

88 Guy Finley, *Relationship Magic: Waking Up Together* (Llewellyn Publications, 2018), 51-52.

89 Leeana Tankersley, *Begin Again: The Brave Practice of Releasing Hurt & Receiving Rest* (Revell, 2018), 27.

90 Ibid., 134.

91 John Gottman, PhD and Nan Silver, *Seven Principles for Making Marriage Work* (Tantor Audio, 2020), Audiobook.

92 Laurie Mintz, *Becoming Cliterate: Why Orgasm Equity matters—And How to Get It* (HarperOne, 2017), 159.

93 Jorie Graham, "The Marriage," *The Dream of the Unified Field: Selected Poems 1974-1994* (The Ecco Press, 1995), 133-134.

94 Francis and Lisa Chan, *You and Me Forever: Marriage in Light of Eternity* (Claire Love Publishing, 2014), 97.

95 Patricia Goedicke, "Compose Yourself," *Invisible Horses* (Milkweed Editions, 1996), 125.

96 Laurie Mintz, *Becoming Cliterate: Why Orgasm Equity matters—And How to Get It* (HarperOne, 2017), 163-164.

97 Dr. Sue Johnson, *Love Sense: The Revolutionary New Science of Romantic Relationships* (Little, Brown and Company, 2013), 215.

98 Patricia Love and Steven Stosny, *How to Improve Your Marriage Without Talking About It* (Harmony Books, 2007), 137.

99 Dr. Sue Johnson, *Hold Me Tight: Seven Conversations for a Lifetime of Love* (Little, Brown Spark, 2008), 66.

100 Carolyn Forché, "Hive," *Blue Hour* (Perennial, 2003), 20.

101 Guy Finley, *Relationship Magic: Waking Up Together* (Llewellyn Publications, 2018), 43.

102 Patterson, Grenny, McMillan, and Switzler, *Crucial Conversations: Tools for Talking When Stakes Are High* (McGraw-Hill, 2012), 57-58.

Kairos: Kind/ness

[103] Bo Stern, *Beautiful Battlefields,* (NavPress, 2013), 143.

[104] Ibid., 149-150.

[105] Guy Finley, *Relationship Magic: Waking Up Together* (Llewellyn Publications, 2018), 70 & 160.

Chronos: February

[106] Harriet Lerner, PhD, *Why Won't You Apologize? Healing Big Betrayals and Everyday Hurts* (Gallery Books, 2017), 2.

[107] Carl Sandburg, "Joy," *Poetry Foundation,* https://www.poetry foundation.org/poetrymagazine/browse?contentId=13232.

[108] Gregg Baden, *The Divine Matrix* (Hay House, 2008), Audiobook.

[109] Patterson, Grenny, McMillan, and Switzler, *Crucial Conversations: Tools for Talking When Stakes Are High* (McGraw-Hill, 2012), 35.

[110] Larry Shushansky, *Independent Enough: A Book About Relationships* (Independent Enough Press, 2018), 7.

[111] Harriet Lerner, PhD, *The Dance of Anger: A Woman's Guide to Changing the Patterns of Intimate Relationships* (HarperAudio, 2016), Audiobook.

[112] Patricia Love and Steven Stosny, *How to Improve Your Marriage Without Talking About It* (Harmony Books, 2007), 31.

[113] Ibid., 168.

[114] Harriet Lerner, PhD, *Why Won't You Apologize? Healing Big Betrayals and Everyday Hurts* (Gallery Books, 2017), 103.

[115] Richard Siken, "Litany in Which Certain Things Are Crossed Out," *Poetry Foundation,* https://www.poetryfoundation.org/poems/48158/litany-in-which-certain-things-are-crossed-out.

[116] John O'Donohue, "For a New Home," *To Bless the Space Between Us: A Book of Blessings* (Doubleday, 2008), 20.

Kairos: The Gasket of Grace

[117] Rob and Kristen Bell, *The Zimzum of Love: A New Way of Understanding Marriage* (HarperAudio, 2014), Audiobook.

Chronos: March

[118] Mona Van Duyn. "The Beginning," *Poetry Foundation,* https://www.poetryfoundation.org/poetrymagazine/browse?contentId=38342.

[119] David K. Wheeler, "Against Acedia," *Contingency Plans* (T. S. Poetry Press, 2010), 95.

120 Amir Levine and Rachel S. F. Heller, *Attached: The New Science of Adult Attachment and How It Can Help You Find—and Keep—Love.* (TarcherPedigree, 2010), 20.

121 Ibid., 21.

122 Ibid., 26.

123 Dana Ward, "Don't Let Me Be Wistful," *Poetry Foundation,* https://www.poetryfoundation.org/poems/55982/dont-let-me-be-wistful.

124 *Princess Bride,* Directed by Rob Reiner (Act III Communications, 1987).

125 Dr. Emerson Eggerichs, *Love & Respect: The Love She Most Desires; the Respect He Desperately Needs* (Thomas Nelson, 2004), 91. *Note:* Eggerichs' claims about the love-and-respect combo, and other topics in his book, have been debated. I won't weigh in on them here. But these quoted lines about acting respectful despite a feeling helped me respect both my husband *and* myself.

126 Ann Voskamp, *One Thousand Gifts: A Dare to Live Fully Right Where You Are* (Zondervan, 2010), 176.

127 Alexandra H. Solomon, *Loving Bravely: 20 Lessons of Self-Discovery to Help You Get the Love You Want* (New Harbinger Publications, 2017), 6.

128 Patricia Love and Steven Stosny, *How to Improve Your Marriage Without Talking About It* (Harmony Books, 2007), 123-124.

129 Gary Thomas, *Sacred Marriage: What if God Designed Marriage to Make Us Holy More than to Make Us Happy?* (Zondervan, 2015), 144.

130 William Stafford, "It's All Right," *The Poetry of Impermanence, Mindfulness, and Joy,* Edited by John Brehm (Wisdom Publications, 2017), 151.

131 Mary Oliver, "I Found a Dead Fox," *White Pine* (Harcourt Brace & Company, 1994), 37.

132 Mary Oliver, "Good-Bye Fox," *A Thousand Mornings* (Penguin Books, 2012), 14.

133 Dr. Harold R. Eberle, *Two Become One: Releasing God's Power for Romance, Sexual Freedom, and Blessings in Marriage, 4th Edition.* Worldcast Publishing, 2018), 87.

Part IV: The Wound That Heals Us

134 *Princess Bride,* Directed by Rob Reiner (Act III Communications, 1987).

[135] M. Scott Peck, *The Road Less Traveled: A New Psychology of Love, Values, and Spiritual Growth, 25th Anniversary Edition* (Simon & Schuster Audio, 2002), Audiobook.

[136] Linda and Charlie Bloom, *101 Things I Wish I Knew When I Got Married: Simple Lessons to Make Love Last* (New World Library, 2004), 232.

[137] Ann Voskamp, *One Thousand Gifts: A Dare to Live Fully Right Where You Are* (Zondervan, 2010), 84.

[138] Simone Weil, *Waiting for God,* Translated by Emma Craufurd (Harper Perennial Modern Classics, 2009), 79.

[139] Terrence Real, *Us: Getting Past You & Me to Build a More Loving Relationship* (Goop Press, 2022), 37.

Chronos: April

[140] Joy Harjo, "The Creation Story," *The Woman Who Fell From the Sky* (Norton, 1996), 3.

[141] Dr. Fred Luskin, *Forgive for Love: The Missing Ingredient for a Healthy and Lasting Relationship* (HarperOne, 2007), 162.

[142] Dan Millman, *Way of the Peaceful Warrior* (New World Library, 1997), Audiobook.

[143] John F. DeMartini, *The Heart of Love: How to Go Beyond Fantasy to Find True Fulfillment* (Hay House, 2007), 28.

[144] Willard F. Harley, Jr., PhD, *His Needs, Her Needs: Building a Marriage That Lasts* (Revell, 2011), 77.

[145] Camille T. Dungy, "Sinner, don't you weep," *What to Eat, What to Drink, What to Leave for Poison* (Red Hen Press, 2006), 47.

[146] Gary Thomas, *Sacred Marriage: What if God Designed Marriage to Make Us Holy More than to Make Us Happy?* (Zondervan, 2015), 218-219.

[147] Laurie Mintz, *Becoming Cliterate: Why Orgasm Equity matters—And How to Get It* (HarperOne, 2017), 156.

[148] Federico García Lorca, "The Poet Tells the Truth," *Federico García Lorca: Collected Poems,* Edited by Christopher Mauer (Farrar, Straus and Giroux, 1991), 835.

[149] Martin Buber, *I and Thou,* Translated by Walter Kaufman (Touchstone, 1996), 95.

[150] Kahlil Gibran, *The Prophet, Poets.org,* https://poets.org/poem/joy-and-sorrow.

[151] Jen Stewart Fueston, "Midlife Valentine," *Madonna, Complex* (Cascade Books, 2020), 57.

[152] Henri J. M. Nouwen, *The Wounded Healer* (Image Books, 1990), 83, 84, & 85.

[153] Harriet Lerner, PhD, *Why Won't You Apologize? Healing Big Betrayals and Everyday Hurts* (Gallery Books, 2017), 61.

[154] Ann Voskamp, *Waymaker: Finding the Way to the Life You've Always Dreamed Of* (W Publishing Group, 2022), 53-54 & 330.

[155] Winifred M. Reilly, *It Takes One to Tango: How I Rescued My Marriage with (Almost) No Help from My Spouse—and How You Can, Too* (Gallery Books, 2017), 141.

[156] Dr. Daniel G. Amen, *Change Your Brain Change Your Life: The Breakthrough Program for Conquering Anxiety, Depression, Obsessiveness, Lake of Focus, Anger, and Memory Problems* (Harmony, 2015), 127.

[157] Octavio Paz, "Concert in the Garden," *The Collected Poems of Octavio Paz 1957-1987,* Translated by Elizabeth Bishop et al. (New Directions Books, 1990), 243.

[158] Gary Thomas, *Sacred Marriage: What if God Designed Marriage to Make Us Holy More than to Make Us Happy?* (Zondervan, 2015), 220.

[159] Molly Peacock, "Sky Inside," *Raw Heaven* (Vintage Books, 1984), 30.

[160] C. S. Lewis, *Surprised By Joy: The Shape of My Early Life* (Harcourt Brace, 1955), No specific page number: I refer to the entire book.

[161] Gary Thomas, *Sacred Marriage: What if God Designed Marriage to Make Us Holy More than to Make Us Happy?* (Zondervan, 2015), 83.

[162] Ibid, 87.

[163] Elizabeth Gilbert, *Committed: A Skeptic Makes Peace with Marriage* (Viking Penguin, 2010), 131.

Kairos: All of the Above

[164] Leeana Tankersley, *Begin Again: The Brave Practice of Releasing Hurt & Receiving Rest* (Revell, 2018), 75.

Chronos: May

[165] Mary Oliver, "Today," *A Thousand Mornings* (Penguin Books, 2012), 23.

[166] Maxine Kumin, "The Long Approach," *The Long Approach* (Viking Penguin, 1985), 79.

[167] Esther Perel, *Mating in Captivity: Unlocking Erotic Intelligence* (Harper, 2006), xiv.

[168] John F. DeMartini, *The Heart of Love: How to Go Beyond Fantasy to Find True Fulfillment* (Hay House, 2007), 91.

[169] Fred Chappell, "Humility," *Spring Garden: New and Selected Poems by Fred Chappell* (Louisiana State University Press, 1995), 134.

[170] Brother Lawrence, *The Practice of the Presence of God,* Revised by Harold J. Chadwick (Bridge-Logos, 1999), 128.

[171] John F. Deane, "A Little Book of Hours," *A Little Book of Hours* (Carcanet, 2008), 64.

[172] Alexandra H. Solomon, *Loving Bravely: 20 Lessons of Self-Discovery to Help You Get the Love You Want* (New Harbinger Publications, 2017), 134.

[173] Patricia Love and Steven Stosny, *How to Improve Your Marriage Without Talking About It* (Harmony Books, 2007), 31.

[174] Ibid., 110-111.

Kairos: Peace Like That

[175] Isaiah 48:18; 66:12.

Chronos: June...And Then Some

[176] Phileena Heuertz, *Mindful Silence: The Heart of Christian Contemplation* (IVP Books, 2018), 170.

[177] Dr. Sue Johnson, *Hold Me Tight: Seven Conversations for a Lifetime of Love* (Little, Brown Spark, 2008), 148.

[178] Wendell Berry, "The Law That Marries All Things," *The Wheel* (North Point Press, 1982), 25.

[179] Dr. Fred Luskin, *Forgive for Love: The Missing Ingredient for a Healthy and Lasting Relationship* (HarperOne, 2007), 130 & 150.

[180] Michelle Peterson, *#staymarried: A Couple's Devotional* (Althea Press, 2017), 190.

[181] Anna Elkins, "A Desire," *Hope of Stones* (Press 53, 2020), 63.

[182] C. S. Lewis, *Letters to Malcolm: Chiefly on Prayer* (Harvest, 1964), 92-93.

[183] Brené Brown, *Atlas of the Heart: Mapping Meaningful Connection and the Language of Human Experience* (Random House, 2021), 206 & 215.

[184] Alim Maghrebi, "After Reading the Love Poems of Dov Ben-Zamir," *Habibi: The Diwan of Alim Maghrebi,* Translated by David Solway (Guernica, 2012), 53.

[185] Dr. Laura Schlessinger, *The Proper Care and Feeding of Husbands.* (HarperCollins, 2004), 94.

[186] Thomas Moore, *Soul Mates: Honoring the Mysteries of Love and Relationship* (HarperCollins, 1994), 35.

[187] Ada Limón, "Notes on the Below," *The Carrying* (Milkweed Editions, 2018), 46.

[188] Bernard of Clairvaux, *On the Song of Songs I* (Cistercian Publications, 1981), 10.

189 Larry Shushansky, *Independent Enough: A Book About Relationships* (Independent Enough Press, 2018), 65.

190 Ibn 'Arabî, *Perfect Harmony,* Calligraphy by Hassan Massoudy, Translation by Shambhala Publications (Shambhala, 2002), No page numbers in this illustrated book.

191 Dr. Caroline Leaf [@drcarolineleaf], *Instagram,* Meme posted August 17, 2022, https://www.instagram.com/p/ChXJoxyu_Bc/.

192 Ibid., Meme posted August 20, 2022, https://www.instagram.com/p/Che2iTSOJOl/.

193 David Whyte, *Consolations: The Solace, Nourishment and Underlying Meaning of Everyday Words* (Many Rivers Press, 2015), 78-79.

194 Stephen Snyder, *Love Worth Making: How to Have Ridiculously Great Sex in a Long-Lasting Relationship* (St. Martin's Essentials, 2018), 161.

195 Wendell Berry, "The Cruel Plumage," *A Country of Marriage* (Counterpoint, 2013), 37.

196 Terrence Real, *The New Rules of Marriage: What You Need to Know to Make Love Work* (Ballantine Books, 2008), 46.

197 Pattiann Rogers, "Place and Proximity," *Eating Bread and Honey* (Milkweed Editions, 1997), 52.

198 Stephen Snyder, *Love Worth Making: How to Have Ridiculously Great Sex in a Long-Lasting Relationship* (St. Martin's Essentials, 2018), 166.

199 Dr. Fred Luskin, *Forgive for Love: The Missing Ingredient for a Healthy and Lasting Relationship* (HarperOne, 2007), 100.

200 Rita Dove, "Geometry," *Rita Dove: Selected Poems* (Vintage Books, 1993), 17.

201 Dr. Fred Luskin, *Forgive for Love: The Missing Ingredient for a Healthy and Lasting Relationship* (HarperOne, 2007), 96 & 97.

202 David Whyte, "What to Remember When Waking," *The House of Belonging* (Many Rivers Press, 2011), 26.

203 Ann Voskamp, *One Thousand Gifts: A Dare to Live Fully Right Where You Are* (Zondervan, 2010), 32-33.

204 Anne Sexton, "Us," *Love Poems* (Houghton Mifflin Company, 1989), 40.

205 Pablo Neruda, "We Have Lost Even," *Twenty Love Poems and a Song of Despair,* Translated by W.S. Merwin (Penguin Books, 2004), 35.

206 Harriet Lerner, PhD, *Why Won't You Apologize? Healing Big Betrayals and Everyday Hurts* (Gallery Books, 2017), 114.

207 Eavan Boland, "What Love Intended," *Outside History: Selected Poems 1980-1990* (W. W. Norton & Company, 1991), 67.

208 Ian Morgan Cron and Suzanne Stabile, *The Road Back to You: An Enneagram Journey to Self-Discovery* (InterVarsity Press, 2016), 166.

209 Emily Nagoski, PhD, *Come As You Are: The Surprising New Science That Will Transform Your Sex Life* (Simon & Schuster Audio, 2021), Audiobook.

210 Eric Fromm, *The Art of Loving* (Recording self-published by the author, 2020), Audiobook.

Kairos: For the Joy

211 Richard Rohr, *Falling Upward: A Spirituality for the Two Halves of Life* (Dreamscape Media, 2011), Audiobook.

The Catch

212 Barbara Brown Taylor, *An Altar in the World: A Geography of Faith* (HarperOne, 2010), 93.

213 Jane Hirshfield, "For What Binds Us," *Of Gravity & Angels* (Wesleyan University Press, 1988), 34.

Resource 3

214 Ian Morgan Cron and Suzanne Stabile, *The Road Back to You: An Enneagram Journey to Self-Discovery* (InterVarsity Press, 2016), 31.

215 Suzanne Stabile, *The Path Between Us: An Enneagram Journey to Healthy Relationships* (InterVarsity Press, 2018), 133 & 169.

216 Suzanne Stabile, *The Journey Toward Wholeness: Enneagram Wisdom for Stress, Balance, and Transformation* (InterVarsity Press, 2021), 130.

217 Christopher L. Heuertz, *The Sacred Enneagram: Finding Your Unique Path to Spiritual Growth* (Zondervan, 2017), 25.

218 Elisabeth Bennett, *The Challenger: Growing as an Enneagram 8* (Whitaker House, 2021), 23.

219 Eve Annunciato and Jackie Brewster, *Hearing God Speak: 52-Week Interactive Enneagram Devotional* (WaterBrook, 2021), 6.

220 Beatrice Chestnut, PhD, *The Complete Enneagram: 27 Paths to Greater Self-Knowledge* (She Writes Press, 2013), 13.

221 Frank De Luca, PhD, *Kindness: A Guide for Humans Based on the Enneagram,* Illustrated by Nancy Bardos. (ARichLife.com, 2021), 3.

357

Made in the USA
Las Vegas, NV
07 December 2022